The Financialisation of Power

The financial crash of 2007–2008 le[illegible] all over the world to ask how far financiers are in control of our lives. To what extent does what they do with our money affect our everyday lives? This book asks whether the crisis, and subsequent use of public subsidies to help the international economy recover, was a unique event, or a symptom of a wider malaise where financiers have effectively usurped the power of governments and are running the political economy themselves.

The Financialisation of Power argues that growth is not always a good thing. The development of more derivatives and faster financial exchanges are draining businesses of investment capital rather than serving to supply it; applying financial logic does not save nature or protect biodiversity and other species. This book outlines the concept of financialisation and how it has been used in various ways to explain the post-2008 crisis and global political economy. There is a particular focus on these issues with reference to Africa, which has a particular dependence on international money. It takes the perspective of the modern state, exploring how the political economy of development actually works in relation to African governance.

This book will be of interest to students of international development and political economy and will be a key source for policy makers interested in African studies and economic development.

Sarah Bracking holds a Department of Science and Technology funded South African Research Chair (SARCHi) Chair in Applied Poverty Reduction Assessment at the University of KwaZulu-Natal, South Africa and is Honorary Director of Research at the Leverhulme Centre for the Study of Value, University of Manchester, UK

Routledge Studies in Development Economics

For a complete list of titles in this series, please visit www.routledge.com

116 **Employment and Inclusive Development**
Rizwanul Islam and Iyanatul Islam

117 **Growth and Institutions in African Development**
Edited by Augustin K. Fosu

118 **Public Finance and Economic Growth in Developing Countries**
Lessons from Ethiopia's reforms
Stephen B. Peterson

119 **Peripheral Visions of Economic Development**
New frontiers in development economics and the history of economic thought
Edited by Mario Garcia-Molina and Hans-Michael Trautwein

120 **The Political Economy of Natural Resources and Development**
From Neoliberalism to resource nationalism
Edited by Paul A. Haslam and Pablo Heidrich

121 **Institutional Innovation and Change in Value Chain Development**
Negotiating tradition, power and fragility in Afghanistan
Holly A. Ritchie

122 **China's War against the Many Faces of Poverty**
Towards a New Long March
Jing Yang and Pundarik Mukhopadhaya

123 **Exploring Civic Innovation for Social and Economic Transformation**
Edited by Kees Biekart, Wendy Harcourt and Peter Knorringa

124 **Trade, Investment and Economic Development in Asia**
Empirical and policy issues
Edited by Debashis Chakraborty and Jaydeep Mukherjee

125 **The Financialisation of Power**
How financiers rule Africa
Sarah Bracking

The Financialisation of Power

How financiers rule Africa

Sarah Bracking

Routledge
Taylor & Francis Group
LONDON AND NEW YORK

First published 2016
by Routledge

2 Park Square, Milton Park, Abingdon, Oxfordshire OX14 4RN
52 Vanderbilt Avenue, New York, NY 10017

Routledge is an imprint of the Taylor & Francis Group, an informa business

First issued in paperback 2018

British Library Cataloguing in Publication Data
A catalogue record for this book is available from the British Library

Library of Congress Cataloging in Publication Data
Names: Bracking, Sarah, 1968- author.
Title: The financialisation of power in Africa / Sarah Bracking.
Description: New York : Routledge, 2016.
Identifiers: LCCN 2015047615| ISBN 9780415538510 (hardback) | ISBN 9780203109274 (ebook)
Subjects: LCSH: Subsidies--Africa. | Economic development--Africa. | Global Financial Crisis, 2008-2009. | Africa--Economic policy.
Classification: LCC HC800 .B697 2016 | DDC 338.96/02--dc23
LC record available at https://lccn.loc.gov/2015047615

ISBN: 978-0-415-53851-0 (hbk)
ISBN: 978-0-367-11076-5 (pbk)

Typeset in Times New Roman
by Fish Books Ltd.

This book is dedicated to Colin, Christine, Louise and Miles

Contents

Acronyms

ABS CDOs	asset backed security collateralized debt obligation (financial derivative)
ADB	African Development Bank
AGRA	Alliance for a Green Revolution in Africa
AIDC	Alternative Information and Development Centre (South Africa)
ANC	African National Congress, South Africa
ANT	actor-network theory
ARC	African Risk Capacity
AT	algorithmic trading
AUC	African Union Commission
BBC	British Broadcasting Corporation, UK
BOP	Back of Port (expansion plan), Durban, South Africa
BRICS	Brazil, Russia, India, China, South Africa (country group)
CBI	Climate Bond Initiative, UK
CBO	Congressional Budget Office, USA
CCRIF	Caribbean Catastrophe Risk Insurance Facility
CDC	Commonwealth Development Corporation, UK
CDM	Clean Development Mechanism (of the UNFCCC)
CDO	collateralized debt obligation (financial derivative)
CERs	certified emission reductions
CFTC	Commodity Futures Trading Commission, USA
COP	Conference of the Parties (to the 1992 United Nations Framework Convention on Climate Change)
CSOs	civil society organisations
DFI	development finance institution
DfID	Department for International Development, UK
EAME	Europe, Africa and Middle East (region)
ECN	electronic communication network (s)
EIA	environmental impact assessment
EIOPA	European Insurance and Occupational Pensions Authority
EOB	electronic order book
ETC	exchange-traded commodities

ETF	exchange-traded fund (s)
ETN	exchange-traded note (s)
ETP	exchange-traded product (s)
EU-ETS	European Union emissions trading system
FBI	Federal Bureau of Investigation, USA
FSA	Financial Services Authority, UK
FSB	Financial Stability Board
GCF	Green Climate Fund
GFI	Global Financial Integrity
GM	genetically modified
HFT	high frequency trading
HFTs	high frequency traders
HNWI	high net worth individuals
IAM	integrated assessment model (s)
IBRD	International Bank for Reconstruction and Development (World Bank)
ICSID	International Centre for Settlement of Investment Disputes
ICSU	International Council for Science (formally International Council of Scientific Unions)
IFC	International Finance Corporation
IFFs	illicit financial flows
IFI	International Financial Institution
IIAG	Ibrahim Index of African Governance
IISD	International Institute for Sustainable Development
ILS	insurance-linked security (ies)
IMF	International Monetary Fund
IOSCO	International Organisation of Securities Commissions
IPCC	Intergovernmental Panel on Climate Change
KZN	KwaZulu-Natal, South Africa (province)
LCSV	Leverhulme Centre for the Study of Value, UK
MEC	Member of the Executive Council, South Africa
NAO	National Audit Office, UK
NGO	non-governmental organization
NMS	National Market System, USA
NSSF	National Social Security Fund, Uganda
NYSE	New York stock exchange
ODA	official development assistance
OECD	Organisation of Economic Co-operation and Development
PEPs	politically exposed persons
PPA	power purchase agreement
PPP	public-private partnership (s)
RE IPPPP	Renewable Energy Independent Power Producer Procurement Programme, South Africa
REDD +	Reducing Emissions from Deforestation and forest Degradation (United Nations)

SDCEA	South Durban Community Environmental Alliance
SEC	Securities and Exchange Commission (USA)
SIBs	systemically important banks
SIPs	Special Infrastructure projects, South Africa
SNALT	socially necessary abstract labour time
SPV	special purpose vehicle (company form)
TITF	'too important to fail' (banks)
TJN	tax justice network
UK	United Kingdom
UNCTAD	United Nations Conference on Trade and Development
UNECA	United Nations Economic Commission for Africa
UNEP	United Nations Environment Programme
UNESCO	United Nations Educational, Scientific and Cultural Organization
UNFCCC	United Nations Framework Convention on Climate Change
WFE	World Federation of Exchanges
XCF	Extreme Climate Facility, Africa

Preface

There were times in the writing of this book when I thought it was only a fictitious commodity, such was the disjoint between the labour required and time available. Real constraints emerged from my life world and the realisation problem was personalised! I thought the book may never exist as a real commodity. But when some people bought it on Amazon I realised I had speculative investors prepared to gamble on my futures position. It spurred me on. I have only gratitude toward my institutional investors at Routledge for their patient capital and contractual flexibility.

I am grateful to the Centre for Civil Society at the University of KwaZulu-Natal for hosting me as a visiting scholar in 2013, during the early part of this work. Also, I am grateful to the Government of the Republic of South Africa for my current Department of Science and Technology funded, National Research Foundation, SARCHi Chair at the University of KwaZulu-Natal. Much of the middle section of the book was completed with generous funding from the Leverhulme Trust, grant RP2012-V-041, entitled Human, non-human and environmental value systems: an impossible frontier? Also, I'd like to thank the Michelsen Institute, Ankor in Norad, SIDA, Trust Africa, and the Southern Africa Trust for variously funding projects and papers which acted as early catalysts or precursors to sections on illicit financial flows, corruption and secrecy jurisdictions.

I would particularly like to thank my colleagues at the Universities of Manchester and KwaZulu-Natal for their constant inspiration, in particular, Dan Brockington, Admos Chimhowu, Philip Woodhouse, Noel Castree, John O'Neill, Tim Jacoby, Aurora Fredriksen, Jonas Bruun, Robbie Watt, Elisa Greco, Fortunate Machingura, Tanja Müller, Tanja Bastia, Anthony Bebbington, Ralitza Dimova, Tomas Frederiksen, Farhad Hossain, Uma Kothari, David Lawson, Beverly Metcalfe, Sharon Morgan, Diana Mitlin, Japhy Wilson, Louise Carver, Kathleen Diga, Stephen Olivier, Glen Robbins, Myriam Velia, Mvuselelo Ngcoya, Siyabonga Ntombela, Thobile Lombo, Mbali Mthembu, Keke Lelethu, Vee Govender, Precious Shezi, Nduta Mbarathi, Ayanda Tshabalala, Mandy Lombo, Nduta Muita, Francie Lund, Cathy Sutherland, Heidi Attwood, Oliver Matapuri and other colleagues from the Leverhulme Centre for the Study of Value, Jim Igoe, Sian Sullivan, Patrick Bond and further afield, but too many to mention, such as Nick Hildyard, Larry Lohmann, Michael K. Dorsey, Oscar

Reyes, Quincy Saul, Amanda Hammar, Anna Zalik, Khadija Sharife, Russell Haggar, Ray Bush, Morris Szeftel, Claire Mercer, Alex Beresford, Jörg Wiegratz, Stefan Ouma, Patrick Bigger, Leigh Johnson, George Harrison, André Standing, Fredrik Eriksson, Barry Winter, Andy Wood, Katia Neves, Lloyd Sachikonye, Joy Mabenge, Freedom Mazwi, Briggs Bomba, Bram Büscher, Ashwin Desai, Ben Cousins, David Neves, David Moore and the late Lionel Cliffe.

1 Introduction

> It would be the same for the children. They would grow up accustomed to senseless cycles … to efforts that could only end up placing them at other people's starting points, to the damning knowledge that the race would always be won by men on stilts, and they had not even been given crutches to help them.
>
> (Armah 1968: 118–119)

A colleague of mine, who is a Marxist political economist, sometimes jokes that he has predicted 15 of the last 9 over-accumulation crises of capitalism. In the joke, the numbers are not important, but the first has to be bigger than the second, and it points to the imprecision of Marxist theory. Indeed, it often appears from this perspective that crisis is ubiquitous, but the crashes that trigger it cannot be forecast, and that the designation of "crisis" proves not so helpful in explaining what is happening and when. Meanwhile, the famous joke about the traditional economist on the desert island who needs to open a can of beans to stay alive, and responds with a "let's assume it's open" piles mirth on mainstream economics and the assumptions behind the models of free and open economies. Neither tradition does well at predicting economic change or the timing of the next crash, and neither is responding well to the need to re-join economics with ecology, climate change and sustainability if we are to survive a warming globe. This book aims, somewhat humbly, to improve this situation slightly by focussing specifically on the financialisation of late capitalism, understood most broadly as the increasing power of the owners of money in the management of economic affairs.

A crisis of red and green

From August 2007 the credit crunch "led to a virtual meltdown of the global financial system and plunged the so-called 'real economy' into an ongoing recession" (Castree 2010c: 185–6). Castree argues that this caused the "coincident" "first" and "second" contradictions of capital to manifest themselves "simultaneously and on a planetary scale" (ibid.: 186). These first and second were identified by O'Connor (1998) as found in the economic over-accumulation tendencies of capital, and the limits of finite resources respectively. Increasing numbers of commentators are now concurring that capitalism, in O'Connor's terms, is facing chronic difficulties in generating its own "conditions of production", due to the finite nature of the biophysical world, and the fact that human economic processes cannot make this universe again (ibid.). Oddly, the crisis has been so protracted that many in the establishment have concurred, such as Andrew Sheng of the China Banking Regulatory Commission and Qatar Financial Centre Regulatory Authority, who wrote in 2009: "the present fiscal trend of rising expenditure and tax cuts to rebuild excess consumption funded by excess leverage, despite limited global resources, is just a race to another crisis" (Sheng 2009: 2). He goes on to argue that in a world of "free capital flows" (associated in this book with "financialisation") "the world is caught in a collective action trap … a global economy without global monetary policy, global financial regulation or a global fiscal system" (ibid.). In short, a world in which the much spoken of "limits to capital" (Harvey 1982), and "limits of Nature" (United Nations Environment Programme (UNEP), 2011) have simultaneously come to a head, threatening the liberal state and a global sustainable future.

However, traditional political economy is only slowly adjusting to the need to theorise holistically across the social and natural science divide, or colloquially across the "red" and "green" agendas. These re-engagements come after a sustained period in which cultural theorists, anthropologists and sociologists have been insisting on a more fluid, less predetermined, and less human-centred theory of agency (Law 1999; Latour 2005: 71; Deleuze and Guattari 1987). The call has been for a "new ontology of the social" (Latour 1999), where predetermined causation gives way to "practices in action rather than settled states" (Fredriksen and Sullivan 2014: 5). Less human-centred implies accepting that non-humans and nature also have agency, rather than that they can be effectively externalised outside capitalist accumulation. As Lohmann summarises

> while the ideal-type capitalist logic explored by Marx involves perpetual, competition-driven attempts to dynamite material "roadblocks" along capital's magical route from investment to payoff, an inevitable "revenge of the finite" highlights capital's own ultimate dependencies on natures that cannot be conceived of as "external".
>
> (Lohmann 2016: 54)

Capitalism advanced through a commodity fetishism that assigned an inanimate state, first to objects and then "Nature" (Nancy 2001: 4; citing Marx 1975: 189). This constituted a "removal of subjectivity and intentionality from nonhuman entities … [in] an historically embedded discursive move that facilitated the creation of a scientifically knowable, exploitable and tradable world of objects" (Sullivan 2014: 26). An attempt to reverse the "Capitalist animism" (Taussig 1987) in which agency was assigned to capital, capitalism and markets has also recently met resistance from theorists of a "post-capitalist animism" (see Holert 2012; also Nancy 2001; Jones 2013; Sullivan 2013a; discussion in Sullivan 2014).

Thus, as the actual global economy is stuttering and choking through 30 years of bubbles and bursts, traditional political economy has struggled to explain social and ecological change beyond the economic dogmas of inevitable crisis and instability. Arguably, this is due to the historical influence of dualism, abstractions, externalities and the legacy of Cartesian and Euclideanism thought. Castree, for example, recounts the history of crisis from the Asian economic meltdown of the late 1990s, the collapse of Long-Term Capital Management in 1998, the demise of Barings Bank, the dot.com bubble and the Argentinian meltdown of the early 2000s as "a long period in which neoliberal policymakers have been seeking to manage ... the chronic over-accumulation tendencies of the capitalist mode of production" (2010c: 189), a "serially rechanneled and diverted" period of crisis dated from the early 1970s, but "entraining ever more peoples and territories" (ibid.: 190; citing Harvey, 1982 and Brenner 2006). It is in this context in which this book has been written. But beyond this "deep" theory, has much of use been said about how to change political economy and political ecology to account for the number of humans, non-humans and nature realms jostling to survive in fragile circumstances? Meanwhile, mainstream economics remains stubbornly insistent that the externalities it doesn't see, the overflows of graphs and models should not matter; yet this is the very life-world in which the rest of us live and hope to prosper.

The purpose here is to deconstruct what "financialisation" means to the challenges of wellbeing, including beyond humans, in the short and longer terms. The effects of the financial crash of 2007–8 are still with us, not just in depressed growth, but in terms of outstanding questions about the configuration of global power. How far are financiers in control of our lives, and in what ways do decisions about finance and investment affect the quality of everyday life? Governments around the world spent hundreds of billions of pounds bailing out banks during the financial crisis of 2007–8. For example, in the United Kingdom alone, taxpayers' direct subsidy was more than £1 trillion (National Audit Office 2011). By the end of 2014, the UK government was still committed to more than £926bn of financial support, a figure that doesn't include the £375bn of money printed and given to banks to ease liquidity constraints (Sikka 2014). Meanwhile in the USA, the government provided US$700 billion to subsidise the banks whose excessive lending had caused the crisis (Congressional Budget Office (CBO) 2013). The legacy is that, with only the aggregate 'European Union' at number 1; the United States and United Kingdom lead the world ranking of total external debt (public and private together) in second and third position, owing US$15.68 trillion (2012 est.) and US$9.58 trillion (2013 est.) respectively (CIA Factbook 2014). While the picture for total public debt as a percentage of GDP is slightly rosier, putting the USA at 71.8 per cent (ranked 36th) and UK at 91.1 per cent (ranked 20th), nonetheless, the countries' liabilities remain significant (CIA Factfile 2014).

The legacy of the biggest gifting to the private sector from ordinary citizens in history is twofold: that the structural relationship between government and banks continues as one of subsidy to this day (Herbst 2013; IMF 2014). Bloomberg News recently calculated that in the USA, taxpayers continue to subsidise banks by US$83bn each year (2013). The National Audit Office (UK), conservatively estimate that the cost of government borrowing of the loans supplied to the financial sector costs £5bn annually, and totalled £20bn to 31st March 2013;

while the shares in Royal Bank of Scotland and Lloyds (directly bailed out) were purchased for £66bn, but were only worth £38bn by 31 March 2013, a total decrease in value of £28bn (National Audit Office (NAO) 2014). The second legacy is that a problem of private sector debt in 2007 had by 2010 been structurally, if not magically, transformed into a problem of sovereign debt in Europe and America (McBride and Merolli 2013), representing the biggest, and least reflected on, heist in capitalist history (see Beetham 2011). Yet where is the public outcry?

By the end of 2014, six years after the crash, the Financial Stability Board (FSB) had developed a list of 30 "systemically important banks" but were still in the process of designing regulation to avoid public bailout of banks deemed "too big to fail". At the time of writing regulators are proposing that banks hold minimum capital of 6 per cent of total assets against losses, a proportion twice the provisional leverage ratio required by Basel III rules. Also the FSB is proposing that banks be required to have capital equal to at least 16 per cent and as much as 20 per cent of their risk-weighted assets, such as loans (FSB 2014; Heller 2014), although part of this could be borrowed (Ewing 2014). It has been estimated that the new capital requirements will cost European banks about US$250bn (BBC News 2014). However, the banking sector has been powerful enough to head off measures designed to curb their profits, excessive remuneration and high costs to lenders in the years 2008–14, and new regulations are already being met with dire warnings of their effects on growth and recovery. Indeed, the very concept of "systemically important" banks ironically enhances their power, as it tacitly accepts the ability of bank failure to be represented as a problem for the taxpayer to solve. Even the IMF has warned of the continuing moral hazard of the creation of the concepts of "too-important-to-fail (TITF) banks" and "systemically important banks (SIBs)" who continue to claim subsidy framed against the idea that if they fail it would be a crisis for us all (IMF 2014). The ability to threaten collapse and disaster is a key mechanism of the power of finance structurally, and is used alongside ideas of the "much-neededness" of foreign direct investment, and the "there is no alternative" tropes of necessary neo-liberalism (Hay 2004; Castree 2006, 2009). It is these ideas that have surprisingly stayed so salient, despite the financial legacies of the crisis, illustrating the surprisingly firm hold that "neoclassical anthropology" or "anthropologics" (Callon 2005: 10; see also Miller, 1998; 2002) – ways of being and doing, which embed a free market order – have on our global discourse to date.

This book is set in the context of the legacy of these events, and the consequential effects for the global poor, not primarily in Europe, but in Africa, where collapses in liquidity in the global Westphalian banking system and overseas development budgets have transformed sovereign lending patterns towards new "BRICS" lenders: China, India, and to a lesser extent Brazil, Russia and creditors from the Middle East (Bond 2014a). But the effects of the crisis are not just empirical and reflected in a new spread of lenders. The most significant consequence is arguably that at a point of crisis in the ideological dominance of private finance and privatised economic accumulation, the global status quo met such a weak resistance, even in the powerful economies of the capitalist core. If billions could be found so suddenly for the largest banks, why were the narratives and mechanisms which frame the "necessary" management of austerity for the global poor left so undisturbed? After all, OECD official development assistance (ODA) remains a miserly US$134.8bn in 2013 (OECD 2014), in comparison with a loss of over US$1.2 trillion in illicit financial flows (IFFs) annually up to 2012, (Kar and Freitas 2012), with over half draining from developing and transitional economies, 90 per cent of which is estimated to constitute a permanent outward transfer (Baker 2005). The answer to the resilience of these iniquitous structures derivative of global neo-liberalism is profoundly constituted in structures of power and inequality.

The consequence of understanding the crisis structurally is that this is unlikely to be a unique event that is unlikely to re-occur, but the product of a wider malaise where financiers have effectively usurped the power of governments and continue to over-determine the rules in the political economy themselves (see Beetham 2011 on the UK). There are likely to be further and larger fiscal "adjustments'"to condition global power structures and patterns of inequality in the near future (Crotty 2009; Goodchild 2012). For Africa, and the least developed countries, which have a particular dependence on international money (Bracking 2009a), the implications of these structural features of a financialised global political economy impact critically and substantively on the lives and very survival of the poor and adversely incorporated. Yet, there is arguably little in mainstream development economics that is of help here, since the axioms and didactic reasoning of "state and economy" and "public and private" remain undisturbed, despite the bluntness of these conceptualisations to designing real structural change. The doxa of the beneficial and unavoidable role of "openness", causing inflows of "much-needed" foreign direct investment (FDI) and job creation remains at the core of Bretton Woods practise, despite problems of empirical verification (Hay 2004). In the past few years this has been joined by a new self-help of resilience to poverty and climate change, which reads as if the ideal neo-liberal subject is the poor person who stays in place and learns to manage their own poverty.

The political economies of Africa

The nature of growth in Africa from 2000 onward has intensified inequality and increased the numbers living in poverty (even if the proportion living in poverty declined slightly) (Graham 2012). High measures of wealth inequality prevail across Africa with 7 African countries registering GINI coefficient scores in the world's worst "top 20" (World Bank 2015). There has been a reversal back to the production structure of the colonial period following substantial deindustrialization from 1990 to 2008, with UNCTAD showing that "the share of manufacturing in Africa's gross domestic product (GDP) fell from 15 per cent in 1990 to 10 per cent in 2008 … and in Southern Africa it fell from 23 to 18 per cent" (Graham 2012: 3; citing UNCTAD 2012). This return to reliance on natural resource exports as opposed to value-added manufactures has stymied economic development and job creation. There is also much evidence that the political economy that results from over-reliance on the extractives sector has negative effects on the quality of governance, democratic accountability and the fiscal base (UNECA and African Union Commission (AUC) 2012b: 25–28).

Financialisation and the offshore economy have facilitated a huge growth in inequality in many African states, with the social orders of Africa growing a "1%" elite class as a consequence. A surprising number of African countries are among the most unequal in the world by Gini coefficient. Seychelles, South Africa, Comoros, Namibia, Botswana, Angola, Central African Republic and Zambia stand (in descending order) as 8 of the top 10 most unequal countries in the world by the World Bank's estimates of Gini coefficient (World Bank 2015). This new elite are versed in the logics of institutionalised graft normalised and legalised through modern financial institutions and vehicles. It is not so much that the 1 per cent can be termed endemically corrupt, although many commentators do so, but that a rapid process of elite formation and wealth accumulation has been facilitated by changes in the global economy in the post-independence era. This new elite has not been passive in this either, as evidence shows how the liberation parties and new one-party states grew their own offshore wealth from the struggle period. For example, the dominant political parties of Angola (Movimento Popular de Libertação de Angola (MPLA)), Zimbabwe (African National Union – Patriotic Front (ZANU-PF)), Botswana (Democratic Party (BDP)) and Namibia (South West Africa People's Organization (SWAPO)) as well as Equatorial Guinea's Obiang dynasty all have corporatised financial structures offshore. In the minerals sector, the dominant parties draw revenue from key strategic partnerships with resource-seeking multinationals – for example, Namibia's Namdeb (with De Beers), Angola's China Sonangol (with China International Fund), Botswana's Debswana (with De Beers) and Zimbabwe's Anjin (with China Anhui); as well as international oil companies invested in Angola and Equatorial Guinea.

The financial structures of ruling regimes consist of a web of firms based in secrecy jurisdictions, but often built with the help of major formal sector banks. For example, Angola's ruling elite has over 200 offshore entities relating to oil and diamonds (Sharife and Grobler 2013), and has assisted Zimbabwe's ZANU-PF to build a similar structure, where ZANU-PF is connected to the Angolan Dos Santos regime through the pursuit of rigged elections (Sharife 2013b) and via aviation secrecy (Sharife 2013a). Meanwhile, in Namibia SWAPO began in the 1960s to set up an offshore structure which led to Jobo Holdings being created at the Banque de Luxembourg. Sharife has investigated this structure and points to the importance of "specialised discretionary units such as the 'Family Office' of the CFG Compagnie Financière de Gestion, part of the Banque de Luxembourg… In 2008, Jobo's assets were sold to clients within the CFG. The company was created elsewhere in Switzerland, and administered by fiduciary trustees, whose CEO, Swiss financial lawyer Maxime Bossy, owns the shares on behalf of a hidden owner" (Sharife 2015). Not satisfied with just one tax haven, however, another conglomerate, Namibia Finance was set up in Curaçao in 1990 – a tax haven belonging to the Netherlands – then shifted to Funchal, Madeira, Portugal's tax haven in 1997, allegedly with the assistance of the Angolan elite. This offshore storage comprises over 100 entities of Namibian mining trading companies at Banif Bank alone, and 2178 companies with "African roots" registered by Madeira's fiduciary trusts.[1]

This offshore economy is facilitated by tax havens and special supranational licence. It can be called dominant in the political economy of Africa in two senses: because of the decision-making powers held by holders of wealth who are based offshore, and due to sheer scale of funds. For example, in 2007 foreign direct investment net inflows globally were US$2.446 trillion, a figure that dropped to US$1.288 trillion in 2009, and recovered to US$1.747 trillion in 2013 (World Bank 2014a). By contrast, a major study found that in 2010 the global super-rich had at least US$21 trillion stored in tax havens, a figure equivalent to the size of the US and Japanese economies combined (Henry 2012).

Thus the need for a continent-wide re-theorisation of the political economy of democratisation is now more critical than ever, given this structural ascendance of finance capital and a group of hegemonic financiers and political elites at the core of Africa's political economy. Joined inexorably to security chiefs within de facto juntas in the executive arm of government, which itself often resembles an imperial presidency, the number of African states facing stolen elections and drops in the quality of governance has grown alongside the role of finance in the management of the economy. For example, the Ibrahim Index of African Governance (IIAG) indicators for 2014 report that the category showing most deterioration (of four in total) within the overall index is "safety and the rule of law", and within that "accountability" is the sub-category showing most deterioration (of a total of 14) (IIAG 2014: 3–6). In the five years to 2014, the IIAG claim that while 25 African countries have improved safety and the rule of law, a larger number, 27, have been measured to have declined in performance in this area, contributing to a second consecutive five-year drop in governance quality in this category for the continent as a whole (8, 17). This includes deterioration in "safety and the rule of law" in three of the top 5 governance performers overall: in Mauritius, South Africa and the Seychelles (with Cape Verde and Botswana the other two of the top five) (12).

Bracking (2005) on the Zimbabwe 2005 elections and Adebanwi and Obadare (2011) more broadly, have pointed to a pattern in which the form of democracy is brazenly used to invalidate its very substance, as in the effective coups following lost elections in Zimbabwe in 2008 and Kenya in 2007. The election in Nigeria in 2007 was also widely criticised (Kerr 2011), although criticism of Museveni's re-election in Uganda in 2011, that ascribed the win to vote-buying and massive pre-election spending on public goods, must be countered by evidence that voters were un-impressed with the opposition slate and satisfaction with macroeconomic growth (Conroy-Krutz and Logan 2011). Meanwhile, a culture of impunity prevailed after the extreme election and post-election violence in Ivory Coast and Mali in 2012 and 2013. Even in Ghana, where relatively high governance quality is perceived, low transparency at the Electoral Commission has led to accusations of rigging after every election since 2000 (Parku 2014). However, despite problems in the results management process spurring claims of rigging, the 2014 Malawian elections were judged largely free and fair, and without significant violence (AUC 2014), while in 2011 in Zambia, it was proved again (the first time being in 1991) that a defeated president (Banda, after just one term) and party (the Movement for Multi-Party Democracy, after twenty years) could leave peacefully once defeated in an election (Iqbal 2011).

Thus democratic processes are varied across the continent, but with a pattern of deeply embedded "party-states" in many of the minerals extractive economies. These national political elites are those most likely to refuse to give up sovereign power and the spoils politics that it enables, even when not fairly elected, and enjoy participation and joint ownership with large corporates in the parallel offshore economy. Their sovereign prerogatives, which enable them to build up sovereign debt and dispose of sovereign assets (Pogge 2002), including minerals, water and now various new green commodities in carbon trading, are commodified to an equity fund in exchange for equity shares, and a place on the invisible board of the special purpose vehicle. Similarly, in a post-crisis bubble, sovereign investments such as infrastructure projects pursued by public private partnerships, are being used to amass further elite wealth. In these, government funds in infrastructure in its many forms provide the means to leverage private capital and generate tenders for those connected to the party state at all levels of government (Hildyard 2016).

Increasingly the economic case for an infrastructural build – traditionally made with projections for growth, employment creation or industrial policy – while still in the narrative, often appear secondary to considerations of the benefits to be enjoyed by the construction companies and contractors. The beneficiaries in this case do not appear as the "public" but as those persons winning the procurement bids. These large build projects are also often accompanied by a rhetoric of national and African pride, notions of bigness and display that again displace both the cost to the public and the financial rewards to be made from the politically connected contractors, financial advisors, fund managers, banks and the infrastructural fund of funds, inevitably offshore, who can profit hugely from building the infrastructure that the multilateral banks – such as the World Bank and IFC – are determined are needed. The economic proof for the role that big projects can play in development, and the growth expected from them is often thin in the publications in which the "infrastructure gap" is espoused, and "assistance" is offered (Bayliss 2009). What is clear however, is that infrastructure can be extremely profitable when structured as "contracted cash flow" with private equity funds often returning between 20 and 25 per cent profits and often more (Hildyard 2016: 36). The data on secondary sales of completed public-private partnership (PPP) project companies shows an average rate of return of 29 per cent between 1998 and 2012 (Whitfield 2014: 5). Hildyard calculates that "$296 billion is extracted every year through 'infrastructure' – over twice as much as the $100.7 billion directly invested by the private sector in actual projects" (2016: 40).

Meanwhile, the poor and socially excluded are left to suffer the non-delivery of public services, and developmental self-help remodelled as 'resilience', 'adaptation' and micro-credit in the shell of the sovereign space. It is the intimate connection between finance, finance capital, money and the commodification of power that this book explores, simultaneously explaining why democratisation in Africa is just so hard to achieve, against a political economy that throws up intractable odds, only seen elsewhere in similarly extractive, often minerals based political economies such as in North Africa and the Middle East, Burma, Saudi Arabia, Russia, China (but of a different political type), Pakistan and the central Caucasus.

The contribution of the book

This book is an effort at critical realism and empiricism designed to sharpen our understanding and awareness of the diminished possibilities and political space into which the financialised global order has entangled civil society and workers. In particular, it concentrates on Africa's global political economy, not from a purely economic point of view, but from the perspective of the political economy of the modern state, and the logics of governmentality that run from it and through it. It asks which of the prerogatives of sovereignty have been eroded, in what way, and how they could be restored and improved on. It also asks what modern sovereignty has made anew and in response to a financialised global economy; how the political economy of development works in relation to African governance. It is a book in the tradition of Foucault that uses concepts of governmentality as logics that condition people in place and time to have available to them only certain possibilities and logics, unless a rupture can be designed.

Nonetheless, the book introduces a number of key concepts that the author has theorised, including "portals of exception" to the canopy of the modern state, where established practise has developed means for the wealthy to avoid public regulation. There is a particular focus on the parallel offshore economy rather than the nation-state authored economic spaces. We will explore "new forms of corruption" jurisdiction shopping, asset grabbing, informality and the role of negotiated, rather than normalised, practises in the ways that firms operate (Bracking 2013a). Portals of exception work vertically to move wealth in a parallel political economy to the measured and the partially regulated spaces of the inter-state system. The work also discusses "spacial political sinks" (Bracking 2007: 15), which provide a context for exceptionalisms to occur, as these latter are socially constructed places and spaces in which all is assumed to be deficient, thus allowing democratic governance to be arrested. These are the borderlands (Duffield 2001) in which biopolitics has subsumed liberalisms and trodden them under foot. The book asks key questions for an African response to a political economy of exception: what has been the political price to the arrest of ongoing processes of democratisation? With global governance norms in effective suspension in many African states, what are the consequences for the poor of participation in a rigged political economy game, where an exceptional right of the wealthy to exploit the poor is remade at every turn, often in the name of development?

The book theorises the later stages of global neoliberalism as a process of privatisation, informalisation and criminalisation of economic regulation and economic rights. It argues that the exceptions provided for by 30 years of neoliberalism have enabled a financialisation of the political economy of Africa. This financialisation has empowered money to become the principle means to exchange and express power, not just by facilitating the exchange of commodities, but by symbolically usurping and calibrating different contexts for people's sovereign citizenship (see Ong 2006). Democracies have been increasingly priced against the needs of international traders, mineral corporations and rapacious elites. Saul famously argues that the ubiquity of the liberal perspective led to a "narrowing of the terms" of the discussion on democracy in Africa, since the hegemonic "political science of democratization" had undermined the essential "political economy of democratization" (1997: 340). Here it is argued that the political economy is not synergistic with the building of democracy – economic and political liberalism are not twins in harmony – but instead economic liberalism conditions against a democratic liberal form. Moreover, democratisation in Africa is a struggle unique to Africa, given the financialised economy and class and social orders that an adverse political economy context has historically built.

Some recent work on democratisation has taken up the challenge dropped by Saul and attempts to use political economy as the conditioning context in which democratisation processes can be theorised. For example, Amy Chua assigns a core importance to political economy in terms of its overall ramifications on the state form and the prospects for democratisation (Chua 2004). A batch of authors, alongside Chua, have taken the evidence of stolen elections to argue that relying on elections at the early stages of democratisation is an error, and that democracies need to mature to manage the power struggles that arise as a consequence of electoral processes (see also Branch and Cheeseman 2008). They term this the "sequencing problem" and yet this linearity forgets that many African countries have had elections in the past with little problem or consequential conflict. The "sequencing problem" remains trapped in a linearity which uncomfortably reverberates with early modernisation work, as in the early American work on the political development of a "backward" Africa (Huntington 1968; Binder *et al.*, 1971). As Carothers (2007) rightly points out, the sequencing problem is misplaced, since there is not a more humane alternative to be found in politics, and nor should processes of democratisation and popular sovereignty be suspended so lightly. Instead, the wider context of why powerful agents seek election theft as a strategic choice must be understood: here it is suggested that it is recent processes of financialisation coupled with the increase in inequality it has wrought that have created the space for elites to be unaccountable, and to seek to hang on to power through a credible threat of violence as has happened in Zimbabwe (2005, 2008 at least), Nigeria (2007) and Kenya (2008) (Bracking 2010), when electoral defeat beckons.

Thus setting aside a sequencing problem, this book draws on the foundational work of Saul (1997) and Ake (1996) on the importance of the political economy of power. It argues further that economic neo-liberalism has undermined the associated discourse and practise of its sibling, political neo-liberalism, to an extent that the resurgence of other non-liberal governance logics, such as authoritarianism and militarism (exercised by juntas hidden just behind liberal democratic shell states), pose a threat to African people's gains from liberation. Indeed, the political economy of economic neo-liberalism is serving to undermine even the narrow "political science of democratisation" giving rise to arbitrary government, non-liberal forms and a resuscitated biopolitics (Mbembe 2003; Murray 2006). Due to the "commercialisation of sovereignty" elites have fought for "the right to make the law" and then to use it for commercial benefit (Palan 2002). Elites have managed to capture parts of a fragmented and liberalised state structure and commercialise the spoils that arise. Often able to run a parallel bureaucratic Weberian structure alongside the captured political economy of the commercialised state, elites are then particularly resistant to leaving the sites of accumulation that they have built.

Beyond neo-liberalism

Commodification, and "generalised commodity production" as Marxian concepts have been successfully used to theorise the frontiers of the capitalist economy, as people and the non-human world have been drawn in to the orbit of capitalist valorisation over the last 500 years (Chomsky 1993). This book reviews this literature and applies it to the last human frontiers: ecology, rights, obligations and solidarity, to explore how the capitalist valuation system has been extended to generate logics of governance within the political systems of the most vulnerable. It has become an established axiom of geopolitics, that international relations reflect nation states as having different statuses, such that dictators will be deposed by external force in places where there is valuable oil or mineral reserves, but international "help" is less likely where there is not. This book develops the themes of financialised political rights, including how these apply within democracies in their variegated, differentiated and everyday forms. It draws on the seminal work of Foucault (1979), Mbembe (2003) and Li (2010) on exceptions to sovereignty justified by governance logics of the allowability of death in the management of surplus populations. What are the particular governance logics and mechanisms used in justification and explanation for the exclusion of millions from effective political life and the sustenance of biological life? How does money come to represent a rarefied mediator of such distinctions, socialising inequality as an apparently just outcome? In this regard, the book will also explore the cultural representations of money as a social regulator and moderator of life chances.

The frontiers of the global political economy as conceptualised here as zones in which commodification is attempting the temporal, spacial (Harvey 1982) and asset expropriation or "stealing" fixes to ameliorate crisis that were first theorised by Harvey (Harvey 2003). But arguably financialisation has entrained a fourth "fix", in the increasing commodification of the virtual and performative (Callon 2007; MacDonald 2008), found in products that denote "care" or "concern" (Bracking 2012a; 2015a), which may be non-material, performative or merely connote spectacle (Igoe 2010; 2013a; 2013b). This proposition draws on the critical geographers' work on the care economy (Mauss 1924; Ahluwalia 2010; Rabbitts 2012; Korf 2007), but also on critical work in conservation and performativity (Büscher 2012; Bracking 2015c). These frontiers, or "edges" of political economy are composed of spaces and things, including aspects of disaggregated and transformed ecology that can be seen and transferred into a commodity form, and this has taken many new forms since the onset of neo-liberalism since the early 1980s, rising particularly rapidly from 2008 onward.

Meanwhile the present is increasingly subject to these processes of expanded commodification: biological patenting, genetic patenting and expropriation (Thompson 2014; Morvaridi 2012) carbon trading, carbon offsetting, biodiversity bonds and the creation of other related nature-based "products" (Holmes 2012; Carver 2015), leading some to argue that we are witnessing a "financialisation of nature" (Sullivan 2014) or even a new type of accumulation catalysed by nature-based products (Holmes 2012; Igoe and Brockington 2007; Igoe *et al.* 2010; Arsel and Büscher 2012; Büscher 2014). New frontiers of the biological are being established, alongside increasingly virtual representations of value in the incessant development of derivatives, CDOs, SPVs, ABS CDOs,[2] and various other imaginative accounting practices in the offshore risk and liability balance sheets of firms. That the value of assets, production, environment and people are increasingly arbitrary and politically negotiated is one central feature of the "financialisation of everything" (Harvey 2005: 24), and here, particularly in Chapter 4, we explore the various genres, fixes and mathematical entrapments to which the real economy has been subjected.

But of particular interest to contemporary theorisation is the meaning and configuration of the relationship between the "real" asset or thing, and the derivative value, income or representation of it (Büscher and Igoe 2013; Sullivan *et al.* 2013; Bracking *et al.* 2014). For example, the underlying "assets" of the financialised global economy and their highly leveraged and securitised derivative income streams may have not merely a distal relationship, but maybe not one at all. For example, in the carbon economy assets can be modifications in factories, or a promise not to build a new dirty facility, while the derivative income from these, or their non-existence, is found in tradable "certified emissions reductions", under the Clean Development Mechanism (CDM). Meanwhile, an "infrastructural asset" could just be a business model or asset-stripping strategy applied by a management service fund or fund group to raid pensions and retrench workers. But as long as the firm emerges as owning an asset with a legally guaranteed derivative income stream the asset is "real". But with so much opacity surrounding the quality or even existence of the fixed asset, how can carbon traders manage risk? Or put conversely, is there a need for this level of opacity in order to generate this type of speculative activity? (Bracking 2015).

It might be, as Büscher argues in relation to nature conserved in place, that not exploiting something, although that does not imply it is not changed or transformed in some other way, can be the basis of value creation. Not in the sense of traditional Marxist value created only from surplus labour and production, but either from value beneficiated in processes of circulation (Büscher 2013), or from singularly virtual valuation processes. For example, Derrida's work on the role of images, pointed to value arising merely in the evocation of emotion, or the performance or spectacle created by an enactment or assemblage of people and things, including electronically (Igoe 2010; Igoe 2013b). The carbon market could be an example of this due to the non-exploitation in place of "conserved nature" and/or the opacity surrounding the actual "fixed assets". The act of creating a biodiversity offset or carbon sequestration project can mean little more than designating it as such, normally by an expert, "donor", consultant in an assemblage with local elites and transnational conservation NGOs. Derivative values or tradable carbon reductions are arguably prosecuting a performance of "care" conjured from the guilt and concern of others. As Anna Tsing theorised, the "global economy of appearances" requires "dramatic performance … [as] an essential prerequisite of economic performance" (2005: 57). As Tsing (2000: 118; cited in Fredriksen *et al.* 2014: 19–20) elaborates:

> In speculative enterprises, profit must be imagined before it can be extracted; the possibility of economic performance must be conjured like a spirit to draw an audience of potential investors. The more spectacular the conjuring, the more possible an investment frenzy. Drama itself can be worth summoning forth. Nor are companies alone in the conjuring business in these times. In order to attract companies, countries, regions, and towns must dramatize their potential as places for investment. Dramatic performance is the prerequisite of their economic performance.

This conjuring also normally involves a reference to scale (Fredriksen 2014), the local and the global and in development and environment the notion of experts working at scale, the carrier of "international best practise" and unique knowledge (Bracking 2014).

Thus building on the early work on commodification and the insights from governmentality theory, the book argues that a new dimension of accumulation, in the form of the virtual and the spectacle, is being strengthened by processes of financialisation. In other words, (1) financialisation affects the past in that the historical accumulation of capital is financialised and mortgaged in a copyright, royalty and intellectual property regime; (2) the future is also financialised in debt repayment schedules, and even collateralised and securitised in relation to future road tolls and earnings from municipal tax payers raised as funds by their political representatives. For example, Thames Water securitised future income streams from its customers in order to increase dividends to shareholders in 2007 (Allen and Pryke 2013). The securitisation in the mortgage market up to the 2008 crash involved raising capital not for the prime purpose of supplying mortgages for people to buy homes, but to make people borrow in order to securitise that borrowing and make profits from its securitisation (MacKensie 2011). Similarly, financing infrastructure is less about "financing development" than "developing finance" with the profits made on derivatives more significant than those on the fixed assets.

But here two further dimensions of accumulation are conceptualised. That is that, (3) financialisation can make an asset or conjure it into existence in the present. Here we are referring to current genres of financialisation in the social, ecological, infrastructural and environmental domains (MacDonald 2008), found in carbon trading, REDD +, payment for environmental services, environmental offsetting and biodiversity banking and sequestration (Sullivan 2014; Nadal and Aguayo 2014; Holmes 2012; Igoe and Brockington 2007; Igoe *et al.* 2010). They are also reflected in social domains where an asset can be a poor person, on whom derivative income streams can be raised for a savvy NGO calculating 'social impact'. And finally, (4) accumulation can progress with only a fictive or virtual asset in any of the past, present or future. Thus the first three temporal spaces for accumulation are also negotiated in a fourth dimension of the virtual.

The book argues that the commensurability of public policy tropes across varied substantive domains – ecological, social and so forth – is not a mere accident or derivation of hegemonic governance norms, but is derivative of a financialisation of power itself across and between these four dimensions. This financialisation of power is itself facilitated by the empirical everyday of a global economy of exception and opacity. In this, politics and politicians are suffering from the collective "self-denying" ordinance (Hay 2004) that paradigmatic or transformationary change is impossible under neo-liberalism, since markets and private capital will withdraw from spaces of democratic regulation, and leave chaos and crisis in their wake. A culture of exemption and exceptionalism – from tariffs and licenses, infrastructural costs, responsibility for environmental and health externalities has grown in many extractives economies (Ong 2006). The culture of exemption also applies to the expectation of making a fair contribution to taxes, and to an increase in illicit flows which avoid or abuse the spirit of a democratic economy (Sharife 2011; Shaxson 2007; Palan *et al.* 2010). Thus, not only does the macro economy fail to produce sufficient employment and wealth to remove 239 million, or one in four Africans, from chronic hunger (a number rising by 2 per cent a year since 2007) (World Hunger Education Service 2013), but there is a substantively proved philosophical case that it undermines the efforts of Africans to do this for themselves (Pogge 2002, 2005, 2008).

In terms of new infrastructural developments, a culture of exemption has also pervaded institutional forms of investment in the form of different types of public–private partnerships (PPPs). While these exist in various different models, they all share the core stipulation that investors have a level of income stream or profit rate guaranteed by government, thus eliminating their exposure to risk while inflating returns to their inevitable secrecy jurisdiction domiciles (Hildyard 2016). Using clauses such as "financial and economic equilibrium clauses" to protect investors from "adverse" public policy decisions, contracts "lock in profits but also lock out democracy, giving private parties a disproportionate influence (enforceable by the courts) over which laws get passed and which do not … stabilisation clauses privatise policy and the law by establishing a regime of investor rights that effectively bypass, supersede or dismantle public interest legislation, placing investors above governments and citizens" (Hildyard 2016; citing Hildyard and Muttitt 2006). For example, a group of investors sued the Argentinian government for freezing water tariffs and devaluing the Peso in response to an economic crisis, and the Argentinian government was ordered to pay them US$405 million in compensation by the International Centre for Settlement of Investment Disputes (ICSID 2010), after the government lost the argument that international human rights law obliged them to protect their citizen's right to water.

Hildyard shows how infrastructure, for example, seen from the world view of the very rich, is not a pipe, or train or hospital, as it would be in a common sense world, but has been reconfigured into anything that constitutes a secure, contracted derivative income stream (ibid.). A similar construction has come to dominate in the way environmental management has grown into an ecosystem service, or conservation into a species bank or REDD + offset. Indeed, in many domains, whether it be infrastructure, health care, agriculture, conservation or social welfare, power over peoples' lives and the service outcomes they can expect have increasingly become conditioned by decisions taken by owners of finance and the types of intervention and programmes that these capital holders prefer. Invariably these involve securing one or a number of derivative income streams from a fixed asset, while managing poverty and non-human species in situ, when the asset can be protected, or by displacement when it faces a risk of income-earning corrosion. In order for this financialised logic of governmentality to succeed, however, sometimes new orders of biopolitics are required, where the tenets of epistemic liberalism and neo-liberalism are discarded in favour of new forms of authoritarians and bare life. I will return to this theme in the conclusion. For now, we will test the proposition that development has become entrained into a global assemblage of finance, in which nodes of democratically authored power – such as formal bureaucratic nation states – have been marginalised in favour of the types of power held by owners of money and those that aspire to that status. This is the central argument of this book, and I will attempt to build the various aspects of the propositions above in the chapters that follow.

Chapter summaries

Chapter 2 discusses the meaning and application of the concept of financialisation and related terms such as neo-liberalism. It argues that financialisation as a concept works at three different scales: as hegemonic ideology; as practices of governance; and as a catalyst and midwife of exceptions beyond liberalism.

Chapter 3 outlines the empirics of financialisation by accounting for the history of money and finance. The figures indicate empirical support for the Marxian idea that crisis is prompted by successive over-accumulation crises, where investment opportunities drop, and money in circulation rises as a proportion of money being used in productive activities (Harvey 1982; Castree 2010c; Büscher 2013). However, the rate of circulation does not also appear to be rising as the storage function of wealth offshore instead generates evermore oppressive income-earning opportunities from the material fixed assets of the onshore economy.

Chapter 4 argues that within valuation processes, values and the emergent prices are co-produced by institutional arrangements, discourse and calculative technologies, such that the division between the virtual and the material is fuzzy with neither appearing solely without the other.

Chapter 5 explores the frontiers of the global political economy, particularly with reference to ecology and theories of commodification and case studies of the infrastructure and weather derivatives asset classes.

Chapter 6 returns to the formal political, the nation state and the growing politics of exceptionalism that the offshore and virtual political economy are generating. That spaces are imagined has been established by critical geographers, but nonetheless the nation state remains iconic and perennial to explanations of development, underdevelopment, growth and poverty. Why is this so? This explores the exceptions to regulation developed by the international financial elite and local power holders. The modern financial class, their corporate clients and associated political elites are building a class system of opaque privilege where the Marxian notion of the "upper echelons" of economy, the financial boards of productive and manufacturing capital, have domiciled their power and privilege in a zone beyond the state. The result is multiple illicit financial flows and a diminishing of the fiscal base available for development.

Chapter 7 discusses further the "problem" of corruption that is closely related to the social orders that are conditioned by the financialisation of power. This chapter looks at the financialisation of government functions in all tiers of government.

Chapter 8 reviews the arguments made in the book about the utility of the concept of financialisation and argues that the potential for political change in Africa is currently constrained by the economic processes it generates.

Conclusion

The normalisation of neo-liberalism was achieved by the late 1990s, and the emasculation of radical ideologies of democracy, social democracy, communism and African socialism was consequential to this hegemony. However, the decreasing role of the IMF and World Bank in Africa and the increasing role of Chinese, Arab, Indian and Middle Eastern investors has exposed elites to an ideological impasse: how to justify wealth in the face of the immiseration of a generation by the last financial crisis. The answer has been a reversal in the Third Wave and a spate of stolen elections, only partially overturned by the revolutions in North Africa, whose long-term fate is still to be determined. The partial financialisation of social welfare in philanthropy has provided a palliative to extractive accumulation for Africa. However, philanthropy has a close relationship to racial "developmental spatial sinks" which exist for the management of the surplus population, enacted without effective social or political contracts to the national state structure. Without state services millions in Africa are consigned to the whims and representations of philanthropy.

The book concludes that the financialisation of power is an immanent and organising governance technology of global capitalism in relation to the political economy of Africa. Nitzan and Bichler famously argued that the capital relation is essentially a relationship of power (2009), but in fact Marx himself conferred on it the role of expressing inequalities of wealth and power through its organisation of class. This book argues that the essential relationship of class has become mediated by financial representations, techniques and technologies in a Foucauldian sense, which manage poor people in an anti-democratic space for the benefit of the wealthy.

Representations of both our problems and the solutions to them by reference to money and its functions is the dominant systemic feature of our post-crisis world view, a world view which offers little hope with respect to building social and economic justice for the poor. The book ends with a review of how the financialisation of power, expressed through the logics of "neoliberal governmentality" (Foucault 1997) and "advanced liberal government" (Dean 2003; Oels 2006: 191–2; inspired by Foucault 2004), has become so embedded in framing our political imaginations that even the proposed "solutions" to our problems, which are largely caused by the hegemonic money form in capitalist accumulation, are themselves imagined within the money form (see Chapters 6 and 7). In the lexicon of modern development and public policy monetised "solutions" across a wide range of policy domains, have dominated, a good exemplar being the near religious passion of the microcredit revolution and its vertiginous fall from grace and refashioning of resilience and self-help for the surplus poor (Kohl-Arenas 2011; Fraser and Gordon 1994; O'Connor 2001).

But since the early 1990s we have increasingly lived adversely with the consequences of the idea that to regulate markets is inherently to disrupt and undermine growth. This ideological belief, and that is all it is, has allowed a privatization of state function, whereby soft codes of conduct, voluntary initiatives, self-certification and weak transparency initiatives have displaced timely, active and preventive government action to regulate the private sector in the public good. Thus Hay (2004: 502) argued that:

> From the 1990s … the normalization and institutionalization of neoliberalism and its depiction as a largely technical set of devices for managing an open economy has served to depoliticise and de-democratize economic policy-making … Politicians use a self-denying ordinance, that external economic imperatives are non-negotiable making domestic political actors powerless so responsibility is [solely] technocratic.

Even in the aftermath of crisis, responses are largely framed in the repertoire of this hegemonic necessary neo-liberalism, excepting the anarchic and spontaneous responses sometimes enacted by the marginalised.

Politicians of the "left", largely still tinker with Keynesianism, but in the context of independent central banks who insist on open markets, this is a somewhat futile policy response. Meanwhile, global civil society, the philanthropy sector, political parties, CSOs, trade unions, churches and faith organisations, and citizens groups has the potential to reinstate ideas of solidarity, the "love of humanity" and the common good into action and practises of government and the private sector, but remain critically fragmented at a global scale. Critiques of the global order resonate with a widespread sense of unease and concern in wider society about the seeming immorality of many corporate practices, even when these are apparently legal, and the cursory nature of the way that everyday life is disrupted and degraded by a private sector that enjoys the freedom of non-regulation afforded it by 30 years of neo-liberal hegemony (Beetham 2011). However, large domains of this global civil society have entrapped themselves into the same financialised logics of governmentality that entrain us all in the global power structure. Environmentalists are busy writing improvements to ecosystem service audit formula; climate justice activists are busy debating the accreditation procedures for offshore funds; while social justice activists calculate the social impact value of the care they give the vulnerable.

A counter-hegemonic perspective is a challenge, particularly since current work on globalization, neo-liberalism and financialisation, as we saw above, is generally in the form of critique, is abstract and somewhat eclectic, not linking well to regulatory regimes, financial knowledge or ideas of social struggle. Harvey's seminal work on accumulation by dispossession (2003), Ferguson's unique insights into investment "hopping" over Africa (2005), and classical Marxist insights over capital's tendency to ever greater commodification of human life and the environment (Castree 2006) have given us the broad spatial coordinates and temporality of the political economy of modern Africa. However, activists are still removed from the praxis of modern accumulation, who does what, and how it is organized. In short there is a need for more empirical research, and this book is a contribution to this effort.

This is required because current calculations of what is acceptable risk to humans, non-humans and nature are set at levels that many of us believe to be unacceptable, as the multiplicity of localized struggles globally indicate. What is efficient to the financier – offshore domicile, no local integration (or accountability), opaque company reporting and a relatively liberal policy on co-investors – is not healthy for the environment. The logic of "unstoppable time" that is intrinsic to the meaning of "growth" in neo-liberal ideology also generates maxims dangerous to people and the environment; such as the argument that everything at the frontier of commodification needs to be "developed" to generate "much needed" growth; or the belief that investment capital is scarce and should be "won" at any cost; or the multiple representations of crisis and calamity with which financiers force acceptance of extractive models (Moore 2008). The means by which power is instrumentalised through processes of financialisation, and how this is represented and justified, needs to be better understood, as a matter of some urgency, if we are to find ways of treasuring (and valuing) nature, human and non-humans outside the capitalist market.

We know from classical liberal theory that social and economic justice requires a democracy that represents the interests of the majority and protects their rights, individually and collectively, in relation to the interests of the wealthy. This particular variant of democratic form aligns well with decreased inequalities at all levels and invokes older ideas of social democracy and socialism. Money cannot buy these commonwealths for humanity, and the transcripts, discourses and academic practises that have been enmeshed ideologically with the rule of money (ultimately a carrier of the interests of the wealthy) will need to be deconstructed in order to properly further the cause of the poor, exploited and excluded (Pogge 2010). But these knowledges come from a liberal era whose central form of governmentality is gone (Dean 2006); and whose assemblage with nature has changed (Lohmann 2015). The concluding chapter asks what knowledge and paradigm shift is required in the discourse and practise of opposition to create effective resistance to a system that can only produce lives for at least 1 billion people alive, that are, in Thomas Hobbes terms, "solitary, poor, nasty, brutish, and short".

Notes

1 K. Sharife, personal communication, 2015.

2 CDOs are collateralized debt obligations, SPVs are legal entities which specialise in acquiring and financing specific assets, while ABS CDOs are a combination of asset backed securities and collateralized debt obligations in one derivatives product.

2 The increasing financialisation of everything?

> A crisis consists precisely in the fact that the old is dying and the new cannot be born: in this interregnum, a great variety of morbid symptoms appear.
>
> (Gramsci 1971: 276)

The concept of financialisation is widely used at an abstract theoretical level, akin to the Marxian notion of the ever greater commodification of life and resources under capitalism, led by an evermore hegemonic group of finance capitalists. It is clustered in a group of like concepts that are "fuzzy" and have imprecise meanings and overlaps, including neo-liberalism, commodification and marketization. In this book we will fix meanings for these, to the extent that this is useful given the highly flexible, situated empirical variations of "actually existing" neo-liberalism and related processes in practice (Castree 2010a; 2010c). We will also explore emerging work on whether a post-neoliberal phase of global political economy is nascent or in evidence (Dean 2003; Castree 2010c; Oels 2006. Neo-liberalism will be discussed in the next chapter, and post-neoliberalism in Chapter 8. But first a few words on the intellectual justification for this book from a risky egocentric perspective, and an exploration of the term "financialisation". In my last book *Money and Power* (2009) I explored the structure of the economy authored and liquidated by development finance to argue that the money provided enabled and conditioned governance in the global South in a Foucauldian "conduct of conduct" sense (Foucault 1979). In this book I am going to do something similar, but for the global economy as a whole, which necessitates a brief stocktaking, not least to avoid writing the same book twice. Also, there is a conundrum in this work that we can set up here and return to in the concluding section, which was raised by my colleague Dan Brockington, around the role of the counterfactual in African political economy. He read *Money and Power* and said it boiled down to six propositions:

1. **Investment in development is profitable**
   This is true in two senses, first in that institutions such as the Commonwealth Development Corporation (CDC), International Monetary Fund (IMF), International Finance Corporation (IFC) and International Bank of Reconstruction and Development (IBRD, or World Bank) make a profit on

their investments for their shareholders (mostly Northern governments and newer sovereign wealth funds and BRICS), and second because of the derivative contracts, procurements and consultancies arising from the business of development.

2. **A lot of 'aid' is in fact money spent in helping firms in the wealthy North West make profitable deals with governments and firms in the South**
   Economic interactions between wealthy countries and poor countries are, in terms of the amount of money changing hands dominated by the Export Credit Guarantee Departments. While their activities are classed as "aid", their primary purpose is to underwrite the costs of risk and thus guarantee profits for the exporting industries of the wealthy Northern countries.

3. **A lot of aid which is not spent supporting the activities of Northern firms is spent transforming societies and economies in the South so that they can become more profitable for Northern firms**
   This is aid spent on conditioning the "soft infrastructure", or what Foucault (1977) called governmentality in "environment policy", or the context in which a firm or person is managed. This is achieved through concessions attached to loans and grants that insist on neo-liberal policy change, the economics of which is questionable (Chang 1994; Rodrik 2008; Stiglitz 1992). Also the "soft infrastructure" has been opened to allow kick-backs for Northern firms in the form of opportunities to buy up privatised companies, reduction of trade tariffs in places they want to export to, and extension of patent rights. In short, the political economy of development promoted and built by "donors" allowed Northern firms an anti-competitive advantage over sovereign firms through tax holidays, export processing zones and other exemptions.

4. **All of this happens because of the powerful lobby of industries in the North who have captured the governments of the North supporting the international financial institutions (IFIs) and institutions of aid**
   There is a powerful web of interconnection between the multilateral, regional and bilateral development finance institutions, which are also sites of regulatory capture. Pro-corporate positions are generally taken by Northern governments in all trade- and investment-related forums.

5. **African elites facilitate the reception of loans and concessional finance for their own profit, but to the detriment of their compatriots**
   African political elites, but not the general population, can join in the extractive type economies that are built as a consequence of this "environment policy" or soft infrastructure intervention. But the loans and finance taken on from the IFIs and DFIs are of questionable benefit to their countries and continue to place their countries in a parlous state financially.

6. **All of this self-serving "aid" business is dressed up in the language of benevolence and debt forgiveness and general munificence**
   This is a modelling of that part of the global economy that is publically underwritten in development finance, but actually it has very fuzzy edges since public money is everywhere used to leverage private, and in contemporary Africa the model of public–private partnership agreements for energy, agriculture and built environment and infrastructure projects are ubiquitous (Foster and Briceno-Garmendia 2010).

Since the late 1990s there has also been a trend that parts of the formal state and political parties within it have themselves corporatised, or been privatised and many of the later have offshore corporate structures, a point we will return to in Chapter 6. However, since the 1990s, the formally aid-authored economy has been declining in size relative to private flows, mostly in the sense that Africa has continued to be a net creditor to the rest of the world (Henry 2012; UNECA and AUC 2012a), while finance from non-OECD countries has risen, particularly from China. For example, China became Africa's largest trading partner in 2009, overtaking the USA, with nearly 2.2 trillion rand (approximately US$ 187 bn) in trade flows in 2013 (Market Realist 2014). In South Africa alone, bilateral trade volume with China grew 40-fold in 15 years, from 12 billion rand (US$1 bn) in 1997, to nearly 660 billion rand (US$56 bn) in trade flows by 2013 (Market Realist 2014).

Despite figures such as these, a quick review of aggregate statistics shows a pattern for the macro economy which is similar to that of the aid-authored economy in the sense that the political economy of Africa is extractive and works to produce poverty. For example, Africa is estimated to have lost between 1.2 and 1.3 trillion dollars in illicit financial flows, 60 to 65 per cent of which is due to corporate mispricing, between 1980 and 2009 (African Development Bank (ADB) and Global Financial Integrity 2013; Christian Aid and TJN 2014). The annual loss to the continent between 2000 and 2008 was estimated at US$50 bn annually (Kar and Cartwright Smith 2010), almost the same as what can be expected annually in foreign direct investments, which were US$38bn in 2008 (Christian Aid and TJN 2014: 29; citing Ndikumana and Boyce 2012), US$62bn in 2009 and US$52.3bn in 2011 (Christian Aid and TJN 2014: 29; citing UNECA and AUC 2012b). Meanwhile, ODA from all donors recorded at the OECD was just US$128bn in 2008; rising to US$133 billion in 2012 (OECD 2014). In other words, ODA struggles to even keep up with illicit flows.

The source of these illicit outflows is primarily corporate but is also via the actions of Africa's own "High Net Wealth Individuals" (HNWIs). For example, Christian Aid and TJN cite a report by Jersey Finance that African nationals banking in Jersey (and there are some 60 other tax havens) have £9.4bn in customer deposits in banks (as compared to £3bn from China) and £31bn in Jersey trusts (as compared to £1bn from China) (cited in Christian Aid and TJN 2014: 7). Adding the people who have completely disappeared from the databases of revenue officers, which for South Africa has been estimated at somewhere between 28,000 and 114,000 HNWI (estimated to lose South Africa US$10.9bn annually in tax) (Christian Aid and TJN 2014: 7, citing AIDC), and the shape of continent-wide structure of extraction comes into view. Tax havens and the illicit economy are discussed further in Chapter 6.

The type of macro-scale analysis of the causes and effects of a political economy of extraction that simultaneously confines subjects into disempowered poverty requires a conceptual map for analysis. Are the aid-authored and "private" economies similarly structured, as the macro data seems to suggest? Or does the mainstream discourse of a capitalism "working" and an Africa "rising", at least in terms of the belief that there is no counterfactual, have some resonance? In this book we will look at the political economy at a continental and global scale, and the shape of some individual nation state formations, and ask how far financialisation has dragged everyone into a habitus where the power of money configures everyday life. But first the conundrum that Dan Brockington broached, when he asked the simple question, so what is the problem? If some metrics of development were rising then perhaps this was capitalism "working", despite the obvious constraints provided for in the six propositions above? My response was weak – I said it's the counterfactual possibility that makes all of this a bad thing. In other words, that there are other developmental pathways that would be better if money didn't transmit through power to constrain and deny them. This of course is empirically difficult to prove. However, in this book I aim to respond to this challenge by showing how the global political economy configures global power in order to deny and to drain resources from the poor. The six propositions above are the starting point from which financialisation more widely can be modelled, since the relationship between states and the leveraged private economy is similar to that between development finance and the private economy it catalyses.

Financialisation: what is it?

In this section I'll begin by trying to work out what is happening in the global political economy as compared to a sketch of the most cited attributes of what "financialisation" refers to in an empirical sense. Then I'll use more generic theory of how capitalism works to analyse what these descriptive and empirical features mean, and how they relate to what we think we know about financialisation processes. In the third section, I will argue that financialisation is best used as a concept in terms of the relationality of power that it can indicate, given the prior empirical account. In the next chapter, we will return to how financialisation exists conceptually in relation to its closest relatives: neo-liberalism, commodification and marketisation.

The term financialisation is a relatively new one and as a concept has been put to work extensively, often inferring a deep structural shift in capitalism itself. Taking Christophers as a starting point, he neatly summarises that the most common understanding of the term is of a financialisation of capitalism itself, whereby "the capitalist economy has changed, becoming more weighted to financial as opposed to non-financial activities and income sources. In short, with financialisation more of the economy is deemed to consist of finance, and more of the wealth it circulates is deemed to be generated through finance" (Christophers 2012: 273). Labban, using a historical account, defines financialisation as a "shift in the creation of value to a relatively autonomous and increasingly dominant financial sphere" (2010: 545). This is the hegemonic view, and dates back to Arrighi's seminal *The Long Twentieth Century* (1994), and was picked up in the work of Stockhammer (2004) and Krippner (2005). However, there are many definitions, with Lee *et al.* (2009: 729) distinguishing 17 separate meanings (see also Guttmann 2008). Apart from the hegemonic one, which is most rooted in traditional political economy, Christophers also usefully isolates two more clusters of meaning: one which "invokes the terms to depict an ascendance in the role of financial concepts, languages and evaluative practises in everyday political and cultural life" (Christophers 2012: 273; see also 2015: 185–187). In this reading finance has "relentlessly colonised all kinds of ostensibly extra-economic lifeworlds, generating financialised cultures and even financialisation identities" (Christophers 2012: 273; citing Martin 2002; Langley 2007, 2008). The third revolves around ideas of shareholders, "shareholder value" and related concepts and the institutions that propagate them as having increasing influence in the business world more generally (Froud, *et al.* 2000; Lazonick and O'Sullivan 2000; Peters 2011).

For reasons that will become clear, the third cluster of work on financialisation is not of particular salience in this book. In terms of the second cluster, of the colonisation of lifeworlds, this definition is of use, particularly in the next two chapters, not as a competing definitional base beyond the political economic (as Christophers (2012) would have it), but as a synergistic approach within a holistic conception of financialisation as a relationship of power in a post-structural episteme. This takes the need for empirical validation as a given but uses this to substantiate an argument for financialisation as a technology of power whereby owners of capital have increasingly deployed it to condition, influence and direct more traditional owners of power such as those in state structures. This firmly embeds a definition of financialisation as within and useful to an account of change in capitalist structures and modes of accumulation in a broad sense. In fact we will arrive, through the discussion, at a definition of financialisation as "a technology of power which uses the money form to quantify human and physical contexts, privilege financial parameters in decision-making, and ultimately return decisions over resources in favour of money-holders in contexts of contested uses and meanings for the non-human world" (Bracking 2012a: 274). Here, the term financialisation signifies a relationship of power in a post-structuralist frame, informed by Nitzan and Bichler's thesis that "capital is not a narrow economic entity, but a symbolic quantification of power … [capital] represents the organized power of dominant capital groups to reshape – or *creorder* – their society" (2009, emphasis added).

Theoretical work has also argued variously that finance, and its institutional assemblage of contemporary neo-liberalism, is fundamentally political: it reforms structures of power within society, as a "non-economic form of regulation"

(Roberts 2010). For Panitch and Gindin (2003) these financial governance mechanisms are authored and promoted by the USA; while for Ayers (2006), civil society is the carrier of institutional arrangements which further and legitimize the economic project of financialisation. I previously explored this international financial architecture in the concessionary aid and development finance system and argued that it is from the "top floor of the house of trade" (citing Arrighi 1994; see also Braudel 1982), where public liquidity is regulated to keep "Southern populations in a permanent austerity cycle" (Bracking 2009a: 3). I argued that it makes sense to see capitalism as a three-tiered structure (following these authors), where finance has an autonomous strategic role from the "Boardroom", directing other circuits of accumulation. Similarly, Johnston and Saad-Filho outline the mechanisms by which finance controls workers and consumers (Johnston and Saad-Filho 2007), while Folkman *et al.* more discretely categorise the financial intermediaries in this regulation of finance in the UK economy (2007: 557).

Taken together it is possible to combine work done in particular sectors and countries, on causes and consequences of these changing processes and construct a composite definition. Thus the theoretical construction of financialisation here is as a process embedded in and enacted using financial instruments working as governance technologies, enabled through accounting mores and sited in the agency of banks and capital markets. In other words, the definition used seeks to identify the critical subject of financialisation rather than defining it by its consequential implications or effects. The global scale phenomena suggest that financialisation can, and does, carry relationships of power that resonate with earlier Marxist understandings of the way capitalism works. For example, Castree (2010c) conducted a useful review of theories of capital accumulation drawing on the work of Marx (1978), Polanyi (2001) and O'Connor (1998). Marx showed that capitalism faces a constant "value-realisation problem" in that the surplus labour embedded in a commodity, representing profit requires that a buyer at that price can be found for the product. At an aggregate scale, if demand doesn't "match the supply of capital looking for profitable returns, various incomplete 'solutions' suggest themselves" (Castree 2010c: 190). During imperialism the solution was to export excess capital abroad and expand the frontiers of market capitalism, and then later, in the post-war period, globalisation remade this as "the financialization of everything" (Castree 2010c: 191: citing Harvey 2005: 33). Castree argues, following Harvey, that this was "backed by powerful ruling parties who captured the state apparatus at the end of the post-war boom" (ibid), resulting in a political economy in which monetary surpluses play a pivotal role in a "new geography of liquidity and investment" (ibid.), where "growing surpluses [are] chasing ever riskier investment and market opportunities" (ibid). These riskier investments are often venture capital and derivatives investments, which, in modern markets, are often reinsured by institutions that work to shore up the power of capital holders with close collaboration between banks and corporations (as we see in the example of "exchange traded funds" (ETFs) below).

Mainstream political economy and financialisation

This holistic view of financialisation as a relationship of power is used throughout this book. However, to justify this we need to explore the mainstream political economy definition, isolate its empirical substantiation and sources of "evidence", in order to arrive at a critical realist view of how financialisation is working to restructure global capitalism – if indeed it is. What of value can we use from mainstream approaches to theorising financialisation? In mainstream political economy, financialisation refers to: (1) the depth and spread of financial markets; (2) combined with new innovative and complex financial instruments, including a spectacular range of short-term and abstracted derivatives and futures products (see Hildyard 2008); (3) accompanied by a growth in all types of debt finance at the global, national, firm, household and individual level; and (4) the consequent dominance of financial over productive capital (Castree 2010c: 189; Stockhammer 2010), and consumption. This latter is seen to signify the dominance over and critical control by banks and financiers over the productive sector and the economy more generally. For example, Krippner, a seminal author in this debate, defines financialisation as a "[p]attern of accumulation in which profit making occurs increasingly through financial channels rather than through trade and commodity trading" (Krippner 2004: 14) resulting in the ascendancy of shareholder value in corporate governance, the greater dominance of capital markets over bank-based financial systems and the explosion of financial trading and instruments and the rentier financial class itself (Krippner 2004; this latter following Hilferding 1910). Similarly, Epstein summarises that "financialisation means the increasing role of financial motives, financial markets, financial actors and financial institutions in the operation of the domestic and international economies" (2005: 3).

Critique of mainstream definitions

Arguably there are three weaknesses in this composite definition from mainstream writers. The first, as Christophers attests, is that empirical evidence remains weak and contested, and insufficient to substantiate the rather grander attached narratives concerning profound structural changes in the nature of capitalism (2012). He noted that the term financialisation has little empirical substantiation, existing with "limited empirical validation and seemingly unlimited conceptual mobilisation" (ibid.: 272). Many authors infer a deep structural shift in capitalism itself, "envisioned less as a contestable hypothesis requiring empirical substantiation, and more as something axiomatic, a taken-for-granted of social-scientific understanding" (ibid.). Christophers, however, notes that for "such a shibboleth of contemporary scholarship" evidence remains "remarkably and curiously thin" (ibid.). Second, many definitions refer as much to the consequences of the greater dominance of finance, than to the causes of, or processes of the same. Third, there is a problem of scale and the space and place at which change is supposed to extrapolate and signify global or structural change.

In terms of the first criticism, there are studies that use the term in relation to specific domains in which empirical evidence is used. For example, Johnston and Saad-Filho uses financialisation to refer to trends in financial investments after 1979, where high interest rates made financial investments and financial activities more attractive (2005: 13). The size of the financial sector increased significantly, while non-financial corporates began trading in financials, and even at the household level financialisation spread as households either became key owners of financial products, such as pensions, or took on historically high levels of household debt, spurred on by easily available personal credit (ibid.: 13–14). Thus finance becomes a mediator of class consumption, as wealth gravitated to holders of financial assets (Epstein 2005: 4). However, these and other sector-based studies are rare, and are also compromised by the second two criticisms, that of distinguishing causes from consequences, and the problematic use of scale and extrapolation. Putting this to one side for a moment, we can begin by empirically testing the key idea, from Krippner, that there has been a shift in where profit is generated to "financial channels rather than through trade and commodity production" (2005: 174). However, even this central premise is itself open to dispute, depending on from where in the world the evidence is taken, and to what extent a global or national scale frames the methodology.

While in the previous section (26) I isolated four attributes of financialisation from within mainstream approaches, Christophers further designates that one of these, the dominance of finance over productive capital, constitutes the "dominant" axiomatic meaning of financialisation. This is the central tenet of Krippner's work, and also of the other two main studies to date that use systematic empirical data: Epstein and Jayadev (2005) on the UK and 13 other OECD countries and Orhangazi (2008) using US data (like Krippner 2005). In Christophers' review of the empirical studies in support of this thesis he then isolates two "indicators": "(1) finance sector profits, and (2) financial sources of non-financial sector income" (2012: 274). He argues that these studies, which rely on data from the USA, UK and OECD show an increase in profits from the financial sector relative to non-financials, but are flawed because they are "geographically anaemic", (a term borrowed from Sparke (1994, 2005)) and don't allow for the fact that the greater scale of domestically registered profits from domestic banks are in fact generated through economic activities abroad. In the UK case, investment income registered domestically is generated largely by the issuance of debt securities by UK listed banks in overseas economic activities. These appear in the balance of payments statistics as increases in investment activities, which attests not to a structural change in the domestic economy (which can be extrapolated to global theory) but to the massive expansion of UK institutions abroad and profits brought back from often non-financialised economies (Christophers 2012). For example, cumulative overseas-sourced investment revenues for UK banks rose from under £20bn in 1980 to £190bn in 2007 (Christophers 2012: 283).

Thus, Christopher's critique of these empirical studies (Krippner 2005; Jayadev 2005; Orhangazi 2008), is that they use a methodology at national scale and then problematically extrapolate to global theory. He uses Sparke's concept of "anaemic geography" to designate this inappropriate use of scale, where the West writes history suggesting that its change happens independently from the non-West, thus conferring a constitutive absence to the latter – following Young's critique of "white mythologies" (1990), and "covertly appropriating the latter into the history of the former" (Christophers 2012: 287; summarising Young 1990). With these, and other renditions of financialisation, this tendency is clear, despite the global nature of accumulation. Relatedly, nationally based studies are seen to also fall into Agnew's "territorial trap" of using the nation state as a point of departure where it is not, in fact, the central or most important scale of use (Christophers 2012: 279; citing Agnew 1994). These studies establish the predominance of finance over productive capital using descriptive statistics. Christophers then shows how just one of these, the rise in the US "share of corporate profits generated in the financial sector … from 10 per cent in the early 1980s to 40 per cent in 2006" (Crotty 2009: 575–6), is then widely cited across a range of derivative studies (Dore 2008: 1098; Gowan 2009: 7; Harvey 2010: 51; all cited in Christophers 2012: 275).

Christophers' correction is that the UK economy has not structurally changed domestically despite huge recorded increases in the contribution of financial corporations to operating profits of "UK plc" (both in absolute terms and relative to non-financials). Thus, whilst the gross operating surplus of UK financial corporations (a proxy for profits) rose from a negligible 2 per cent in 1980 to 22 per cent in 2009 expressed as a share of total UK corporate surplus – a gross operating surplus of 1 billion in 1980 rising to 67 billion pounds in 2009 for financial corporations – he notes that much of this apparent domestic increase was contributed to by income earned overseas (2012, 281–286).

However, when data for total investment revenue is used, as opposed to operating surplus, the overseas component did not grow relative to the domestic component, standing at 33 per cent in 1987, and 34 per cent in 2008, "showing no increase in the relative overseas contribution to UK financial corporations investment earnings" (284). This is a conundrum that Christophers then "solves" by looking at, as far as the data allows, what constitutes "domestic" and its relation to where the economic activity takes place. When a London-based investment vehicle invests in shares of a company listed in London, share dividends earned are recorded as domestic investment revenue. Similarly, statistical recording norms also register investment in UK-issued financial assets as "domestic", despite these relating to the raising of finance by overseas economic entities.

It is worth relating his work in some detail. In the UK from the early 1980s, there is a context of rising domestic financial "profits" absolutely and relatively to non-financials. But Christophers' conundrum is that while operating output of UK-listed firms is rising synergistically to this, overseas investment revenue is apparently stagnant. To try to explain this, he breaks down the nature of the overseas activity which is generating the rises in domestic financials' contribution to the UK economy, noting that:

> Perhaps surprisingly (given the large number of foreign companies pursuing often high-profile share listings in London), it is not in fact equity-based securities that account for the bulk of the growth in value of international fund-raising in the UK. It is, rather, in the UK debt market that the increasing relative importance of international issuers has been most apparent, and most material to the investment revenue growth of UK financial corporations.

Apparently, between 1989 and 2009, domestic debt securities rose by 7.7 per cent, while international ones grew by 18.9 per cent in the same period "with the strongest period of growth coinciding with that of domestic investment earnings of UK-resident financial corporations" (285). He concludes that a "significant and growing share of what appears in the UK national accounts simply as 'domestic' investment is, in reality, domestically realised investment in international economies" (ibid.).

From this evidence Christophers argues that the proof of financialisation based in structural change is weak: in fact he points out that the value of financial services supplied domestically has only kept pace with the overall expansion of the UK economy over the past 20 years. Thus the argument that financialisation can be indicated by a "demonstrably growing share of overall UK private sector surpluses accruing to financial corporations" is not there. While "UK financial corporations have been generating increased revenues and profits in both absolute and relative terms … this growth has been driven in large part by increased demand from overseas – both for financial services (the output revenue data) and for finance per se (the investment revenue data)" (286). For him then, the supply side might have financialised, but not the demand side.

The problem here is that Christophers is using a nationally based case study to critique a theory of financialisation that he criticises for being inappropriately nationally based. The strange conundrum he finds, of increasing overseas issuance of debt is probably an indicator of the City of London's widespread use of secrecy jurisdictions, the avoidance of tax of its major listed companies and the practise of "thin-capitalisation" where offshore indebtedness to a shell company from a "domestic" facilitates tax reductions and illicit financial flows (more below). Exploring these types of explanations would add to a global scale theory of financialisation: these data could be explained by deducing that they are consequential to the role of secrecy jurisdictions since the former (operating output) is not taxed, and the latter (investment revenue) might be. Indeed, Christophers notes that since financialisation is a global process its substantiation and demonstration should also be at global scale (288). He leaves this challenge, but we can take it up here using truly global data from the World Federation of stock Exchanges (WFE).

An empirical examination of financialisation

Moving to a global scale of empirical data can help us test the "financialisation" proposition further. In fact, there is empirical data to support the first proposition about financialisation, concerning the depth and spread of financial markets and their dominance over production. This is mirrored in fact in the Marxist proposition that capital as value is increasingly stored in circulation rather than in production. Taking these propositions together, there is empirical data on the growth and use of money that can be referred to in order to test how far processes of "financialisation" are in evidence. Although there are forms of virtual money developing, such as bitcoin, the vast majority of global money remains government-backed mediums of exchange, although in advanced economies, "public" money can be a much smaller proportion of total money, much of which is produced privately. We can measure that more value is being stored as money by using the established conception of global money supply measured in four "buckets", M0, M1, M2 and M3. M0 is currency in circulation and is sometimes called base money or public money (Hanke 2012). M1 is M0 plus demand deposits, and M2 is these plus savings accounts and small time deposits, and M3 is all of these plus large time deposits and money market funds. M3 is also known as broad money and includes institutional money market funds, repurchase agreements and other large liquid assets.[1]

In 1971, when the US dollar effectively left the gold standard, the total amount of M0 globally was equivalent to US$171 bn. By the end of 2010 there were 920 billion in US dollars, more than US$1 trillion circulating in Japanese yen; US$1.1 trillion in euros; and then another 131 currencies which together with these three (which singularly represent 60 per cent of all money in circulation) takes the total figure to US$5.2 trillion of physical paper money in circulation. The fourth largest currency is the Chinese renminbi. This total figure means that circulating money has grown by over 30 times since 1971 (Hewitt 2011). But though this is a huge rise, when global demand deposits are added in (thus making M1) the figure for circulating money shoots to US$25 trillion since the amount held in deposits is nearly four times greater than currency in circulation. Adding savings accounts and small time deposits (to make M2) take the figures into the high US$50 trillions (as there is even more in M2 than M1). Finally, capturing all assets considered liquid (M3) takes the total amount of money to over US$75 trillion. In other words, broad money too has risen by the order of a similar magnitude of 30 times (Hewitt 2011). Interestingly, after the crash of 2008, broad money expressed as a per cent of GDP rose rapidly by 116.8 per cent globally, in a short period to 2013, while in the East Asia and Pacific region (all country income levels) it rose by a massive 186.3 per cent (Word Bank 2014b).

It can be considered that M0 and M1 are money being used as a medium of exchange, and liquid, while M2 and M3 are less so and can be considered as a store of value. M1 (which includes M0) in 2010 was globally about US$25 trillion and represents money in circulation, while M3 minus M1 was about US$45 trillion, representing value being stored as money (Kelleher 2014; citing Hewitt 2011). Adding in US$2.1 trillion as an estimate of gold being officially stored as private and official bullion stocks (Kelleher 2014; citing Butterman and Amey 2002) gives a global value of stores of value, including savings accounts, small and large time deposits, money market funds and gold bullion of US$47.1 trillion. Thus a total estimate of global value of mediums of exchange and stores of value would be US$72 trillion. Four years on, given the extent of recent "quantitative easing", this figure can be considered even larger, particularly because of the recognised data problems in adding in offshore and hidden wealth. In fact, recent figures since the crash support the view that financialisation has not been a victim of crisis, but has been catalysed to further deepening as a consequence. Thus, more value than ever appears to be "stuck" in circulation in the post 2007–8 period. The headline global supply of broad money (M4), for example, stood at US$102.1 trillion in 2008. Then rose to US$113.4 in 2009 and remained at US$116.8 in 2013 (World Bank 2014).

Thus we have empirical evidence for 3 of the 4 propositions above, numbered in our model of the mainstream definition of financialisation (page 26), that (1) financial markets have grown exponentially since the 1970s in depth and spread; and that (2) much of this is in speculative products, debt and derivatives. There is also empirical data to support the third proposition about financialisation: (3) that capital as value has been increasingly stored as money, debt and capitalised stock. In fact, here (in 3) we have evidence for a proposition that is shared by both maistream definitions of financialisation (Krippner; 2005; Epstein 2006) and Marxian accounts (Moore 2010; Marazzi 2011). Money in circulation has certainly grown dramatically over the last 40 years (by a factor of 30 times), as has the overall money supply (by an equivalent proportion). But how do these figures relate to money in production? Are these value forms a substitute, or an addition to other choices to invest in production? In other words, is there empirical evidence for the fourth proposition above, (4) that finance capital grows increasingly to dominate over productive capital in both scale and organisational form?

In terms of scale, money in production can be proxied by the value of global stocks and shares listed. The value of these has not risen as steeply as the increased value in money and liquid forms. If we look at the indicator of market capitalisation (also known as market value) we have a measurement of the value of listed companies, formed from the share price times the number of shares outstanding. Investment funds, unit trusts, and companies whose only business goal is to hold shares of other listed companies are excluded. Market capitalisation before the crash in 2007 for listed companies globally (in current US$) was $64.47 trillion, which dropped (nearly in half!) to $34.87 trillion in 2008 and recovered to $53.16 trillion in 2012, less than half the value of broad money (World Bank 2014c). Of this, $18.69 trillion was domiciled in the USA alone in 2012 (World Bank 2014c). According to the World Federation of Exchanges (with later data), in 2013 global market capitalisation for equity stock rose by more than 17 per cent between 2012 and 2013 to over US$64 trillion, "the level observed during the first period of 2008 before Lehman Brothers bankruptcy" (World Federation of Exchanges 2014: 1). Figures for narrow and broad money supply, as compared to market capitalisation are reproduced in Table 2.1.

Table 2.1 A comparison of the magnitudes of different types of value (est. US$ trillion)

	2010	*2011*	*2012*	*2013*
Stock of narrow money			26.67	27.49
Stock of broad money			79.31	82.84
Stock of domestic credit			86.03	97.9
Market value of publicly traded shares	54.61	47.13	53.87	
Debt – external[a]			69.87	72.97
Stock of direct foreign investment – at home			22.85	24.7
Stock of direct foreign investment – abroad			23.64	25.2

[a] this figure is the sum total of all countries' external debt, both public and private.
Source: www.indexmundi.com/world/economy_profile.html citing CIA World Factbook.

However, we do not have evidence for a widely professed view that the scale of money in circulation is accompanied by increases in the velocity of circulation, as asserted by authors such as Moore (2010) Marazzi (2011a) and Büscher (2013). Interestingly, for the argument that follows, the total value of the stocks traded in the recent period, given as a percentage of GDP, an indicator that shows whether market size is matched by trading, dropped significantly from 2008 and hasn't recovered to date. Thus, in 2005 stocks traded globally were 102.8 per cent of GDP, rising to 177.1 per cent in both the years 2007 and 2008, after which they dropped every year to just 69.4 per cent of global GDP in 2012 (World Bank 2014d). World Federation of Exchanges (WFE) note that the value of share trading rose by 12 per cent globally between 2012 and 2013 to US$55 trillion. However, this was extremely uneven by region, such that despite rises in capitalisation, Electronic Order Book (EOB) turnover value only increased by 1 per cent in the Americas and Europe, Africa and Middle East (EAME) region but surged by 47 per cent in the Asia Pacific (in local currency terms) (WFE 2014: 2).

These observations relate to the types of monetary and fiscal policy adopted globally since 2008: As the Index Mundi index summarises (Index Mundi 2014), using CIA Factbook data:

> Financial stabilization and stimulus programs that started in 2009–11, combined with lower tax revenues in 2009–10, required most countries to run large budget deficits. Treasuries issued new public debt – totaling $9.1 trillion since 2008 – to pay for the additional expenditures. To keep interest rates low, most central banks monetized that debt, injecting large sums of money into their economies – between December 2008 and December 2013 the global money supply increased by more than 35%.

Thus, while exaggerated by crisis, monetising debt has been a historic feature of the past 40 years (affirming proposition 3) above). However, there is not strong empirical evidence for the proposition that an increasing liquid money supply (relative to value in production) is accompanied by a greater velocity of circulation (as posited by Marx 1978; and reviewed in Büscher 2013).

Types of value and how they relate

It is apposite now to break up the global supply of value in a different way, according to the type of product or form that the value is contained, in order to further consider the idea that finance 'dominates' production. For example, against a global money supply of US$75 trillion in 2011 (Hewitt 2011), market capitalisation in equity markets was US$64 trillion in 2013, with the value of shares traded in that year at US$55 trillion. This compares to total cash markets in bonds with a turnover value of US$22.4 trillion in 2013; ETFs had a turnover value of US$11.9 trillion; and securitized derivatives US$0.632 trillion (WFE 2014: 1–4). Thus, liquid money is nearly twice the order of magnitude of "money in process" or invested in stocks and shares, a proxy for value being used in production. Also, financialised money products, of bonds, ETFs and securitised assets, are more than half the value taken together of the total capitalised stock. To understand what this means in terms of analysis requires us to examine this data historically. In Figure 2.1, the figures of bonds, derivatives, ETFs, equities and securitised derivatives are mapped together for the historical period 1995 to 2013. The plotted data shows that the value of money stored is rising relative to that in cash circulation; and that the value of money in circulation is indeed rising relative to that "in process" or directly related to investments in production. Money is progressively moving from (1) production to circulation; and (2) from liquidity into abstract securities, derivatives and ETFs, here termed storage.[2]

This both confirms and problematizes Marxian understandings of accumulation. While the Harvey observation of a crisis of accumulation is supported by the first of these tendencies; the movement of money into stores is not, particularly if we add in the observation that the figures we have are missing many offshore

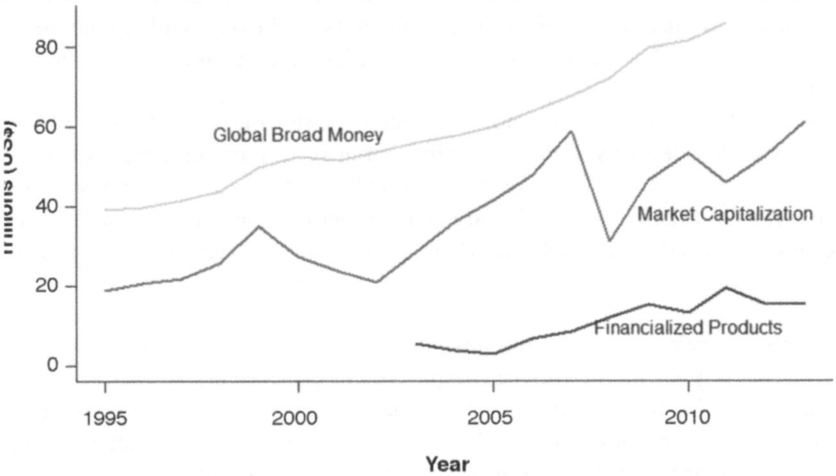

Figure 2.1 The financialisation of power

Source: Data from World Federation of Exchanges (various years). Graph computed by Stephen Olivier, University of KwaZulu-Natal.

stores of value. For example, the entries in the WFE data sheets for Mauritius and other tax havens are strangely empty. How does this relate to the premise of a growing fourth dimension in capitalism of a virtual "stored" world of value? This might reflect, author and reproduce a regime of class power and inequality, in the sense that the money is removed from use? Or it might reflect that the offshore economy, where many of these instruments are domiciled, has allowed financialisation to author patterns of power and authority globally, not least by undermining traditional nation states and the regulatory power contained in base money? Is this stored money used to make further virtual money, or used to structure ever increasing derivative income streams for the already wealthy in relation to a fixed stock of assets? The relative opacity of these stores allows their owners to not only avoid tax but also to gamble on when and where the value reappears in circulation, avoiding downturns, slumps and high investment rents and charges. It portends a boardroom for the global economy that has escaped even the docile regulation of the lattice of nation states that makes up the global international relations landscape. We know from theories of money that the ability of the owners of money to regulate its supply allows its value to be raised, and the offshore economy allows the private holders of money to do just that, even outside the measuring instruments for money supply widely in use by states and their central banks.

Harvey might argue that this represents a classic "temporal fix" allowing financialisation to author patterns of power and authority globally, by effectively removing surplus value temporally from circulation. Certainly, one political economy effect of an increase in privately issued and stored liquidity is that the regulatory power of traditional nation states contained in "Tier 1" money, base money authored and reinsured by nation states, is undermined. In other words, power in the global economy is tipped in favour of financiers, as finance capital increasingly dominates, whether it chooses to invest in substantive production at any particular moment or not. Returning to insights on the nature of "moneyness" might help explain these changing means by which value is moved and stored in accumulation.

Hanke (2012) explains that money created by the money authority (notes, coins and banks' deposits at the monetary authority) are the underlying base of the economy, and are "high-powered", "imbued with the most moneyness of the various types of financial assets that are called money". They are base money, and can quickly be used in transactions where goods and services are exchanged for money. Other assets

> possess varying degrees of moneyness – a characteristic which can be measured by the ease of and the opportunity costs associated with exchanging them for base money. These other assets are, in varying degrees, substitutes for money. That is why they should not receive the same weights when they are summed to obtain a broad money supply measure. Instead, those assets that are the closest substitutes for base money should receive higher weights than those that possess a lower degree of moneyness.
>
> (Hanke 2012)

The amount of base money supplied by nation states has been in demand since 2008, and governments have indeed raised liquid money, but have had difficulty finding buyers for government-backed bonds, particularly in Europe. As one fund manager at the Conference of the Parties to the UN Framework Convention on Climate Change (UNFCCC) in Lima reportedly remarked "Funds are paying to invest money in European sovereign bonds" (Williams 2014). The data confirms this remark. According to the WFE, between 2011 to 2012 bonds dropped by 20 per cent, and between 2012 to 2013 they dropped by a further 15 per cent globally, with EAME exchanges registering the biggest trading losses in 2012–13 of minus 18 per cent (WFE 2014: 4, 8).

Hanke has recently provided a critique of Volcker's money supply measures in the early 1970s and the policy response to the crisis of 2007 and 2008, that places these differences in "moneyness" at its centre. He argues that the monetary authorities contracted the money supply too much in response to the 2008 crisis, because they are using conventional money measures of M2, which imbue each type of money with an equally weighted "moneyness" or "usefulness in immediate transactions where money is exchanged between buyer and seller" (Hanke 2012). He has a preferred Divisia M4 measure (produced by the Centre for Financial Stability in New York), which weights these other types of financial assets differentially. In terms of the 1971–2 crisis when policy makers sought to limit money in circulation to stop inflation – raising interest rates and restricting M2 – Hanke shows how they inadvertently restricted it too far because they used the M2 measurement, which gives different types of money the same value. However, the differences in moneyness make the standard M2 measure and the Divisia measure diverge, as time deposits and funds become more attractive (as interest rates rise) than cash deposits, and money supply, in effect contracts quicker (than the M2 shows) as private producers of money withhold production. In contrast, the Diversia measure shows more accurately the actual money supply.

By 2007–8, the chance of error in fiscal policy is arguably greater, due to the historical decline in the proportion of total money that is accounted for by government. When policy makers seek to limit money supply, or indeed grow it, they only have base money or M0 to use. In the USA, M0 base money is only 15 per cent of total broad money (M4), with a huge 85 per cent of money produced by the private banking system (Hanke 2012). Before the crisis the proportion of base money, or publically produced money accounted for by the Federal Reserve Bank, was even less, at 5 per cent, but this tripled between August 2008, a month before Lehman Brothers collapsed, and July 2012. In the same period, privately produced money shrunk by 12.5 per cent, leading to a contraction of 2 per cent in the total money supply (M4). In other words, and conversely, the authorities were trying to grow the money supply, but the actions of the private sector in withdrawing money – partly in response to quantitative easing – meant the money supply didn't grow as much as would be predicted by M2 measurement. Thus Hanke concludes by criticising the US Dodd-Frank legislation, and new (more stringent) Basel III capital and liquidity requirements for arresting private financial asset production.

Marxian forms of value

We can leave policy debate here, suffice to say that there has not been a normal trend to overly restrict money supply or related financialised paper products in the long term. But the issue of what form these types of money take, and whether we can change our idea of their form depending on how we theorise the production or accumulation process is a difficult one. Marxists have long held a distinction between "money in circulation" and "money in production" (more in Chapter 3). However, this is not easily fixed, and not as clear as the Marxist account might suggest, which in turn makes it hard to measure the increasing role of circulation upon which the "over-accumulation" thesis depends – that is the idea that productive capital generates surpluses that can't be easily absorbed back into production so they circulate as surplus in financial markets. This Marxian thesis lends itself well to the axiomatic condition of financialisation: that finance tends to increasingly dominate production.

We saw above how there is empirical evidence of the growth of circulating and stored money relative to production, a proxy for finance being dominant. However, organisationally and institutionally, it is hard to separate money exclusively doing any of these things in the singular – either "circulating" or "being invested" – due to the complexity and merging of value forms and institutional instruments. This insight flows from the third cluster of meanings given to financialisation by Christophers of it relating to changes in organisational form and the increased role of shareholders (see page 24). The merging of value forms was also noted in Hilferding's early rendering of financialisation as a progressive merging of industrial, merchant and financial interests (developed by Arrighi (1994)). Where finance and corporates are directly linked, the power of finance can be seen as institutionally embedded, but it means that classifying value as either in storage, in process or in circulation becomes epistemologically impossible, although we have attempted a proxy of this categorisation above. First, money shifts between categories in a very short period of time. For example, the rapid recent growth of exchange traded funds (ETFs) illustrates this proximity well, but given their recent rapid growth might also suggest that ETFs have a particular role in changing the organisational form of control within the various structures of circulating and stored money, in favour of financial managers, such that the proposition that financialisation leads to the domination of money in process can be better illustrated by changing institutional forms, rather than just proxied by values in the traditional categories of circulation or process. In 2013, for example, while European bonds were collecting negative returns, the NASDAQ OMX exchange registered a per cent change year on year of 132 in trading volumes of ETFs; the Japan Exchange Group a somewhat astonishing year on year increase of 329 per cent (WFE 2014: 9). Regionally, while EAME registered a minus 30 per cent decrease in trading volumes, Asia-Pacific rose by 109 per cent (ibid).

ETFs are investment funds, which own underlying assets of stocks, commodities and bonds, which are traded on stock markets by pre-authorised broker-dealers. These broker-dealers are usually only the largest banks, who have a prior agreement with the ETF's distributor to buy and sell directly with the ETF in creation units, large blocks of tens of thousands of shares, usually traded in kind with baskets of the underlying securities typically held by the ETF. These authorised participants exchange these creation units and thus provide liquidity to the fund. They also provide an arbitrage function, since the ETF, unlike traditional mutual funds or unit investment trusts, does not trade simply on its net asset value, but is allowed to trade around this figure, more like a closed-end fund. The logic is that if there is strong investor demand, the financial institutions will buy more creation units, in order to sell the ETF in the open market. Increased supply reduces market price and reduces the premium over net asset value. When there is weak investor demand, ETF shares trade at a discount from net asset value, but financial institutions have a motivation to buy them and exchange them with the ETF for a basket of net assets worth more. Futures and options are available for the largest ETFs.

ETFs have been available in the USA since 1993 and in Europe since 1999, and were originally operated like traditional index funds or index trackers, also collective investment schemes, which rise and fall alongside a stock measuring index. However, from 2008, the US Securities and Exchange Commission (SEC) began to authorise actively managed ETFs, where fund managers can make specific investments in particular stock, with the goal of outperforming an investment benchmark index, or the one they used to simply track in the index fund. Although the SEC Rule of 2008 mandated full transparency of the underlying assets, it also allowed that this rule might be made less stringent in future (SEC 2008). In essence, ETFs allow people with money "exposure" to risky investments such as commodities, while the banks ensure that the returns are delivered – through the arbitrage function – while also retaining the possibility of market transactions with the underlying assets. While this could be viewed as a conflict of interest, or price setting behaviour, it is presented as risk management, and the customers are allowed to avoid tax by the ultimate offshore domicile of most of the ETFs.

To illustrate, Source UK Services is of particular interest in development terms as its profits are generated by trading in many of Africa's key exports: minerals, metals, agricultural commodities. It was founded in 2008 by Bank of America Merrill Lynch, Goldman Sachs, J.P Morgan and Morgan Stanley and is a British-based provider of exchange-traded funds (ETFs) and exchange-traded commodities (ETCs), joined in 2014 by Warburg Pincus who purchased 51 per cent. It has raised US$20bn in assets with a product range of 53 equities, 31 commodities, 3 fixed income and 4 alternative products, although at its website it refers to "84 expertly engineered ETPs [exchange –traded products]" and "current partners" of "CSOP Asset Management, LGIM, Man GLG, PIMCO, Bank of America Merrill Lynch, Goldman Sachs, JP Morgan, Morgan Stanley and Nomura" (Source UK 2014) with current products in gold, palladium, platinum and silver. Source UK Services has its parent, Source Holdings Limited incorporated in the Cayman Islands and is an Irish tax registered company, with two subsidiaries – Source Investment Management Limited, an Irish UCITS Management Company ("Source Investment Management") and Source UK Services Limited, a Financial Services Authority (FSA) regulated company ("Source UK"). "Source" is used to refer to group entities as a whole. For UK-based retail customers this generates avoidance of income, capital gains and inheritance tax.

However, ETFs have been criticised even by some regulators and industry insiders as contributing to a number of risks that could be potentially destabilising for financial markets. There are risks related to a tracking error, particularly for commodities ETFs, because the physical assets cannot be easily stored or independently valued. The commodity ETFs are consumers of their own target commodities, which can affect the underlying price (Rubino 2011), such that "Some market participants believe the growing popularity of exchange-traded funds (ETFs) may have contributed to equity price appreciation in some emerging economies, and warn that leverage embedded in ETFs could pose financial stability risks if equity prices were to decline for a protracted period" (IMF 2011: 41). Rubino points to Active ETFs, which manage assets rather than just composing representative baskets, as contributing to commodity price volatility, by first noting the three-fold increase in the price of silver since the first silver ETF, SLV, was introduced in 2006 (2011: 31). He then cites Christopher Aldous, CEO of London investment firm Evercore Pan Asset commenting "You could say that [physical commodity ETFs] just take productive assets out of the system for no other reason than speculation … Recently, something like 80 percent of UK copper stocks was stuck in London Metal Exchange warehouses. I think it's bad for the economy and for the reputation of the whole market" (Rubino 2011: 31). ETFs have also generated criticism of regulatory risk, with areas of concern including the lack of transparency in products, also related to the underlying assets, their increasing complexity; that some are failing in regulatory compliance and that they embody conflicts of interest (FSB 2011; IMF 2011; Ramaswamy 2011), particularly when they are "synthetic" ETFs, which are related to "physical ETFs", but do not own a basket of underlying physical assets (Rubino 2011: 31–33). This latter regulatory problem is connected with stability risk, because of inherent counterparty risk.

For example, as Rubino explains, a traditional ETF buys and holds a basket of stocks but synthetic ETFs enter a swap with them: "A fund's creator produces collateral of some sort and then executes a swap with a counter-party in which the fund gets the future return on its target index (say, the FTSE 100), and the counterparty gets the return on the collateral or some other agreed upon cash stream" (Rubino 2011: 31). In these arrangements the synthetic ETF hopes to track the index more accurately, thus helping to reduce tracking error and it is cheaper because it doesn't need to buy a representative list of stock. But there are issues of conflicts of interest, opacity, investor confusion and regulatory compliance (Rubino 2011: 32–33; FSB 2011). An investor in a synthetic ETF theoretically has both the counterparty committed to matching the return of the underlying index and the collateral. But "one possible synthetic-ETF configuration has an investment bank using its own assets for collateral and its own trading desk as the swap counterparty" (Rubino 2011: 32). It can then choose collateral of dubious quality, and gets Tier 1 capital, high-quality capital in return. If the counterparty failed and an ETF is forced to sell collateral this probably low quality paper would probably be worth a fraction of its face value. If the bank's own trading desk is the counterparty the same firm owns the collateral and the obligation for the total-return swap, making the investor an unsecured creditor of the bank.

In other words an investor might think an ETF buys stock and commodities and that they had a right to a share of these, but someone else is handling the management and storage, "an attitude woefully outdated and potentially dangerous in a world of ETNs [exchange-traded notes], leverage, and swaps" (Rubino 2011: 32) . Original ETFs then were where the assets were held by a custodian, a bank which swaps them for shares in the ETF. But the ETF acronym is useful for banks to use to imply less risk, while actually the assets are on the banks own balance sheet, a risk concentration similar to that generated by securitization, where "With Lehman and the other banks, the structured products just disappeared. It wasn't that their value fell like a mutual fund with the market. It's that they had no value" (Rubino 2011: 32, quoting Julie Patterson, UK Investment Management Association, Director of authorised funds and tax). The European Undertakings for Collective Investment in Transferable Securities (UCITS) regulatory regime doesn't allow the provider to own the counterparty or collateral, but a number of synthetic ETFs are not UCITS compliant and are issued by "reputable" banks such as the iPath S & P 500, by Barclays Bank. In short, and in Marxian terms, ETFs represent yet another abstraction in the money form that benefits the holders of capital above those that do not hold capital, as income streams are squeezed from the values embedded in underlying assets. In terms of our discussion, the ETF effects 'dominance' in its simultaneous management of the storage, circulation and investment in production of its value units, and swaps between them.

Conclusion

What does this description of recent macro changes mean to relationality and power in the global political economy: the proposition (4) that financial capital dominates other forms of value, and in particular productive capital? In this chapter we have established that liquid money is nearly twice the order of magnitude of "money in process" or invested in stocks and shares, a proxy for value being used in production, and that financialised money products, of bonds, ETFs and securitised assets, are more than half the value taken together of total capitalised stock, with values of liquid value rising faster than productive stock (WFE 2014: 1–4; Hewitt 2011). It means that the value of money in circulation is indeed rising relative to that "in process" or directly related to investments in production, but that the value of money stored, in a somewhat contradictory tendency, might be also rising in relation to that in circulation. Money is progressively moving from (1) production to circulation; and (2) from circulating liquidity into abstract, and mostly offshore (Bracking 2012b), "storage" in securities, derivatives and exchange traded funds (ETFs). Thus Marxian premises on financialisation appear correct empirically, excepting the proposition of ever faster circulation, which we return to in the next chapter.

The chapter also noted the growth in derivatives as a form of value and the greater commensurability of exchange between different types of value form, from commodities, to money, assets, asset classes, ETFs, indexes and the trading on them, and synthetic indexes and products that track indexes. This is potentially significant in terms of the way financialisation has affected state power and political structures with a parallel offshore "storage economy" facilitating the circulation and trading of new complex products. All of these imply a level of complexity in the global economy that the Maxist term "generalised commodity production" doesn't quite capture. These expanded value forms constitute a rarefied value system which allows financiers to lock down the value leakage to workers and the owners of productive assets, non-humans and nature. As regulators admitted after the 2007–8 crash, the innovations of financial institutions in off-balance accounting and securitised risk had gone unregulated despite borrowing and debt liabilities being outside the norms of regulatory gearing ratios and risk practices. Banks instead delivered a complexity of calculation to the pricing of derivatives products that escaped regulators' powers. This illustrates the centrality of money to power, and the greater dominance of finance, which has also more holistic effects, framing "possible actions" and policy debate in social, cultural and nature worlds.

In this chapter we noted three related criticisms of the term financialisation in common use: its empirical evidence; its failure to separate cause from consequence; and the problem of scale. This chapter has not explored the latter, suffice to say that some of the conundrums and confusions that arise from national-scale data could be echoes of the offshore economy and its effects. To date, theories of financialisation have existed on several levels whose interconnections are not well built: the abstract theoretical where it is closely entwined with work on neo-liberalism; and the micro, where it is discussed in specific financial instruments and policy. Castree (2011) made a similar point in his epic review of the literature on neo-liberalism and conservation, where the bridge between the grand theory of "everything", and the empirical practices that financialisation may lead to or embody is weak and problematic. In short, there is a dearth of the empirical work necessary to identify the structure and agency of the relationships that carry financialisation into human lives as power, something that Brockington and Duffy (2010) found when they applied the term to conservation.

Globalisation theorising has not helped here: there is much written generally about the speed and spread of economic interconnection, but little on who does what, ownership or power. But three promising subgroups of political economists offer a lead. First, from work on conservation, accumulation and ecology there is a robust literature that theorises the relationships between neo-liberalism, financialisation and the constitution of nature and frontiers of valuation. Second, the connected but wider interdisciplinary work on imagined communities and sovereignty regimes informs our knowledge of the (informalised) institutional nexus in which financialisation occurs (Cameron and Palan 2004; Agnew 2005; Ong 2006; Leander 2008), using spaces of exception as much as legal sovereign domains. Third, a smaller group of writers who have, somewhat inadvertently, produced a better conceptual map of financialisation through empirical work on tax havens (Palan 2002; Palan *et al.* 2010; Bracking 2010; Shaxson 2011). Indeed the subtitle 'How globalisation really works' of Palan, Murphy and Chavagneux's book *Tax Havens* (2010) acknowledges this connection. We return to these three bodies of work in Chapters 4, 5 and 6.

Notes

1 "Different measures of money supply. Not all of them are widely used and the exact classifications depend on the country. M0 and M1, also called narrow money, normally include coins and notes in circulation and other money equivalents that are easily convertible into cash. M2 includes M1 plus short-term time deposits in banks and 24-hour money market funds. M3 includes M2 plus longer-term time deposits and money market funds with more than 24-hour maturity. The exact definitions of the three measures depend on the country. M4 includes M3 plus other deposits. The term broad money is used to describe M2, M3 or M4, depending on the local practice" *Financial Times* (2016).

2 Some might object to the use of the term 'storage' to refer to the function of derivatives products, especially as many offshore funds also simultaneously invest their money in short-term markets as a hedge. My defense is that a derivative, spot or option freezes investments in real time in expectation of future payout. While invested there, money is not in circulation per se, although it may be earning premiums on short-term positions.

3 Financialisation

How and why is it happening?

> You cannot build an entire social cosmology [economics] on the assumptions of individual rationality, equilibrium and perfect markets – and then blame the failures of this cosmology on irrationality, disequilibrium and imperfections. In science, these excuses and blame-shifting are tantamount to self-refutation.
>
> (Bichler and Nitzan 2015: 67)

Financialisation is not a describable consequence of mechanic processes in markets but is "a technology of power which uses the money form to quantify human and physical contexts, privilege financial parameters in decision-making, and ultimately return decisions over resources in favour of money-holders in contexts of contested uses and meanings for the non-human world" (Bracking 2012a: 274). As a technology of power, financialisation can be conceptualised at many scales and in different domains or life worlds, but invariably as an *in situ* embedded process of vibrant contestation and change, if the whole assemblage of that which is entrained by financialisation is the unit of analysis. In fact, financialisation as a concept works in five different modes: as an empirically observable set of propositions about the changing structure of the global economy; as a hegemonic ideology; as practices of governance; as a catalyst and midwife of exceptions beyond liberalism; and as a process that values the previously unpriced at capitalism's spatial frontiers. We will return to the last four of these modes in the next few chapters. On the first, we established in the last chapter that there is a large store of value, in real and historical terms, which is currently largely stored in funds, derivatives and pseudo-virtual products, which, (as we will see in Chapter 6), are predominantly stored in secrecy jurisdictions.

In this chapter we keep the focus at an aggregate scale of analysis. This is not to say that there is an *a priori* reason to privilege the definition of financialisation at any particular scale: either as a macro process that arises in neo-liberalism and extends that logic; or as a logic building new techniques of power and commodity processes at a micro level. In fact the linkages between the scales at which the concept is used have themselves problematic connections: the bridge between the grand theory of "everything", and the practices that financialisation may lead to or embody is problematic, a point also made by Castree in his epic review of the neo-liberalism and environment literature (2011). But for now we need to continue the analysis of the relationship, empirically and theoretically, between finance and money, and the "real" or productive economy and the observable changes in the relationship between the two that the concept is seeking to capture. This chapter argues that financialisation creates a relationship between future time (denominated in derivative income streams) and current production and extraction in place.

Marxist theories of circulation

Marxian political economy gives us additional insights about why financialisation is happening, which, as summarised recently by Büscher (2013), begins with capitalist circulation. Marx theorised that when a capitalist "throws money into circulation, in order to withdraw it again by the sale of the same commodity" he/she makes "money in process" or '"value in process" or capital, such that "the circulation of money as capital is an end in itself, for the valorization of value takes place only within this constantly renewed movement" (Marx 1976: 249, 253; cited in Büscher 2013). The realisation problem, that of recovering the value of investment embedded in a commodity by realizing that value in circulation and sale, has been managed historically by the insurance and reinsurance regimes (Haufler 1997). But circulation itself is not stable or predictable. As Harvey pointed out, circulation, and the credit system it builds is both essential for the stability of productive capitalism, but also a source of instability in itself, as "credit can be used to accelerate production and consumption simultaneously" (Harvey 2006: 285). The credit system is adjusted to attempt the coordination of fixed and circulating capital through time (ibid.). However, this in turn generates "fictitious capital", defined as "money that is thrown into circulation as capital without any material basis in commodities or productive activity" (ibid.: 95). For Harvey, "fictitious capital" derives from the money form, where the holder of money holds a piece of paper "the value of which is backed by an unsold commodity", representing "fictitious value", or "credit money" that circulates without reference to an underlying commodity. "A gap is thereby opened up between credit moneys … and 'real' moneys tied directly to a money commodity … If this credit money is loaned out as capital, then it becomes fictitious capital" (ibid.: 267).

Financialisation often refers, as we saw in the last chapter, to this growth of money-based instruments in relation to actual production, a point first discussed by Marx in relation to real capital counted in labour time, and fictitious capital, or capitalization, defined as "the magnitude of expected future income discounted to its present value" (Bichler and Nitzan 2015: 50). However, the expected future income was seen by Marx as fictitious in three senses: that there may be no principle to call on (the ADS CDOs of the last crash); "capitalization is based on changing income expectations that may or may not materialize", and "even if the expected income is given, its capitalized value varies with the discount rate" (ibid.). For Marx the divergence between these two values meant "everything appears turned upside down here, since no real prices and their real basis appear in this paper world, but only bullion, metal coin, notes, bills of exchange, securities.

Particularly in the centers, in which the whole money business of the country is crowded together, like London, this reversion becomes apparent; the entire process becomes unintelligible" (Marx 1894: 576). Thus the idea of "fictitious capital" is useful for us here in this sense that it is directly linked in Marxism to accounts of financialisation. This allows for the empirical test contained in the last chapter of the relationship between money and production, and a similar one by Bichler and Nitzen (see pp. 60–1 and Figure 3.1) of comparing the market value of corporate equities and bonds with the current costs of corporate fixed assets.

However, according to traditional Marxists, accumulation crises are not solved by the generation of fictitious capital. Rather, the contradictions are contained at a new level, "for over-production and over-speculation" (Harvey 2006: 288), such that the "velocity of accumulation must continuously increase" (Büscher 2013: 24), to maintain the "value" of fictitious capital, such that "with its further institutionalization capitalism becomes progressively dependent on the circulation and proliferation of this type of capital" (ibid.). An imperative is introduced "to reduce the time and cost of capitalism so that capital can be returned more quickly to the sphere of production and accumulation can proceed more rapidly" (Smith 2008: 126). Critical writers concur that financial markets have grown exponentially, with the intensity and velocity of capital circulation rising accordingly (Moore 2010; Marazzi 2011a). However, from the data in Chapter 2 it is unclear whether capital is returned to accumulation or stored in banks and offshore in order for a non-productive class to profit from it. There is also no proof that the velocity of circulation actually rises over time. Certainly the value of capital traded on exchanges rises historically in the *longue durée*, but the non-recovery of trading volumes since 2008, alongside the invention of new derivatives and the "revolution" (Rubino 2011: 31) of exchange-traded products does not necessarily mean that the shares in underlying assets need to be circulated more often – merely the paper derived from them, and that not necessarily so.

Velocity of circulation

Perhaps the problem of providing empirical validation of the increases in the velocity of circulation thesis, which is the sub-component of the way that Marxist writers have explored financialisation as a process related to the "over-accumulation crisis" of capitalism, is that there are a number of ways of measuring velocity of circulation. There is also a potentially bigger problem that none of them are sufficient, as we see below. Above and in Chapter 2, the volume of shares traded was used as a proxy of how fast capital was circulating between and returning to production. However, a more literal definition of velocity might relate to the speed at which trades occur in a machinic or technological sense. Certainly, the emerging literature on liquidity and high-frequency trading is suggesting that inbuilt in the agency of the technologies being used are moral and distributional issues that change the nature of accumulation (Muniesa 2007; MacKenzie *et al.* 2012). This work began in social studies of finance on the automation of stock exchanges (Muniesa 2005, 2007; Pardo-Guerra 2010); on manual "point and click" trading within automated exchanges (Zaloom 2006; Preda 2009), and has been added to by writers on fully automated trading (Lenglet 2011; Durbin 2010) and aspects of fully automated trading (Muniesa 2007), notably price formation (Beunza and Stark 2004), arbitrage and the "ideology of impersonal efficiency" (Beunza *et al.* 2011).

The growth of high-frequency trading was catalysed not only by technological changes but by two key changes in US SEC regulations, prompted by the mid 1990s scandal of price fixing on the Nasdaq exchange. The first in 1999 was Regulation Alternative Trading system (ATS) which allowed electronic communication networks (ECNs) to operate as market centres without having to register as exchanges. ECNs like Island and Archipelago had taken about one third of market makers volumes in Nasdaq listed stock (Peltz 2010). The compulsory mandate for exchanges to move from fractions to decimals in 2001, contributed to the growth of electronic trading. Then came the 2005 rule by SEC Regulation NMS (National Market System) or the "trade-through rule", which prohibits an exchange executing an order at an inferior price to one quoted at another trading venue. This is a precondition for successful high-frequency trading as it ensures that if they are the first to post the best price for a stock they will get the trade (Peltz 2010). For some, including the general manager of Equinix in 2012, high-frequency traders are therefore the "democratic enforcers" of this regulation (quoted in Peltz 2010). However, the issue of how technology changes social and institutional structures and vice versa is complex and crosses science and technology and social sciences.

The study by MacKenzie *et al.* (2012) reviews the earlier work from the social studies of finance literature beginning from the seminal work of Carruthers and Stinchcombe on the social structure of liquidity as "exchange which occurs easily and frequently" (1999: 353) given "three basic mechanisms": continuous competitive auctions; traders able to maintain a continuous price by their ability to transfer large trades for a small margin; and the existence of homogenous and standardized commodities such as "legal instruments with equal claims on an income stream" (Carruthers and Stinchcombe 1999: 353; cited in MacKenzie, *et al.* 2012: 2). The work of producing these is what is happening at the frontier of accumulation when a thing must be measured, pacified and turned into an asset or commodity with a legally contracted derivative income stream. The work of capital holders to make Southern governments bound to honour these is done at aggregate scale in corresponding investment environments and investment protection guarantees, which guarantee even future governments against legislating change in policy environments which would adversely affect the income stream or status of the asset. This latter entraining of the things and people at the place of production requires the ideological work of neo-liberal discourse around financialisation, and assists in controlling the present with respect to future income streams that investors increasingly insist are legally guaranteed in contract agreements in individual projects.

Since Carruthers and Stincombe first worked on liquidity, and their focus was principally on how commodities were made homogenous, continuous auctions and market makers prepared to trade have been greatly changed by the introduction of fully automated trading in automatic, ultra-fast high-frequency trading. Carruthers and Stincombe argued that "central to liquidity" is "the agreement of a large number of buyers and sellers that a given commodity has a given price, at which they could all buy it or sell it" (1999: 379). However, MacKenzie *et al.* argue that subsequent technological developments make that agreement "precarious", or the truth statement of an established price misleading (MacKenzie *et al.* 2012: 3). Underlying stock markets are public-limit order books in which orders to buy and sell commodities at certain stated prices, or the best available market price, are recorded. These public limit orders are maintained on computer systems called "matching engines" which execute a trade when they find a bid to buy and an offer to sell that match. Although traders used to execute the actual exchange, automation developed through the 1990s to make exchanges quicker.

Then computer software was developed for computers not just to execute deals electronically, but to pursue trade themselves. This can now be done using various automated programs that are of two types: "proprietary-trading systems", which make profits by identifying small arbitrage margins generated by different exchanges in time and space and as trading rises and falls in price; and "execution algorithms" which search for liquidity, usually for large institutional investors, where the scale of large orders is likely to have adverse "market impact" effects on the price (prices increase as a large investor buys and falls as it sells). Because of the adverse market impact of these large trades by mutual funds, pension funds and so forth, execution algorithms break up large orders into smaller tranches and then seek to execute parts of them at favourable times in a "distributed execution" (Pitluck 2011). This copied the behaviour of human traders who for some time had sort arbitrage opportunities by buying or selling on the quiet to use market information effectively. The first generation of software merely broke up orders and executed them at pre set distributed time intervals (Leinweber 2009: 74), but were easy for other traders to spot, and made no effort to choose the most profitable time to trade. Second generation programmes were developed that sought to buy and sell in relation to patterns of traded volume at optimum times, either as a proportion of observed volume just before the execution of the trade, or in anticipation of volume patterns over a trading period, in "volume-weighted average price" or VWAP programmes, respectively.

MacKenzie *et al.* explain that the current third generation of automated trading programmes are "non-scheduled 'liquidity seekers', which, in the words of an interviewee 'go out and get [liquidity], and hide at the same time'" (2012: 8). These execution algorithms are "ranged against" the other "camp" of proprietary-trading from which they try to "hide" (this language is taken from interviews with traders according to MacKenzie *et al.* (2012: 8)). These proprietary algorithms are seeking to make a small margin, or the bid-offer "spread", by buying securities at the best bid and selling at the best offer from data captured by the underlying public-order books held in exchanges and in other "trading venues" such as ECNs that can trade in stocks but can't themselves list companies. Proprietary algorithms work in various ways, such as first, a "market-making algorithm", which "continuously quotes a price at which it will buy and a higher price at which it will sell", thus "providing liquidity" by posting orders that others may execute (ibid.: 8–9). A second type of proprietary algorithms seek arbitrage between different markets or between equity derivatives and the underlying assets, while a third type in "statistical arbitrage" seek to identify persistent patterns between prices or related shares and bet that patterns will return to these if they have diverged, such as between Coca Cola and Pepsi (ibid.: 9). MacKensie *et al.* identify a fourth type called "order-anticipation strategies" or "algo-sniffing" that "seek to identify and exploit execution algorithms whose already-executed trades are simply the tip of a hidden, yet-to-be-executed larger 'iceberg'" (ibid.). Apparently, the profits from this derive from "towing an iceberg" (ibid.: 9; citing Durbin 2010: 66–68). The last fifth type of proprietary algorithm is illegal if detected and is called "momentum ignition" where large numbers of orders are placed, many of which will be cancelled before they are executed, with the intention of changing a price and then profiting from the change (ibid.; see SEC 2010: 3609–10). These algorithms require high-frequency trading, which grew in the United States from a 26 per cent share in equity trading in 2006 to 61 per cent in 2009, while around 75 per cent of these high frequency trades in 2010 were generated by electronic market-making algorithms (cited in MacKenzie *et al.* 2012: 9).

In terms of our examination of the velocity of circulation it is interesting that high frequency trade (HFT) makes most profit when trading volumes and volatility are high, such as in periods of crisis, and risk can be reduced by trading less frequently in other time periods. Because of HFT, spreads – the difference between the highest bid to buy and the lowest bid to sell – have also reduced rapidly (Brogaard 2010; Hendershott *et al.* 2011). This spread is the most widely used measure of liquidity, and is often at the lowest value in the current pricing regime of one cent (MacKenzie *et al.* 2012: 10). Thus BATS, the USA's largest trading venue for exchange traded products, can boast that its quality is proven in that it had the lowest effective spread in 64 of the top 100 exchange-traded products in August 2015. BATS gives incentive rebates to electronic markets makers using BATS that issue or remove liquidity in exchange traded products (ETPs). Thus, as MacKenzie *et al.* show, new venues live in a symbiotic relation - ship to electronic market makers with the former often significant shareholders in the latter, with, for example, the Chicago-based Tradebot HFT "market maker", which issues liquidity also creating BATS in 2006, which by 2010 had attracted 10 per cent of all US share trading (MacKenzie *et al.* 2012: 11). By October 2015, BATS had the largest 28.06 per cent share in the USA in ETF market volume, with the NYSE trailing at 21.4 per cent, the NASDAQ at 14.68 per cent and "others" making up the difference at 0.98 per cent; the number 2 spot for trading in overall equities trading in the US; while its European equities trading venue BATS Chi-X Europe recorded a 25 per cent overall European market share in August 2015 (BATS 2015a, 2015b). With a surprising synergy to the performative economics literature the BATS tagline is "making markets better", which mirrors a language of "market making" evident in other parts of the market architecture, such as NYSE floor specialists who are now termed "designated market makers" (Peltz 2010).

As MacKenzie *et al.* explain, the speed of light in a vacuum provides a physical limit to the speed of price signals in high-frequency trading such that there are implications for profitability in a time advantage of a thousandth of a second. Traders at a distance from matching engines only learn "what the price is" more slowly than those with servers next to the exchange, known as co-locators, which are often in the same building. As automation has reduced the time it takes for a matching engine to respond to a signal to well below a millisecond, distance/space has become more important, given that even at the speed of light it would still take 4 milliseconds for a signal sent from Chicago to reach Nasdaq's matching engine in Carteret NJ, giving say BATS, "a hopeless disadvantage compared to one [a matching engine] close to Carteret" (Mackenzie *et al.* 2012: 12). Thus BATs keeps its servers in Equinix New York colocation facilities, along with other high frequency trading firms, who co-locate their computers in the same building as the matching machines of the main exchanges and electronic trading venues.

This importance of latency and its close relationship to technologies in proximity can be read from a brief review of trade announcements made by leading technology companies to their customers. For example, in January 2014, BATS Global Markets (BATS) merged with Direct Edge, another electronic trading provider, and then partnered with Equinic Inc, a global interconnection and data centre provider to locate its combined exchange platforms optimally. The data centres are termed "trading ecosystems" and are named by initials of their host city and numbered. In a press release in February 2014, it was announced that the Direct Edge exchanges (EDGA and EDGX) would be moved in early 2015 from Equinix's NY4 data centre in Secaucus New Jersey (NJ), to BATS technology in Equinix's NY5. Then the BATS BZX and BYX exchanges and BATS Options would move to join them in NY5 from NJ2 in Weehawken, NJ. Commenting on the move, Karl Strohmeyer, president of Equinix in the "Americas", confirms in a press release that "BATS understands that one of the keys to success lies not just in what you deploy, but where you deploy" (Equinix 2014). This is the critical issue of where you deploy affecting the management of trading time and its financialisation in latency risk. Thus, Mr Strohmeyer continues that "In today's networked world, financial services companies need to position their systems for maximum connectivity, performance and agility in order to keep ahead of fast moving trends."

However, a change like this could potentially ruffle the map of competitiveness across BATS' client base due to the sensitivity of the time and space dimensions. Two hints of this come from the press release: first BATS is quick to reassure customers that it would also "maintain a network Point-of-Presence (PoP) in NY4 and NJ2 indefinitely" to "allow current Direct Edge Member connections in NY4 and BATS Member connections in NJ2 to access all BATS/Direct Edge Exchanges without interruption once they are moved to NY5". It also promises to keep latency constant across its customer base during the change: "To ensure a seamless transition to NY5 while preserving the ecosystem in NY4, BATS will engineer connectivity from both NY4 and NY5 to all BATS/Direct Edge matching engines in NY5 to be equal latency for the foreseeable future." In other words, it will make a temporary and artificial suspension of the advantages of speed embedded in its technology to keep current customers happier, but then change latency rates in future at an unspecified time, thus restoring to itself the profitability opportunities of arbitrage caused by minute differences in cable length and technology (which it can sell to customers). But most tellingly the press release has a disclaimer attached warning of the risks and uncertainties contained in "forward-looking statements", noting that actual results might differ and it assumes no obligation to update the press release. In other words, the effect of the changes will alter members' respective profitabilities, but Equinix will not be held responsible if the plan is carried out differently. Data centres are normally quite secretive about who their customers are.

These reassurances to the customer base illustrate that the synergistic relationship between time and space is not the only determinant of profitability. It is also the connections these hubs foster between firms. Strohmeyer continues his comment (on the merger and machine integration) that "With the global network of Equinix data centers, BATS can achieve proximity hosting requirements while tapping into a financial services ecosystem with all the major market players." It is the "major market players" that are significant for utilising the advantages of time and space, and being close to them in an "ecosystem" of computers reflects the continued importance of being close to them as traders with the best market information. In effect, what was once referred to as "insider trading", or dealing on information ahead of other people is institutionalized in a technological and human assemblage or network. Also, it would be hard theoretically to work out where the frontier is between insider and outsider since major banks and firms coproduce trading environments and then simultaneously trade in stock and the derivatives of stock that may also be owned by themselves. For example, the same press release also reminds us that "In addition to Secaucus [where NY2, NY4, NY5 and NY6 are located], BATS utilizes Equinix's London Slough data centre campus LD4 which provides a secure, low-latency, high-performance trading environment for BATS Chi-X Europe's integrated and dark electronic trading books." We see below that "dark" here refers to transactions done with customers away from the public record of public order limit notices. By October 2015, Equinix, offered nine "NY" exchanges, a full four of which are in Secaucus at its "campus". Alongside the technical specificities it boasts of "data center expertise and our unmatched ability to connect [companies] to a large and diverse mix of business partners" (Equinix 2015a), and "communities of interest" (Equinix 2015b). "Platform Equinox" is "where opportunity connects" to "Change the economics of IT" in more than 100 data centres in 33 metropolitan areas globally (Equinix 2015c). But critically, membership of this community allows privileged access to trades, and for critics a two-tiered stock market.

Thus major high frequency traders (HFTs) co-locate their computers in the same building as the matching engine of the trading venue in data centres.

Colocation facilities are linked by faster cables to reduce latency, while specialist software supplies traders with data feeds. By 2015, fibre optic cables were being replaced by microwave technologies. For example, Interxion Holdings, "a leading European provider of cloud- and carrier-neutral colocation data centre services" has a central London "data centre campus" and joined with McKay Brothers International, who produce "the lowest known latency connections", to join the City of London and Slough and the City of London and Frankfurt. Slough is the home of a significant number of London-based trading firms' servers and key exchanges' matching machines. McKay Brothers also provides low latency microwave networks and millimetre metro networks between Illinois and New Jersey, also colocation hubs in the USA. Apparently, "Microwave typically offers a better-than 40 per cent improvement in latency over fibre connections" (The Trading Mesh 2015). But the theoretical question remains of whether this physical increase in the velocity of circulation, enabled by technological features such as new high-speed cables, changes the relationship between owners of investment and those affected by economic assets in their daily lives.

The answer to this question is yes, in relation to stopping time and using relationships of power between firms to fix a deal. Just as "circuit breakers" have been used to halt exchanges in times of high price volatility, particularly drops, HFTs have generated their own form of "circuit breaker" in the form of "dark pools". High-frequency trading, somewhat ironically, has generated an increased volume of trades in "dark pools" where investors meet in private and away from public exchanges where the sale or purchase would instantly appear on the raw data ticker, and adverse price effects for large investors would follow. This appears on the face of it to exclude and prevent the types of sharp practices that high-frequency traders have been accused of, of spying on orders and subtly manipulating prices against large investors (Duhigg 2009). However, it turns out that many of the dark pool meetings are sponsored by trading venues who pursue HFT and who then have the capacity to bid against the dark pool participants or benefit from price changes that come into effect later, when the news does go public, by holding a stock position at that time. Also, the issue of what is the "right price" is subject to a divergence between the "private" deals and what stock is listed in public order books, such that the general public or remote investor will pay a disproportionate cost to changes in position that are known about by HFT venues and by the large institutional investors. Thus on the one hand, HFT and the growth of new stock trading venues, combined with a lower volume and price for deals and a lowering of fees, democratizes trading somewhat and makes it easier for the less wealthy to join in; but on the other hand large deals have reverted to secrecy, with time lags in raw data flow and the manipulation of time acting as revenue generating skills.

In times of extreme price volatility "market makers" may also withdraw all liquidity from the market, and the technological context does not change this. Just as traders in the 1987 crash stopped answering their telephones, traders in the "flash crash" of 6th May 2010 withdrew orders from the public limit order books or turned off their servers. The "flash crash" is widely believed to have been started by an algorithmic trade of $4.1 billion entered by a mutual fund company at an electronic futures market (where traders bet on the direction of markets without actually buying or selling stock) causing a rapid price drop that quickly travelled to trigger a wave of selling in the actual stock market (Commodity Futures Trading Commission (CFTC) and SEC 2010; Goldfarb 2010). The Dow Jones industrial index dropped over 600 points in a matter of a few minutes (Goldfarb 2010), wiping more than a half a trillion dollars in equity value from the market, only to restore it a few minutes later, with 19.3 billion worth of equity shares changing hands in the day, or more than twice the average daily market volume rate for the United States in 2012 (Peltz 2012). Events such as these have caused a slew of public and private litigation cases in the USA over high-frequency trading, including a private plaintiff case against CME and CBOT; and *City of Providence, Rhode Island* v. *BATS Global Markets, Inc. et al.* ("*City of Providence*"), in which private plaintiffs sued 12 high-frequency proprietary trading firms, 14 national securities exchanges and 15 brokerage firms in a federal class action for "purportedly violating the anti-fraud provisions of the federal securities laws" and conducting insider dealing (Rossi 2014). The controversy here concerns the sale of deal information to preferred HFT firms before it is made public. SEC, CFTC and FBI are also investigating other practices such as spoofing and layering (creating fake orders), marking the close (ordering to change the close of day price), painting the tape (sequence of small fake orders), order stuffing and price fade (artificially stimulating the appearance of demand or decline in it), all of which are pursued to manipulate prices (Rossi 2014).

Space, time and "fairness"

In short, space and time have a direct effect on the "fairness" of the market, with distance from the matching machine generating "latency arbitrage", where latency is the time elapsed between the sending of a signal and its receipt, which confers on high frequency traders an advantage due to co-location and sophisticated processing programmes for raw data feeds (Arnuk and Saluzzi 2009). While some commentators see this as an inevitable competitive advantage which compresses profit margins and reduces costs (Narang 2010: 3), the advantage of direct data feed access, and the incorporated software to process and automatically respond to it, means that HFTs can place intermarket sweep orders faster than some institutional investors when their servers indicate a price change (MacKenzie *et al.* 2012: 19–20). Some market participants enjoy advantages related to the technicality of trading and the technology in play (International Organisation of Securities Commissions (IOSCO) 2011), just as pit traders did before automation. Traders in open-outcry pits used to "bounce" prices on small trades in order to encourage outside customers to issue "stop loss orders", just as HFT firms can now practice momentum ignition (MacKenzie *et al.* 2012: 20). The generic inequalities of markets have always generated differential access, but now "[b]ecause information can only travel at the speed of [light], the current state of the market will appear differently in different geographic locations" (Angel 2011: 11). Practices such as "flash trading" where exchanges "flash" information to HFT firms a few fractions of a second before the information appears in the order book and feeds allows those firms to trade ahead of pending orders, construed as "front running" a practice that creates a two-tier system that disadvantages retail and institutional investors relative to HFT firms (for this reason US Senator Charles Schumer requested it be banned to the SEC in July 2009) (Picardo 2014b).

The issue of dark pools is a consequence of this. These are private forums for trading securities where neither the identity of the trade or its size is known to the public investor until it is executed in order for large investors to avoid "market impact" on large deals, which would have been traditionally broken up into tranches. They have been widely criticized for fairness (Lewis 2015; Picardo 2014a). While dark pools began in the 1980s they have grown to account for some 40 per cent of all US stock trades in 2014, compared to 15 per cent in 2008 (Picardo 2014a). On an exchange an institutional investor wanting to sell a large share block would be visible to others, and even if broken up this would generate price effects. In a dark pool the lack of transparency can work in the investor's favour as the trading intention is not posted to the order book prior to execution but only to the consolidated tape after a delay (ibid.). However, the investor only benefits if there is no information leakage. HFT dealers "ping" the market to look for dark pools in order to practice "front running", where pinging is the placement of small marketable orders, usually bids and offers in 100-share lots for every listed stock, to seek out large hidden orders (Picardo 2014b). Once the firm receives a ping that a small order has been executed, or a series of them, it can engage in predatory trading, or electronic front running, against that large buy-side order by rapidly buying up all the available stock and then selling it at a higher price to the original order. If the large order is a sell order, the HFTs can "hit" all the bids across multiple exchanges, to lower the price, and then executing (as in buying) the original large sell order at a lower price.

There are three types of dark pools – broker-dealer owned to facilitate their clients' sales, where the price is discovered from order flow; agency broker or exchange owned, where the venue acts as agent and uses a price derived from exchanges such as National Best Bid and Offer (NBBO); and electronic market makers, who "discover" prices from their own feeds and act as principals for their own account (Picardo 2014a). Thus a brokerage can use a public exchange, a dark pool or "internalize" a customer's order, matching buy and sell orders from its own customer base. Top internalizers include units of KCG Holdings (KCG.N), Citadel, UBS UBSN.VX, and Citigroup (C.N). Dark pools include Credit Suisse (CSGN.VX) and Morgan Stanley (MS.N), Citadel Dark Pool, BIDS Trading Dark Pool, Liquidnet Dark Pool, Credit Suisse Dark Pool, Wolverine WEX Dark Pool, Virtu Financial Dark Pool, Henning & Carey Dark Pool and IEX, a buyside darkpool in NY5. There are around 45 dark pools and as many as 200 internalizers competing with 13 public exchanges in the USA (McCrank 2014). Dark pools are responsible for between 35 and 40 per cent of trading volume typically (Mamudi 2015), and it has been argued that "The exchanges have basically become the liquidity venue of last resort" (McCrank 2014, quoting Manoj Narang, chief executive of HFT firm and technology vendor Tradeworx.) In times of price tranquillity, a dark pool offers cheaper fees for transactions than public exchanges. Over time, the average size of orders in dark pools has shrunk to around 200 shares, similar to public exchanges (McCrank 2014). However, when prices are volatile, traders tend to go back to public exchanges in order to execute the trade quickly. For example, on 24 August 2015, when there was a stock market rout in the USA, dark pools "handled less than 30 per cent of equity volume, their smallest share of trading since August 2012" (Mamudi 2015).

However, dark pools are controversial. It has been calculated that when off-exchange trading in a security is as little as 10 per cent it can start to corrode the price discovery process of open exchange (Comerton-Forde and Putnins 2015; but see also Zhu 2013), while when dark venues account for more than 50 per cent it is hard to establish a price (Preece 2012). The problem is that a large sale in a dark pool will disadvantage a public investor who has just bought that stock as it would be likely to cause a price drop when it is made public, such that exchange prices diverge from the "real" market. There is also the risk that investors in the dark pool are disadvantaged by the actions of the broker dealer, particularly when the institutions' proprietary traders are simultaneously trading against pool clients or if the institution sells special access to the pool to HFT firms (Lewis 2015), both of which represent conflicts of interest (Picardo 2014a). Lewis pointed out that pool clients are vulnerable to predatory behaviour by HFT firms who use various programs to ping and unearth large hidden orders and then engage in front running or latency arbitrage.

Dark pools and fairness

Meanwhile, since the publication of Lewis's *Flash Boys*, there has been a slew of court cases in the USA over dark pools including Barclays LX, although most were eventually dismissed by a District Judge in August 2015. New York State Attorney General Eric Schneiderman, alleged in 2014 that "Barclays demonstrated a disturbing disregard for its investors in a systematic pattern of fraud and deceit." Apparently Barclays failed to communicate to its institutional investors that its dark pool included Tradebot, an HFT known for aggressive and predatory behaviour. According to Mr Schneiderman "Barclays grew its dark pool by telling investors they were diving into safe waters. Barclays' dark pool was full of predators – there at Barclays' invitation." (Trotman 2015). By January 2015, the Attorney General announced he had "uncovered significant and additional wrongdoing" (ibid.).

However, dismissing the cases against 7 exchanges and Barclays, the United States District Judge, Jesse Furman, ruled on 26 August 2015 that:

> Lewis's book may well highlight inequities in the structure of the nation's financial system and the desirability for, or necessity of, reform. For the most part, however, those questions are not for the courts, but for commentators, private and semi-public entities (including the stock exchanges), and the political branches of government.
>
> (US DC 2015)

The reasons the cases were eventually dismissed are enlightening about the protection that large exchanges and Barclays LX have under current US law. A number of cases were read together and the plaintiffs challenged the legality of the provision of co-location services, the proprietary data feeds and complex order types as disadvantaging funds and investors in relation to HFTs. The complex order receiving the most attention was "hide-and-light" orders, where traders place orders that remain hidden until a price change triggers them to "light", thereby "ensuring that the trader that places a hide-and-light order is always at the front of the order queue, enabling the trader to trade ahead of ordinary investors" (US DC 2015: 10). In the attached cases against Barclays, the funds tested the legality of the way it managed its dark pool alleging price manipulation was caused as it failed to tell investors of its hidden HFT clients, particularly Tradebot, representing it instead as "safe", with low proportions of "aggressive" HFTs trading. Meanwhile it was recruiting HFTs, allowed them the "codes" from its dark pool servers, and "by providing proprietary feeds and co-location services at prices that only HFT firms could afford, Barclays set out to capture this trading volume by rigging its dark pool in favor of the HFT firms" (ibid.).

However, the Judge ruled that the exchanges held immunity from private law suits and money damages since they were discharging the regulatory duties conferred on them by the US SEC; and ruled the plaintiffs had not proved their claims of price manipulation. On the first, an exchange is entitled to this immunity "when it engages in conduct consistent with the quasigovernmental powers delegated to it pursuant to the Exchange Act and the regulations and rules promulgated thereunder'" (US DC 2015: 16). Significantly for the exchanges, "the motive or reasonableness of the actions in question is irrelevant to the analysis" (ibid.). The fact that the exchanges are for-profit corporations seeking to profit from their proprietary feeds does not matter since they are simultaneously carrying out a regulatory function of providing price data consistent with SEC regulation. While ruling that the colocation issue was not one which contained any element of regulatory function (thus not attracting immunity since it had an exclusive commercial purpose, or "non-regulatory function"), the Judge ruled that the proprietary feeds and complex order types enjoyed absolute immunity since they related to the "plainly proper functioning of the regulatory system" (ibid.: 18). The plaintiffs had argued that these complex order types were "products", however the Judge responded:

> These contentions, however, amount to little more than an argument that the Exchanges should be denied absolute immunity because they acted with an improper motive – whether it be to profit or to satisfy the HFT firms (and thereby, presumably, profit). But, as noted, motive is irrelevant to the absolute immunity question.
>
> (US DC 2015: 19)

In this way the exchanges are not mandated to provide all order data in the same way to all customers at the same time, and they have protection from prosecution.

Thus, "Where – as is the case with the complex order types at issue here – the act of creating a product has a regulatory dimension, an exchange is immune from suit based on that product" (ibid.).

On the issue of proprietary data feeds, he also rules that they are consistent with quasi-governmental powers delegated from the SEC when exchanges "stand in its stead", arguing that "the nature of the function performed" is not "materially different when the Exchanges disseminate data through a proprietary data feed rather than the consolidated feed" (ibid.: 20). Thus, any aspect of an Exchange which has an element of regulatory function, however small, confers on it immunity from private prosecution, even though in this case it privileges one group of customers, who can pay for superior data, over another group.

> At bottom, Congress and the SEC have delegated to the Exchanges the task of disseminating market data as part of a national market system. In doing so through proprietary data feeds, the Exchanges are performing that task no less than when they do so through the consolidated feed. That is, the dissemination of market data through the propriety data feeds is "consistent with" the quasi-governmental powers delegated to the Exchanges pursuant to the Exchange Act and SEC regulations [DL Capital Grp., 409 F.3d at 97 d]. It follows that the Exchanges are entitled to absolute immunity for the proprietary data feeds.
>
> (US DC 2015: 20)

Thus while the plaintiffs viewed data feed products as manipulative devices, the Judge argued this turned on issues of motive which were "irrelevant". The clear implication is that a regulatory function does not have to be provided for all the public equally.

The Judge notes that SEC does not choose to regulate the content of proprietary data feeds, since "Congress wanted as much of the regulatory regime as possible dictated by the market rather than regulatory fiat" (2015: 21; see Exchange Act Release No. 34-59039, 73 Fed. Reg. 74,770, 74,771 (Dec. 9, 2008); see also Regulation NMS, 70 Fed. Reg. at 37, 566–68.). But then he rather contorts what would normally be viewed as "regulation", by arguing that purely private data feeds are "commensurate with market-based" regulation, (and SEC regulatory mandates) despite an absence of actual SEC rules. He argues that

> There is no reason to conclude that the SEC's choice of regulatory paradigm – market-based regulation rather than rulemaking – renders the dissemination of data by propriety data feed exclusively non-regulatory. And it is not the case that an action must be mandated by the SEC in order for it to be regulatory; otherwise, the absolute-immunity inquiry would turn, first and foremost, on whether an action was pursuant to an SEC directive and not, as it does, simply on the nature of the action in question.
>
> (US DC 2015: 21)

On the issue of de facto exclusivity of the data to high-paying HFTs, he notes:

> That complaint goes to the manner in which the Exchanges' exercise their authority, not to the character of that authority itself, and the Second Circuit has made clear that the "manner" in which an SRO exercises its authority is not relevant to whether that exercise of authority is regulatory.
>
> (US DC 2015: 22)

He concludes that since the dissemination of data in either feed type "is not exclusively non-regulatory in nature" the exchanges have immunity (22).

The Judge viewing the feeds as merely a string of data, rather than ways of structuring markets would not be commensurate with the work of actor-network theory (ANT) specialists. But it does enable him to dismiss the case on the second grounds of not proving price manipulation. He argues that the plaintiffs

> fail to explain how merely enabling a party to react more quickly to information can constitute a manipulative act, at least where the services at issue are publicly known and available to any customer willing to pay … to the extent that the SDNY Plaintiffs allege an artificial effect on the market, that effect was caused by the HFT firms' trades themselves, not by the Exchanges' provision of co-location services, proprietary data feeds, and complex order types to the HFT … Put simply, without the trades, there would be no effect on the market at all.
>
> (US DC 2015: 27–28)

In the Barclays case he rules similarly that the manipulative act cannot be attributed to Barclays since the information they provided on the dark pool could not be proved to have changed the market price either in the split second of trading or in traders' decisions to trade (ibid.: 29–45). This is technically true and allows the Exchanges to distance themselves from the decisions their customers make, but it also protects all parties from collective responsibility, particularly given the extremely close connections, including cross ownerships between exchanges, trading venues, HFTs and shared software companies and cloud providers and associated software. Exchanges are in effect not being held responsible for the fairness of trades held in their venues, or for the insider trades they can deal on their own accounts, and this is currently in accordance to US law, if the Judge here is correct.

Managing time, space and connection

Thus the issue of velocity of circulation being inevitably quickened in capitalist markets emerges as more complex in that speed has indeed become a source of profit, but in more complex scenarios: it is an ability to manage time in one's favour, as investors in dark pools are doing, that is critical, particularly given the physical limits to the speed of latency. Also, the interests of investors in a fund diverge from those trading in indexes, ETPs and in HFT venues and give "market makers" and fund managers a clear chance to profit even at the expense of their own clients, with investor returns the "elephant in the room" (*Morningstar Advisor* 2011: 56). The travel of profits is then across investment classes toward those fund managers working at the most central investment banks and trading venues, who can build "structured vehicles" and trade on their own positions, determining in effect the returns allowed for other classes of investors in lower tranches. For example, most retirement savings, ultimately owned by workers, are invested in mutual funds, many of which in turn invest in index funds which track a particular commodity or asset classes by issuing securities against an underlying representative sample of listed stock, which they sometimes own, or if "synthetic" do not own. These indexes then have to periodically rebalance their value against the adjusted value of the underlying listed stock and its market capitalization. Just before this point profits are transferred from investors to algorithmic traders who can bet ahead of the adjustment (Petajisto 2011). While greater velocity is an attribute in this latter example which co-determines profits, the ability to withdraw stock from time, such as to a dark pool, or to the consolidated data feed can also be a means to generate profit. The power to manage time and space have a symbiotic relationship to the generation of profit.

The fact that it was not higher speed alone which was the source of the profits of HFTs, but their ability to use their position in the management of time to disadvantage others was born out by events (Philips 2013). As more entered the market, and as the efficiency of tracking small spreads in which to move volume and profit from arbitrage, were pursued with increasing vigour, spreads reduced, and earnings collapsed in 2012–13. Philips summarized that they reduced "volatility, suffocating their two most common strategies: market making and statistical arbitrage" (2013). Thus in 2010, HFT accounted for more than 60 per of all US equity volume, and approximately two-thirds of all stock trades from 2008 to 2011, but by 2013, when stock markets were relatively tranquil and price volatility had halved, trades sank to just about half, with average profits falling from about a tenth of a penny per share to a twentieth (Philips 2013). While HFT and algorithmic trading illustrate the speeding up of circulation of money, trading volumes actually fluctuate, and were similar in 2013 as they were in 2006. Thus to proxy the actual speed of circulation literally to the Marxian notion of "velocity of circulation" would miss the peaks and troughs of volume trading. Thus the doubt must remain that the "velocity of circulation" must always rise, when proxied by trading volume, or when viewed against its actual physical limits.

Algorithmic trading

Given the scale of global derivatives trading it can be argued that the most generalized and abstracted form of value is not a commodity as such, but a type of standardized "base unit" of collectivized derivative income on an indexed batch of funds, without a necessary ownership stake in any real thing or object (such as positions held on synthetic indexes which track indexes of "energy in

Asia", or "health services in Central America"). An HFT firm may make billions a day but end with no owned stock. In other words, while people, non-humans and nature are entrained in nationally based economies, a relatively small group of persons are enabled to become multi-millionaires by an automated computer-world of matching machines, algorithms and raw data feeds transmitting over 4 million public listed trade orders a second, without having to actually own anything. The argument that market makers and HFTs generate "liquidity" and serve a public good, at least for investors, must be considered against the actual nature of a "trade" where for a fraction of a second a computer generates a public order bid and a public order ask and captures part of the market "bid-ask" spread at that moment, only for both signals to disappear a second later. The vernacular term for this is "scalping" and algorithmic programs developed by the world's largest banks reflect the extractive nature of the activity, such as "stealth" (Deutsche Bank), "Sniper" (used to detect dark pools of liquidity) and "Guerilla" (Credit Suisse), "Iceberg" and "Dagger" (Quod Financial). Likewise "sniffers" are used to detect algorithmic trading from others, given that an algorithm might generate a bid order given a certain rise in price and if widely used, simultaneously generate a better market price into which to sell.

How does this level of abstraction relate to how capitalism actually operates? Particularly as this change in the technology of finance has the rather ironic consequence of decreasing opportunities for arbitrage. Chaboud *et al.* find that "AT [algorithmic trading] activity causes a reduction in the number of triangular arbitrage opportunities" (2014: 2048). In other words, because computers can search out the smallest price differences across global exchanges so rapidly, these disappear and the price spread becomes extremely small. Historically, derivatives and futures markets have generated profits by a human's ability to make profit from asymmetrical information or information gaps, or indeed insider information. Now, this opportunity has devolved to those banks who have developed smart technologies (which have significant costs in R&D) at the expense of non-algorithmic traders. Chaboud *et al.*, using a large data set of foreign exchanges trades from 2003–7 also find that "algorithmic traders reduce arbitrage opportunities more by acting on the quotes posted by nonalgorithmic traders than by posting quotes that are then traded upon" a result which they say is consistent with the theoretical models of Biais *et al.* (2011) and Martinez and Roşu (2011), that "AT improves informational efficiency by speeding up price discovery, but it increases the adverse selection costs to slower traders" (Chaboud *et al.* 2014: 2048).

Also, other work on AT might suggest that the level of financial abstraction in trading, combined with the increased efficiency of price discovery contributed by AT, makes information from beyond the market, and interestingly, information which impacts on the underlying production and asset quality, of a heightened importance. For example, Hendershott *et al.* (2011), used the flow of electronic messages on the NYSE after the implementation of Autoquote as their dataset, and showed that AT improves liquidity in terms of its standard measure, of a reduced quoted and effective bid-ask spread. Hasbrouck and Saar (2013) also concluded that HFT reduced short-term volatility and bid-ask spreads while increasing displayed depth in the limit order book. Hendershott *et al.* attribute lower spreads to "a sharp decline in adverse selection, or equivalently a decrease in the amount of price discovery associated with trades. AT increases the amount of price discovery that occurs without trading, implying that quotes become more informative" (2011: 3). The authors argue that computers enhance the informativeness of quotes by more quickly resetting their quotes after news arrivals. Similarly, Brogaard *et al.* (2014) use NASDAQ data from 2008 and 2009 to show that HFTs trade in the direction of permanent price changes during news announcements of macroeconomic conditions, thus facilitating price efficiency. The idea that HFTs are the "informed" traders is reinforced by a study by Hirschey (2013), who finds that aggressive purchases (sales) by HFTs predict future aggressive purchases (sales) by non-HFTs. In other words, what is happening in the world is reflecting quicker in the prices of stock, but since this speed will again produce arbitrage opportunities, even as the time reduces for it to do so, it is not surprising that major newsfeeds that impact finance are being packaged into software that can communicate automatically with the AT algorithms.

One strange finding of Hendershott *et al.* was that "Surprisingly, we find that AT increases realized spreads and other measures of liquidity supplier revenues. This is surprising because we initially expected that if AT improved liquidity, the mechanism would be competition between liquidity providers. However, the evidence clearly indicates that liquidity suppliers are capturing some of the surplus for themselves. The most natural explanation is that, at least during the introduction of Autoquote, algorithms had market power. Over a longer time period liquidity supplier revenues decline, suggesting that any market power was temporary, perhaps because new algorithms require considerable investment and time to build." (2011: 4). The amount of surplus captured by the HFT companies and new venues over time has certainly capitalized them well as their share of trades continues to grow.

Has financialisation caused structural changes in capitalism?

The rate of technological change depicted above makes it hard to work out what capital is "fictitious" in a virtual sense, and how much is "real" and related to actual fixed assets and stock. Bichler and Nitzan have addressed this theoretically in terms of the economic categories of financial and real capital, categories shared by neoclassical economists and Marxist economists, where financial assets are not "real" but are simply "claims on wealth". Both classical liberals and Marxist share the view that crises occur when the prices of nominal or financial capital diverge from "real" values, which Bichler and Nitzan refer to as the "mismatch thesis". In the Marxist case, a crisis forces an inevitable adjustment to bring financial capital back in line with the "proper" valuation of productive capital, while in the neoclassical case the real/nominal duality starts in balance but distortions occur (which need solving). While coming to the idea of mismatch from different directions, the former starts with a mismatch, the latter with a match, they share the same duality. These authors reject this thesis on the grounds that the "classical dichotomy" of dividing the economy into "two parallel worlds: real and nominal" must be rejected in favour of an epistemology which recognises that this a priori division of "real" and "nominal" capital cannot be empirically established, or at least has not been successfully established to date by either school (Bichler and Nitzan 2015). While both schools start from the "benchmark" of real or actual capital, that finance either matches or mismatches, the benchmark is a measure of the "material quantity of capital goods. The only problem is that nobody knows what this quantity is or how to measure it" (ibid.: 52).

Bichler and Nitzan discuss the way economists measure quantified real capital and concur with the original "Cambridge Controversy" of the 1960s that in actual fact there is no adequate means to do it. They argue that "capital goods can have many prices and there is no way of knowing which of them, if any, is the 'true' one" (Bichler and Nitzan 2015: 48). In neoclassical theory, there is supposedly a situation of perfect competitive equilibrium from which the value of quantified capital can be measured, but depending on how this is proxied, different results emerge. The most common way of measuring "real" capital, is as the money price of capital goods while nominal or "financial" capital is the value of capitalized stock. This problem of the differing values of capitalized stock and underlying physical capital/assets, seen as generic to processes of financialisation, then has an august history, and was solved by Marxists who assume that the labour theory of value is an iron law, and that because of this there must inevitably be a "financial crisis" to bring capitalized values back into line with underlying values in production, denominated in socially necessary abstract labour time or SNALT (which also can't be measured).

The problem of deriving the value of current production from future expectations of income stream is reflected in the "future disclaimer" of Equinix, and is at the root of why financialisation as a process is so fundamental to our lives, in that since financiers have the ability to define the value of the future, they also have the power to control fundamental relations between people and ecology in the present. The same issue of deducing value from the future was also discovered by Irving Fisher in the neoclassical school in 1907, who wrote "The orchard produces the apples; but the value of the apples produces the value of the orchard … We see, then, that present capital-*wealth* produces future income-*services*, but future income-*value* produces present capital-*value*" (Fisher 1907: 13–14, original emphasis) For Bichler and Nitzan this process is what "contemporary commentators refer to as financialisation" (2015: 51). This confounds perfect equilibrium by causing distortions and imperfections as finance deviates from "real" values. However, it again cannot be measured since neoclassical economics lacks a means to measure its utils, a base unit of capital conceived through an act of theoretical reduction which generates a commensurable hedonic pleasure to be found in each commodity. Commodities have util-generating capacities that can only be derived from prices. Thus, as Bichler and Nitzan summarise, just as "God is revealed to us through his miracles, and the same, argue the economists, holds true for the fundamental quantities of economics: they reveal themselves to us through their prices" (2015: 53). Since neither Marxists or neoclassicists can measure their base units – SNALTS and utils respectively – the main component of financialisation cannot be measured, since "the real price that the mismatch diverges from is itself 'totally nominal'" (ibid.: 58).

But importantly for our discussion of financialisation, Bichler and Nitzan also present incredible empirical data that tests the mismatch hypothesis, and shows that "financial accumulation not only deviates from and distorts real accumulation … it also follows an opposite trajectory" (ibid.: 48). Thus, while economists have argued that capitalism is thriving when "real investments" grow, the most profitable periods for financialised capital, or at least those in which its value is rising the most, are those periods when "real accumulation" is in decline. In fact, when the market value of equities and bonds (fiction) is compared to the current cost of corporate fixed assets (fact) the graphs move in inverse relationship to each other (ibid.: 66). Bichler and Nitzan argue that "if the US case is representative and the growth rates of capitalization and "real capital" move not together but inversely, the interests of the capitalist rulers are pitted against those of society" (ibid.: 66).

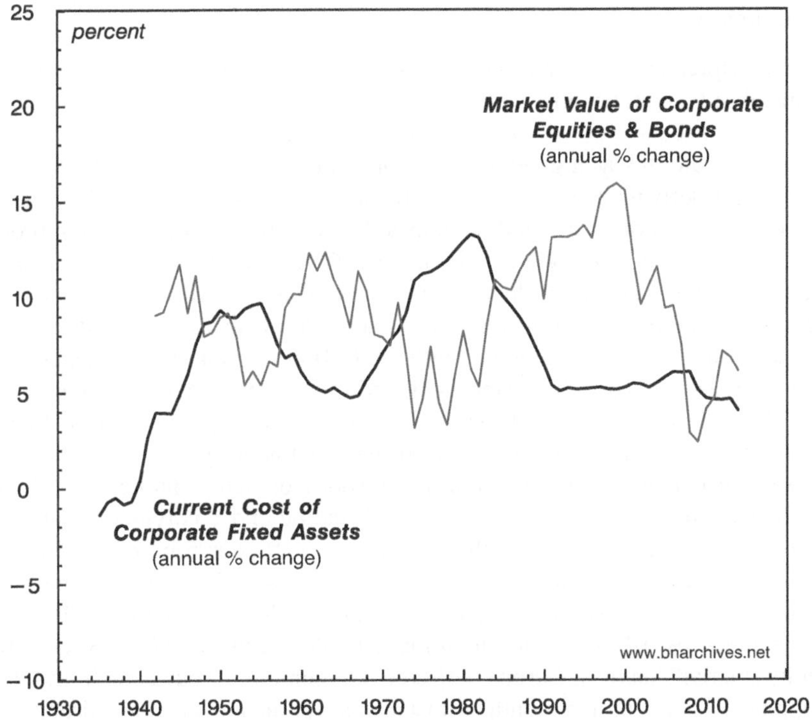

Figure 3.1 U.S. Capital Accumulation: Fiction vs. Reality

Source: Figure 7 in "U.S. Capital Accumulation: Fiction vs. Reality" from real-world economics review, issue no. 72, 47 Capital accumulation: fiction and reality? p. 66.

This pattern appears commensurate with how financialisation, as a process defining an actual assemblage in production, could lead to this swap between value in production and value in financial assets. It is conceivable that as capitalisation rises, along with the claims on derivative income streams, more investors are seeking more wealth from the underlying asset, which in turn is squeezed in order to provide it. The history of PPPs that Hildyard describes (2016), and their shifting of super profits to private equity funds from degraded assets, and from price rises to customers could cause such a divergence. Moreover, Bichler and Nitzan's comparison between capitalised stock and the underlying costs of capital problematises the financialisation thesis further, since this posits that the former always rises in relation to the latter, but in their figure (see Figure 3.1) this relationship is cyclical, and the costs of corporate fixed assets can also rise in inverse relationship to capitalization. Obviously their model does not include derivatives and broad money so it is limited to the more technical definition of financialisation derived from Marxist theory. However, in relation to financialisation working as a relation of power it does illustrate the transfer of wealth from firms to stock holders, particularly facilitated in periods of "boom", even as the stock of productive assets is devalued.

Conclusion

In this chapter we reviewed the management of time and space in the world of financialised capitalisation and the equity market and started to explore the possible consequences of these for other investors and the economy at an aggregate scale. It was argued that developments in financial markets in terms of futures and derivatives and a greater abstraction of products on indexes creates different patterns of distributed outcomes. It also reflects on the historic problem that within accumulation the future income of productive capital is that which is used to manage current production processes. This is a tricky art. In fact, even market regulators are noting that participants don't necessarily understand the processes that they are producing, with the FSB noting that ETFs "generate new types of risks, linked to the complexity and relative opacity of the newest breed of ETFs. The impact of such innovations on market liquidity and on financial institutions servicing the management of the fund is not yet fully understood by market participants, especially during episodes of acute market stress" (FSB 2011). Sometimes circuit breakers suspend trading and this type of capital does not proliferate but reduces. But this tinkering is a tenuous form of control.

Further crashes have followed the 2008 meltdown. For example, the biggest one-day slide in almost four years occurred in the UK on 15 October 2014, where UK markets lost £46bn of their total market value in just one day (Straus 2014). Equity markets across Europe suffered "a complete rout", with the FTSE dropping 10 per cent in a month, with Japan's Nikkei stock average dropping 2.2 per cent and the Shanghai Composite Index down 0.7 per cent and Wall Street showing steep falls, with the Athens exchange suffering most and Greek ten-year bonds rising above the critical 7 per cent level, signalling to many that the

European debt crisis was far from over (Straus 2014). On 24 August 2015, the Chinese Shanghai composite index dropped 8.5 per cent in a single day, the biggest selloff since 2007 in an aftershock of the crash of 12 June, which caused a third of the value of A-rated shares to be wiped off in the month that followed. The strange conundrum since 2007 is how bond and equity markets are not apparently recovering while ETFs and the new "Green Bond" markets (see next chapter) are apparently booming, even though in the case of the latter no one really knows, and it is certainly not legally defined, what exactly "climate finance" is or constitutes. The question arises as to whether this degree of ambiguity in new issue products has become a necessary or structural feature, an inbuilt requirement for the level of abstraction required to circulate "fictitious capital" at a higher "velocity of circulation".

This chapter examined the material frontiers of the embeddedness of value creation in situ, and the constraints faced to profit creation by a finite world where money "stuck" in circulation has increasingly been banked in complex financial derivatives. We see in the next chapter how some of this has increasingly been denominated as "units of Nature". Pacified derivatives of Nature assemblages have the potential for political elites to spin income from sovereign assets on a scale unprecedented. This development works coevally with the emergence over the last 40 years of an entirely non-state based political economy offshore, the dimensions of which are only just becoming apparent. It is the premise of this book that financialisation processes, and the management of this future/present generation of derivative income streams for capital holders, has helped perform a new assemblage and entrainment of social relations and power at the interface of people and capital. In the next chapter these frontiers will be explored further, in particular in terms of how space and time dimensions have been joined by the dimension of virtuality. This is the contemporary tendency of value units emerging globally to be simultaneously conjured at the 'new frontiers' of accumulation (as outlined in Chapter 1, p. 14, point 3), and generated virtually (as in 4). In this latter category we can include knowledge products, expertise, technical and consulting reports and calculative technologies which assist in the subscription and abjection of new materialities, and ideas about them, into valuation systems.

4 The relationship between the virtual and the material

In the last chapter it was established that the velocity of circulation expressed in time is approaching the speed of light, while many HFTs hold stock for only a few minutes. However, it was also established that powerful market-makers manage time and space in their favour, making decisions about where and when to trade, which may also involve opacity and time lag. Examining patterns of shift in and out of different forms of capital and money it was also noted that there is a shift between value held in capitalized stock and value held in underlying assets where "booms" are associated with time periods when capital is most extracted from production, values diverge from it, with financial profits soaring as firms' stock depreciates. Data suggests that in periods of financial boom firms are also becoming increasingly indebted and profits can drop (Roberts 2015). These observations are somewhat mysterious and have proved historically challenging for economists to decipher or predict. Thus, in this chapter it is useful, as a complimentary methodology, to explore the processes of how values are made within different time and space constraints and by people entrained in place as an ever-shifting and indeterminate process, in order to see how changes in place might be contributing to changes in the value of money products. It will be argued here that within valuation processes, values and the emergent prices are co-produced by institutional arrangements, discourse, calculative technologies, such that the division between the virtual and the material is fuzzy with neither appearing solely without the other.

Circulating values

Many contemporary Marxists, such as Harvey or Smith, retain the idea that "the circulation of value requires also a physical circulation of material objects in which value is embodied or represented" (Smith 2008: 126; cited in Büscher 2013: 24; Lohmann 2016: 54–55; McNally 2003: 12). Others are debating how far fictitious capital is just that, disconnected from units of production such that circulation is an ill-connected distal system, or even an autonomous one (Igoe 2013b; LiPuma and Lee 2004; Boltanski and Chiapello 2007). For example, LiPuma and Lee argue that "connectivity itself has become the significant socio-structuring value, leading to the emergence of circulation as a relatively autonomous realm, now endowed with its own social institutions, interpretative culture, and socially mediating forms" (2004: 19). For LiPuma and Lee, the increased autonomy of circulation is because financial derivatives changed their nature from the 1970s from being "production-focused and functionally geared to hedging" (ibid.: 97), to being organised around "wagering on circulation" (ibid.: 99) with consequential effects on the means of realization of circulating value (ibid.: 54; cited in Büscher 2013: 24), and presumably on the character of the production system itself. In short, this shift has created a circulation system where "the goal of financial circulation increasingly shapes the means of its realisation" (ibid.).

Meanwhile Büscher concurs with Graham that Marx's theory of value still forms the "deep structure" of capital, but that

> today it is not the muscle-power of people that provides the most highly valued labor forms. Far more intimate aspects of human activity have become technologized and exposed to the logic of commodification. Correspondingly abstract forms of value have developed. Value production, in turn, has become more obviously "situated" in the valorized dialectics of "sacred" and powerful institutions, such as legislatures, universities, and transnational corporations … located today predominantly in "expert" ways of meaning and, more importantly, in their institutional contexts of production.
>
> (Graham 2007: 174; cited in Büscher 2013: 25)

These expert ways of meaning and institutional contexts of production seem to promise a post-production economy, with value embodied in "reports, policy briefs, think tanks, brands, marketing, and so on" (Büscher 2013: 25; citing Goldman and Papson 2006). But in Büscher's work he puts this form of "new" value together with financial derivatives, futures and other financial constructs (citing Lee and LiPuma 2002) and classifies both as fictitious capital according to Harvey's definition of not directly having "any material basis in commodities or productive activity" (Harvey 2006: 95). He cites Graham to the effect that "what we call 'values' are more or less ephemeral products of evaluation", which "like all aspects of meaning … are socially produced and mediated" (2007: 4).

Understanding valuation

There is a theoretical problem to solve here in the relationship between valuation processes and what Marxists conceive of as "value", which requires a short detour into newer theories, in order for the question to be addressed of how far can a value be virtual, or in other words, created solely from the valuation process in which it is made without altering a material thing in place. From this, we can then progress to understanding how far different values in different domains can be viewed as commensurate. A value is created in a valuation system, which itself is composed of work of calculation and rationality. Work on this has a long genealogy, with Weber persuasively writing of the "calculating rationality" associated with the emergence and consolidation of capitalism (Weber 1930). Foucault argued that states employ "governmentality" using such devices to abstract, measure and rationalize bodies and nature (1980); while Deleuze and Guattari's isolated productive "striations" (of time, space, bodies, nature etc.) associated with the formulations of state or royal science (1987). Indeed "calculative rationality" is immensely important in shaping society, culture and economy, and is associated with, and generates, particular power-effects (Bracking *et al.* 2014). The power/knowledge concept used by Foucault, for example, speaks to the idea that in knowing about something we can have power in relation to it, or control it, and vice versa, and that in controlling something we have to come to know about it. In the effort of capital holders to make profit there is an effort involved in controlling the resources that are needed and a rationality applied to measurement and order as a consequence. The rapid spread of ideas of green economy and natural capital refer only to the last of these efforts to know in order to take control, and arguably in the process of moving from the first to the second is a process or act of valuation.

At the Leverhulme Centre for the Study of Value, the relationship between how value is created and how evaluation systems work generated a research protocol with three components: institutional assemblages, calculative technologies, and discursive framings which together define a particular valuation system in place (Bracking *et al.* 2014; Fredriksen *et al.* 2014; Fredriksen 2014). It draws from Callon (2007, 320), that "Agencements [mostly translated into English as 'assemblages'] are arrangements endowed with the capacity of acting in different ways depending on their configuration". The calculative technologies in a marketization or valuation process are the mathematical formula, the software in the trading machines and so forth, which condition how price emerges, while the discursive framing is the overall understanding of market participants of what is being sold. Using the protocol we can identify that an actor's power over a particular configuration of the three elements – institutional assemblage, discursive framing and calculative entity – leads to different patterns of co-production of value by the real and the virtual, or by the material limits of things and the way humans relate and explain them.

For example, in a study of the diamond market in South Africa, a marketization process was described in which value is largely performed, or has been historically, by the key power-holder, De Beers (Bracking and Sharife 2014). In this oligopolistic market it is hard to ascertain how much value is being passed through any particular jurisdiction, or indeed how much the price of a natural resource that is exported has an assigned "fair" price in relation to any empirical or materially independent measurement of value. It describes how an institutional assemblage is contributed to and conditioned by a single company, wherein a calculative entity, in this case "The [diamond] Price Book", records the value of a particular quality of diamond carat; while a discursive framing assists in making diamonds, which have little intrinsic value, into a luxury good (Bracking and Sharife 2014). The study argued that De Beers were culpable of trade mispricing and tax avoidance. However, the problem noted by this study was that there is an epistemological challenge in how to understand the real in relation to the performed, and that the implications of the analysis for the notion of "mis" pricing of diamonds required further theorization. Given the analysis above it should be clear that "mis" cannot be understood as a "wrong" price in relation to a "correct" price that actually exists somewhere, which would conform to a positivist epistemology, even though the tax justice discourse relies on this being a possibility.

Economic sociology and performativity

The performativity of value has been variously theorised by Callon (2005; 2007), Miller (1997; 1998; 2002) and MacKenzie (2009; 2011) and authors of the wider school of economic sociology. Callon (1998; 2007) and Callon and Muniesa (2005) describe the processes of framing, standardisation, and disentanglement and then re-entanglement (Callon 2005) that commodities undergo in order to enable the homogenisation referred to by Carruthers and Stinchcombe (1999). Callon (2005) widens agency to include technologies, framings, evaluative processes within a socio-technical arrangement or "agencement" within which the various projects of economists in the wild, traders, firms, marketing agencies and so forth all compete and jostle for power over the way the eventual commodity emerges and is priced. Miller critiqued this analysis by arguing that Callon was unnecessarily privileging the power of the abstract market of economic theory over evidence of the continued centrality of a "highly entangled" world of exchange, citing his own theory of virtualism to describe "the increasing ability of economists and other agents of abstract models such as audit and consultancy to transform the world into close approximations of their theory and models" (Miller 2002: 218). His argument with Callon seems to be that he does not see this as inexorable or inevitable, whereas he depicts Callon as assuming it is (although maybe not correctly so, as evidenced in Callon's reply (2005)). Essentially, according to Miller, "[f]or Callon, what lies within the frame is the market system, indeed it is the frame that helps define and preserve it as a market system. In my case – by direct contrast – what lies inside the frame is a ritual system, which is supported and defined by its opposition to that which lies outside the frame, which is the market system" (2005: 223). The "confusion" is that this ritual and ideological system is called "the market" (Miller 2005: 224) in Callon, while all actual markets are instead understood as historical and ethnographic entanglements in Miller. However, since Miller does not then further theorise what he means by "inside" and "outside" the distinction and difference between the two authors seems somewhat pedantic.

But both authors point to the power of evaluative practice in making markets: for Callon this is termed "neoclassical anthropology" or "anthropologics" (2005: 10); while Miller sees neoclassical economics itself as essentially a form of anthropology and an ideological model associated with neo-liberalism (2005: 219; 224). Both see the evaluative practice as serving to make the world increasingly in its own image. The concepts of performativity and neo-classical "anthropologics" (ibid.: 10) contribute to analysing ways of being and doing, which embed a free-market order. Performativity is also closely related to MacKenzie's use of "reactivity" invoked in his remarkable work on how evaluative practice in the securities and derivatives markets in the 2000s contributed to the financial crash of 2008 (2011). Here, the ratings agencies of securities became market makers as traders conformed to their conventions on measurements of default, recovery, risk and most importantly correlation (the likeness of different underlying assets to react similarly to economy wide risks) in order to achieve ratings that would attract investors. The calculation of risk related to ratings conventions was undertaken instead of employing more accurate mathematical models of actual structural risk to assets, (although many claimed that the latter option was operationally and/or mathematically impossible in any case). The "evaluation practises crystallized in ratings reduce a difficult problem of evaluation … (of complex debt instruments) … to a simple one, by establishing a rough equivalence among debt instruments of different kinds and with different particularities" (MacKenzie 2011: 1784).

The ABS CDO example explained by MacKenzie shows how the constructors of the instruments could anticipate the reaction to them from the ratings agencies and then construct key parameters, such as the rating and spread, in order to achieve certain ratings and thus buyer demand for the product. In other words, the design was informed by how ratings agencies would evaluate them, "in a clear manifestation of what Espeland and Sauder call 'reactivity': the effects of evaluation or ranking on what is being evaluated and ranked" (MacKenzie 2011: 1786). In the case of ABS CDOs, this evaluative practice allowed the quality of the underlying asset, most often mortgages, to become less significant than it should have been mathematically. This was in a context where securitisation had switched from a means to increase lending (to customers to buy homes) to a means to make profit through arbitrage, or "lending in order to securitise" (so that traders could make profit) (ibid.: 1823).

From the above demonstration (Bichler and Nitzan 2015) of the way the value of underlying assets and their financial capitalisation can diverge over time, it is possible to suggest that the interests of those owning and trading in securities conflict with those affected and related to the underlying assets when this performativity is in play. In other words, they are not merely helpfully supplying liquidity and investment, but are extracting value from stock by the way that the products are measured and valued. Values can be made and discursively mobilised, but also dispensed with and constrained systemically in derivatives markets. But this virtuality is not without material effect – in fact far from it – in that it works to enable certain power holders to gain strategic access and control over workers and natural resource assets. In short, values are co-produced by holders of money and the calculative technologies that emerge in the context of the overall assemblage of capitalist accumulation. This resonates with older Gramscian approaches to understanding the capitalist class as composed of distinct factions that can have conflicting interests, not as a homogeneous group with a uniform "interest". Also, these interests may not be known and are constantly contested and changing, rather than being read from history as epiphenomenal of outcomes in a teleological way, as a functionalist reading of Marx might imply. The battle in the New York District Court between the HFTs and the private equity funds would illustrate this. Market participants often do not know what is happening, or might happen, and then interpretations can differ.

Understanding indeterminacy

As Castree recounts, "fictitious capital" was also used by Polanyi (2001) as one of four new insights on the nature of capital accumulation under liberal capitalism, and describes "any commodity whose social, cultural and/or ecological value exceeds the market value placed upon it within a capitalist system" (Castree 2010c: 192). It has what Polanyi termed "doubleness" or "duality", inhabiting "a world both within and beyond "the market" (Castree 2010c: 192). This fictive nature of value, and its "doubleness" are then contextualized in Polanyi's concept of "embeddedness". This expresses his view "that a capitalist economy must exist in a more-than-capitalist world … of social, cultural, economic, political and biophysical diversity that confronts capitalist economies as both opportunities and barriers: "outsides" that can be made profitable given the right conditions but whose non-commodification may also be necessary to capitalism's survival" (Castree 2010c: 192) This insight, in turn, prompted Polanyi to coin the term "the double movement" to apply to the resistance of the outsides in the face of expansion of capitalist commodification, leading to Polanyi's "fourth insight" that a "market society" required engineering to house the market economy: a society that learns to live with the "creative destruction" of markets (Castree 2010c: 192–93). Here we can note that the pressure to expand money is created within the context of the ever-fluid societal context (and non-human/nature, or ecological context, in the next chapter) in which capital finds itself. Rather than one didactic "double movement" it is the politics of embedding financialisation (within a pattern of constant resistances) as the "new normal" that prompts and makes the materiality and associated discourse and spectacle of political economy, and which generates the coding of advanced liberal government technologies that embed financialised norms as ruling political orthodoxies.

For our purposes here it is acceptable that capital cannot be measured in a fixed time or space against its own material units that can be isolated into one category or another of real or fictitious (as Bishler and Nitzan argue (2015)). This is commensurate to viewing the world as one in which complexity and indeterminacy are constantly remade in the power struggles between different actors. This ontology also helps to manage the empirical challenges of proving the underlying economics. Chapter 2 illustrated the difficulties of proxying forms of measurement of money and stock into the theoretical categories of Marxian thought, given the complexity of stock and the connectedness between financial derivatives, capitalized products and underlying assets. For example, the purpose of a securities index is to provide liquidity to a sector, such as energy or infra - structure, where firms list their productive assets and the income they generate on the list in the form of underlying funds or ETPs, in order to balance the values of the securities and the firm capitalization over time. However, it is not a case of discovering the balance between them that is of interest here, but the way in which values of underlying assets, people and nature are co-produced in such mechanisms, insofar as the owners of the stocks can enforce legal and contractual agreements to have power over the context, people and things which are required for their assets to generate income.

It is for this reason that production in general can be seen to have been made subordinate to circulation, as a consequence of structures of power that have become advantageous over time to the one faction of money-holders who trade using private equity funds and derivatives, rather than those owning assets. These have developed along five axis: (1) with financialisation continuing a historical process of reforming the historical assemblage or "regime of accumulation" in place, most notably with regard to the non-human and ecological; (2) that this includes the production of evermore "fictitious" value in the sense first described by Marx and Harvey of value related to as yet unsold commodities adding to money in circulation; (3) that fictitious capital has itself split and morphed into a higher order value category of the non-material, an ideational form of virtual value found in spectacle and narrative and embedded in intangible "products"; (4) that accumulation continues to breach and incorporate new temporal and spatial "frontiers" for value creation; and finally (5) that there is a significant contemporary overlap in terms of value units which are simultaneously generated as virtual (as in 3), and generated at the "new frontiers" of accumulation (as in 4). In this latter category we can include knowledge products, expertise, technical and consulting reports and calculative technologies which assist in the subscription and abjection of new materialities, and ideas about them, into valuation systems. We return to these in the next chapter.

Calculative technologies and value entities

Within accumulation assemblages, and often particularly in evidence at their frontiers, there is a valuation system or "calculative technology" (which is the collective term for a statistical package, a software program, an equation, a pro forma, audit technology and so forth that accounts for a thing or person) which acts to create entities in these different contexts in forms that can be priced and marketed. These assist in the technical production of "value" through the creation of new "value entities" that can be accounted for, costed and also circulated in monetised/financialised forms, for example with prices. In the previous chapter, examples of new calculative technologies would be the algorithmic trading engines inside the machines which use programing to make decisions on trades which affect prices and profits. The new valued entities they generate are units of capital extracted from catching a portion of the spread in a trade. Not only are these calculative technologies developed by programers to be sold to trading companies or exchanges and then embedded in the overall sociotechnical arrangement that conditions the market, in this case the market for capital, but once in place they serve to act on that environment. The District Judge who saw merely data travelling down a cable underappreciated that the data was organized by mathematical models, with raw data not passively transmitted, but actively organised to generate differentiated market outcomes (or if he did, this was immaterial to his decision to dismiss the case against HFTs). The data flow was not just numbers, but numbers organized with triggers and instructions, just as in the "hide and light" orders and proprietary ordering systems. Calculative technologies then have a consequential effect of changing the way that aspects of the world are valued in relation to one another, with arbitrage opportunities exploited, which change the values of different regions and people, and values between asset classes.

The important contribution of the concept of "calculative technologies" is that it provides a way of critically theorising and investigating how new entities such as these are able to be created and *accounted for*, such that they can assume "market values". In this way, a prior value of an exogenous "economic x" (as in conventional economics), is not there waiting to be discovered, as the economic sociologists and performativity theorists insist (Bracking *et al.* 2014: 10). In fact it is produced by the valuation system in which it is made acting as a means of representation of "real world" facts and production structures. That the "real" price of something is often thought to be waiting to be discovered is instead an appearance generated by processes in which "experts" work. Prudham argued that "the alienation, individuation and abstraction involved in constructing the discrete 'thingness' of genes and organisms" makes these bits mutually equivalent and exchangeable "but also as if they had been 'invented' by experts and investors" (Prudham 2007: 418). However, these experts often claim that their discoveries reflect an inherent value that needed to be known. In short, values at frontiers are constantly in the process of being made, such that an epistemology which can explain how these discoveries happen is one of *how* "economic x is made" (see Callon *et al.* 2007).

Moving away from money markets to other places of accumulation, there are also calculative technologies that are embedded in institutional arrangements that assist in the making of new valued entities, individual examples of which would be carbon credits, species credits, biodiversity offsets, marketable title deeds, water allowances and development impact scores. The creation of the carbon economy, eco-system services, and biodiversity habitats provide three contemporary examples of this struggle in the context of building a new architecture for capital accumulation in which nature is abstracted into fluid circulating units of value, or in Büscher's terms "liquid nature". Freed from context and place these can be exchanged for commensurate forms of derivatives in other, also made commensurable "markets". The spectacle or "theatres of persuasion" are often international conventions and conferences where experts meet to solve humanity's problems, which the experts pacify, measure and define. The UNFCCC, the International Union for Conservation of Nature (IUCN) World Conservation Congress and other examples, are thus powerful sites in which organizing rationality is produced, becoming themselves subject to ever greater levels of spectacle by those who would wish to buy and sell transferable circulating nature units.

Thus, much of the current literature on "discovering" the value of nature through applying the calculative technologies of ecosystem services experts is a well-intentioned effort to apply prices to things in order that people, and in particular, planning departments and politicians, will value them more and conserve, preserve or restore them. Similarly, the calculative technology of "natural capital accounting" seeks to "discover" and then account for the value of minerals and oil when they have not been removed from the ground by giving those stores full current market value (as if they had already been sold) in order to argue that they should be left in the ground because current returns to a country are too low. The World Bank produced some of the earliest calculations, and authors such as Patrick Bond use this logic to argue for a reduction in minerals extraction, particularly in the context of climate change (Bond 2014b; 2014c). But here the calculative technology (natural capital accounting) has created a new valued entity in the form of a unit of mineral in the ground, which is discovered to be the same unit of itself, but in a new form that could be instantly traded for a realized price. Thus the "accounted for" natural capital is a virtual representation of its thingness that is still in the ground.

For example, in the generation of carbon units to be traded, the underlying asset that is "made" is a valuation denominated in CO_2 equivalence of an historical act of pollution of methane, sulphur, nitric oxide and so forth, which is to be (now) abated. It was not priced before, but via carbon calculation, can now be turned into certified emission reductions (CERs), which can be traded and transformed into money, moving through a certification process, to a market launching process, underwriting, securitization and then trade. In this process, the originating company, and then the carbon trader, can become quite boastful in company texts in their exaggerated claims of how much their prior pollution is worth now it can be monetized and "discovered", and the lack of shame attached. It is a conversion from harm to care that simultaneously conjures CERs into the carbon economy. However, the evidence from the European Union emissions trading system (EU-ETS), and the relative lack of investment in "green" assets suggests that this "liquid nature", or more accurately in this case, "liquid care" has a limited demand curve, rather than that it is the prime focus of value creation.

However, knowing how market-oriented technologies, calculative rationality, accounting "devices", notional values and value framings are increasingly incorporating evermore entities into socially articulated markets and spaces (Bracking *et al.* 2014), does not necessarily give them central agency in determining value. As Lohmann reminds us, it is not the calculative technology per se that makes new exploitable zones or assets for capital, for these latter are not

> pre-existing objects whose appropriation came about only at the point at which they happened to be measured or exchanged for money. Nor were they imaginary objects created by a reductionist "politics of knowledge"

> involving numbers and calculations, nor a sort of "superstructure" built on a separate base of purely "economic" relations.
>
> (Lohmann 2016: 45)

Also, no technique of measurement rises to,

> prominence because a few isolated geniuses decided to throw off encrusted bias and face the physical world as it "really is", but through intensive alliance-building involving what Bruno Latour calls theatres of persuasion, in which far-flung inscriptions and visualizations of all kinds … [are] assembled in a single framework and technologies built for comparing and manipulating them
>
> (Lohmann 2016: 50; citing Latour 1986)

These mapping and calculative techniques to make ever new "externals" from the complex entwined mess of human/non-human/nature places, involves "hard work and intensive struggle" by protagonists (Lohmann 2016: 50), and is arguably never fully "won".

It may be that the constant development of new measuring devices and calculative technologies is itself a consequence of a foundational problem that biological processes do not lend themselves easily to capitalist logics, such that capitalist agriculture embeds rationalities in order to have the most advantageous position in relation to risks. An earlier generation of authors in fact wrote extensively on this. Burbach and Flynn defined the "problem of (capitalist) agriculture" as "how to make nature step to the tune of the capitalist clock, that is, how to revolutionize the biological processes themselves" (1980: 28). Similarly Goodman *et al.* argued that an uneasy alliance is formed, where, "agro-industrial capitals are the protagonists of an unstable and constantly redefined alliance between rural, land-based or nature-based, processes and capitalist industrial production processes" (1984: 197). The companies involved partially appropriate aspects of production, while the direct rural producers combine what has not yet been incorporated, and manage the technological applications (ibid.: 196). This analysis helps explain how agro-industrial companies can increase their level of profits relative to the rural producer, by managing those links in the product chain that are the most profitable, that is, inputs, processing, distribution and retail, while leaving the producer with the least profitable, biologically-embedded, and consequently most risky part of the chain, which is growing the crop.

Assemblages

To understand the emergent financialisation of nature into new and virtual commodities it is useful to use theoretical approaches that can understand indeterminacy, unsettled or not yet finished processes and things in motion. The history of the European Union emissions trading system for carbon (EU-ETS) for example, arose, peaked and collapsed as a marketization system with contested entities, agency and materiality. That said, it also served a core of corporate interests well: the carbon speculators and the European coal-fired power stations. It is useful to understand such experiments as emergent assemblages, assemblage theory being derivative of the literature on "vibrant materialisms". Assemblage accounts are constructivist understandings of socio-spatial relations which "blur divisions of social-material, near-far and structure-agency to explain extended social formations comprised of heterogeneous interacting elements" (Nel 2015: citing DeLanda 2006). This theorisation of near, but not concrete, sets of social and nature relations has fluidity and sees change as a variable. Thus:

> The aim is not a totalisation, a definitive tracing of limits, or a final theory of everything. It is rather an expression of possibilities, an invention of new methods and new perspectives, an active "entertainment" of things, feelings, ideas, and propositions that were previously unavailable to us.
>
> (Shaviro 2009: 148; on Deleuze and Guattari's idea of assemblage; cited in Nel 2015: 3)

In assemblage theory an entity can be a thing, a body, a machine, a city, state or in our case a system of financialisation composed of cognate logics, practices and relationships that bind people, things and nature into an emergent, immanent, historical domain of finance. This has a spatial, territorial and discursive form, a gathering of cognate logics, beliefs and practices which then acts upon the world to reproduce and subject other people, animals and natures. In a sense, it has accumulation logic, not just in terms of capital, but in terms of calculative practises, recruiting and calling other spaces and prior rationalities into itself.

As summarised by Nel there are two axes of "co-functioning" in assemblages: "first between the *material (machinic content*) and *virtual (collective expressions*); and secondly between (re)territorialising and deterritorialising" (2015: 4, emphasis in original). Parts of the assemblage come together and move apart between these two moments, such that between them "everything happens" (ibid.; citing Anderson and McFarlane 2011: 149). The first moment is that defined by the tension of the material relative to the normative or ideational; while the latter shapes the spatial and territorial fixity or destabilisation and disassembly. The territorial footprint or otherwise of the assemblage is conditioned by the second moment, but can also be seen as over determined by the first. For example, the idea that a financialisation of eco-system services or biodiversity offsets is possible can act to incorporate evermore hectares of land from which new valued entities can be extracted. Thus global organisational practices in conservation and ecology, are articulated in specific places and spaces, "or territorialised in assemblages – they define new material, collective and discursive relationships. These 'global assemblages' … are domains in which the forms and values of individual and collective existence are problematized or at stake, in the sense that they are subject to technological, political and ethical reflection and intervention" (Collier and Ong 2008: 4; cited in Nel 2015: 5).

Green Bonds

The role of ideas and materialities co-producing value is well illustrated in the example of "Green Bonds". Issuance in the green bond market grew from US$11bn in 2013, to US$34.2bn on 20 November 2014, and is predicted to be at US$300bn by 2018 (Environmental Finance 2014a). The Climate Bond Initiative (CBI) estimates that in 2014 the "total universe of bonds linked to key climate changes solutions" stood at US$502.6bn, compared to US$346bn in 2013 (CBI 2014: 3) with US$7.2bn in new green bonds issued in the first quarter of 2015 (ibid.). These figures appear large when compared to public OECD members' global expenditure in grants on climate change of US$9bn in financial year 2013–2014 (OECD 2014), and as of May 2015 a Green Climate Fund (GCF), which had generated US$10.19bn in pledges, of which US$3.97bn had been signed into contracts (GCF 2015). The GCF is a new specialist entity of the UNFCCC dedicated to attracting and spending climate finance. Also, in Chapter 2, it was established that money in the global economy, conservatively measured, is at least US$117 trillion. In other words, green economy assets remain a small fraction of the global economy, and yet are seen as central in financing climate change mitigation and adaptation.

As of July 2015, there were five main green bond indexes listing these bonds, where an index is used to track performance of green bonds that are included in the index: Solactive (the first index in March 2014), MSCI/Barclays (October 2014), Standard and Poor's (S&P) (one in July and another in September 2014), Bank of America Merrill Lynch (BAML) (in October 2014) (Environmental Finance 2014d). Two further indexes exist, Nikko Asset Management (from 2010, but restricted to World Bank issues) and Calvert (October 2014, but extremely broad). The possibility of increased derivatives trading was then enhanced by the launch of the world's first index-linked green bond fund, the State Street Global Green Bond Index Fund for institutional investors by State Street Global Advisors in April 2015, which tracks the Barclays/MSCI green bond index launched in 2014 (Environmental Finance 2015b). The indexes vary in size but the MSCI/Barclays is viewed as the "most green" as it includes post-issuance verification.

However, the determination of green is left to industry experts and third-party bodies closely connected to the issuing bank, and market rules are still voluntary rather than mandated. Each index is different, having a "unique selling point", summarised by Sean Kidney, CEO of NGO the CBI as "It's all quality ice cream, but investors can still pick the flavour they want" (Environmental Finance 2014b). Most significant are differing inclusion rules (for bonds to be listed on the index), which derive from the lack of standardisation in this relatively new market, and the lack of a determinate definition of "what is green?" (Environmental Finance 2014a). Thus the green bond market privileges what appear to be quite ad hoc evaluation and verification procedures, with the subsequent rating, "Gold Standard", or inclusion in an index, having immense consequences for the demand for the bond or ABS. For example, of five current indexes for green bonds in 2015, one uses an NGO, Climate Bonds Initiative (CBI), one Bloomberg and the others in-house "specialists" (Environmental Finance 2014d; 2015a).

In the absence of market rules, "green" is currently determined by two main qualifications: either the proceeds of the bond are (supposed to) be ring-fenced for environmentally beneficial projects – called "use of proceeds" bonds; and/or the issuers themselves badge them as "green" with an accompanying narrative – called "self-labelled" bonds (Environmental Finance 2014b). Some indexes, like the carbon traders before them in the "Gold Standard" brand, use external market verifiers. Solactive uses the Carbon Bond Initiative (an NGO) to decide what is "green" and includes self-labelled use of proceeds issued above US$100m in size, but excludes asset-backed notes, that is securities, (which meant that Toyota's US$1.75bn ABS to support leases for its hybrid cars was excluded), and is agnostic on project bonds. Project bonds are dedicated to a classified green activity, such a solar power, in their entirety but are not seen to generate much profit. The CBI provides a universe of approved issues from which the index's constituents are drawn, and Solactive then assesses them on the quality of the issuers' own explanation for the "use of proceeds", with 65 included by October 2014, whose identities are not disclosed except to customers. Meanwhile Barclays and MSCI have written their own rules and methodology, and are still debating eligibility thresholds for large hydro projects, annual reporting requirements and the "use of proceeds" category (Environmental Finance 2015a).

The S&P Dow Jones has two indexes, one for labelled use-of-proceeds of bonds (S&P Green Bond Index), and the other for project bonds (S&P's Green Project Bond Index), and assesses the "use-of proceeds" narratives in both indexes to decide on inclusion. The latter included 21 bonds (as of November 2014), which were products of special purpose entities, asset-backed securities linked to green assets, or corporate bonds from "pure-play" firms, where "pure-play" means all the money is invested in the thing that is "green" rather than just a part of it (which is termed "non pure-play"). Thus, in the latter there is "no self-labelling requirement, but proceeds must be used entirely for green projects, and notes must be serviced by revenue generated by those projects", generally over a 20-year period with an average size of just under US$400m in a single bond (Environmental Finance 2014d). Meanwhile, for consideration of inclusion in the BAML's Green Bond Index a bond must first be tagged as green by Bloomberg (190 bonds were in 2014), and then BAML uses the use of proceeds criterion, with reference to the Green Bond Principles (first launched in 2011, revised from January 2015), to select 51 bonds (as of November 2014), collectively valued at US$31bn and accounting for 77 per cent of the overall capitalisation of the market (ibid.).

In practice, many assets designated as "green" would be of dubious quality to environmental scientists. For example, in the HSBC Global Climate Change Index (CCI), there are "pure play" companies, which are "those deriving more than half their revenues from climate-related activities" and "non-pure plays", which have presumably less revenue invested in this way, although down to what benchmark remains opaque. Also, a history of controversial "green bond" investments is already growing, with early examples notably including GDF Suez's "green" bond that financed the controversial Jirau Dam in Brazil, which with its neighbour Santo Antônio Dam, both on the Madeira River, the largest tributary of the Amazon, had "serious and perhaps irreversible impacts on freshwater ecology and nearby communities". It also threatens the survival of migratory fish, some indigenous communities in the area were not even contacted, there are toxic effects on the river, and flooding has been exacerbated leading to thousands of displaced persons (Environmental Finance 2014b).

This last example illustrates the messiness of assets on the ground in relation to their pacified securities and derivatives products. It suggests that in the green bond market, the act of valuation which confers "greenness" can add to the profitability of an underlying asset in the derivatives markets, which have principle correspondence to it – such as in "forestry" "infrastructure" "energy" or "transport" – but the profitability of the asset is still also co-produced through its materiality in place. Also, the quality of the place can deteriorate as a result of the economic activities financed from the investments.

New value entities

Answering the question of what is, and what is not a green economy asset is a matter of standpoint, in the absence of legal regulation, not least because this judgement is a product of differing evaluation processes. There is also a form of virtuality that can be isolated in reference to profits made in pure arbitrage opportunities based in the reinsurance and credit default swap markets of green bonds, supported by the fact that nothing has actually changed in the productive economy outside the world of derivatives. Thus, while it is obvious that not all economic activities invested in by green stock are fictive, it cannot be established how far investments are "real" or "performed" when benchmarked against their real existence or scientific contribution to averting climate change. Instead, the real and virtual are coproduced and 'discovered' within evaluation practice (even if we cannot establish to what exact degree they mix). This conditions "how far" investments cause changes in the material world, and how far the asset comes into existence as a consequence of a written or discursive framing and an associated virtual life-world, often as an acronym listed on an index, which also has an acronym. Thus there emerge three questions from the sections above.

(1) Is this configuration of markets for newly valued and pacified nature-based products generated because circulation is dominant over production due to financialisation?
(2) Are financialised products standardised from different human and ecological domains, including from the money market itself, commensurate with each other?
(3) How far is this dependent on structures of expertism, knowledge, power and privilege in the institutions in which values are made?

In terms of the first question, the answer must be no. Büscher has argued that the institutional demands of "liquid capital" require circulation to determine production (also Marazzi 2011: 48–49). Or as LiPuma and Lee (2005: 424) argue, we are living in

> an era where speculative capital, a socio-historically specific concept of risk and derivatives products have become the centre of the financial clockwork that turns the hands of contemporary capitalism. There is reason to believe that circulation-based risk represents a new self-structuring dynamic that is superimposed upon and structurally supersedes an earlier form grounded in production-based labour.

Büscher argues that this isn't new, but what is, is that "the valorisation of production is increasingly alienated from the act of production" (2013: 25). In other words, production in general, as a Marxist category, "is relegated to producing 'underlying assets' for the financialised derivative structure that is the prime focus for value creation in contemporary capitalism" (ibid.: 26). He then argues further, that these two propositions are the precursors for his idea that "liquid nature" then circulates as capital, where nature is not necessarily moved or used but conserved: the two propositions require the circulation of "liquid nature" as capital.

However, given the importance of financialisation to entraining people in place in particular ways, we can concur with Büscher's first proposition that valorisation is carried out in an interdependent, but related domain to production, if this is akin to his notion of "alienation from", in the markets we have described above. His second assertion, that production in general "is relegated to producing 'underlying assets'" (ibid.) is more of a cognitive challenge. Arguably it is not that one dominates "over" the other, such that production is "relegated" by circulation. Rather there is a constant indeterminacy concerning whether the act of making a legally safe and contracted derivative income stream from an asset will work. For example, the market for timber and the market for ABS CDOs, in terms of a risk agency rating, would not be seen to have much correlation, or risk from an aggregate economic event. The calculative technologies in each would be different with market intelligence around risks covering different events, from the weather, biological reports to data on individuals' incomes and risks. However, the markets are nonetheless connected in the structure of power and economy overall, particularly in places where houses are built from wood and house prices are sensitive to new build costs, or where timber plantations and forests are taking land needed for houses. In other words, value production is triggered through an indeterminate network of partially commensurate market environments, not by a *deux ex machina* of one "Market".

Also, with the generic trends in global financialisation, capital may differ when applied at another scale, or to economic activities whose designation as "green" is even more ephemeral than those of "conservation". The answer to this dilemma may be that when a green economy asset directly guarantees access to scarce, exploitable resources in a more conventional mode of accumulation, acting in effect as a "gateway asset", it generates derivative income streams in the wider regime, or people/ecology assemblage. For example, a REDD + generated carbon mitigation unit may struggle to find a buyer, since "care" itself is a luxury commodity whose purchase lacks immediacy or compulsion, whereas ownership of the REDD + carbon mitigation unit, as part of a wider forestry assemblage (see Nel 2014) could quite readily generate for its owner other income streams, such as access to land and "renewable" timber concessions where the REDD + scheme acts as offset. Thus, whether circulation comes to dominate production – as Büscher (2013), Marazzi (2011: 48-49), and LiPuma and Lee (2005: 424) argue – may be critically determined by the nature of the particular green economy asset in question, and its social, economic and ecological entrainments and entanglements in place. Just as the windfarms in the Clean Development Mechanism (CDM) portfolio in South Africa gave energy conglomerates access to public subsidy and control over their "competitor" energy substitutes, and thus a leverage on the energy regime as a whole, ownership of a carbon sequestration (added to the CDM structure in 2011), can generate overall control over timber supply and competitor suppliers in a particular situated natural resource economy.

The second question asks whether it is plausible to view financial derivatives, knowledge-based products, or units of underlying contracted infrastructure as acting the same in accumulation. New commodities derived from knowledge, or calibrated in environmental care or repair, certainly may share with financial derivatives an element of evaluative expertise provided by persons or algorithmic programmes in discrete institutional contexts (see Bracking *et al.* 2014). However, as "gateway assets" units of value related to the environment are arguably different, in that their means to attract profit requires attachment or embedding in a material regime of accumulation, which may or not be a given. In other words, a calculative technology contributes to a valuation system within an overall assemblage, and in that sense has agency, but it is the overall assemblage that guarantees command over resources and which as a holistic whole expropriates profit from the commoner (see Lohmann 2014, 2016). We return to this question of financialised nature in the next chapter.

The answer to the third question, of whether both ecology and knowledge-based valued entities rely for their successful circulation on the power of expertise and evaluation itself, has been answered using the examples above. It is not that values are simple ephemeral products of evaluation, but that value is co-produced between the virtual and the material in different combinations depending on the nature of the "thing" itself, which has agency, and the power relationships between participants in the market. Over time, there has been a tendency for the financiers and owners of investment to become more powerful in relation to owners of corporate capital and over workers and people in the entrained assemblage that their investments condition. However, this is not necessarily inevitable as the periodic crashes in global accumulation prove. And yet, even in a crash it seems that finance can do well: it is extractive in a boom and reinsured in a crash. In short, and using market vernacular, it is financiers who are "towing the iceberg" of the peoples' economic and social lives.

Conclusion

There is a fairly recent insight from the "vibrant materiality" literature on conservation that humans, non-humans and nature combine into constellations of resistance to new financialisation processes, and that none need to be eminently privileged in terms of agency (see Lohmann 2016; Sullivan 2014; Nel 2015). This goes further than O'Connor's ideas of "double contradictions", (of economy and ecology providing resistances to accumulation). Here power derivative of human structures and institutions is not seen as acting in a unidirectional manner toward "external structures" but flowing in assemblages of human and non-human elements which all act in certain ways on other elements. In this consideration the dimension of the imagined, the virtual and ideational is also performative of the way power operates and values are made in financial framings of human/ecology assemblages. Using economic sociology in this way may perhaps also assist in the older problem of how to understand crisis and the expansion and contraction cycles of value empirically. Marxist economics provides an annoyance of laws, tendencies, counter-tendencies and "fly-in" explanations used to "best fit" moments of financial crisis and class struggle, but generally is hopeless in either predicting a crash or empirically explaining "what just happened". In short, it is time, for political economy to open up the draw-bridge to the "framed out" non-existence of its traditional utils and SNALTs, and establish a critical and empirical account of financialisation "at work".

5 Frontiers of accumulation and ecology

> Africa needs solutions. The XCF will offer African nations a new financing mechanism to manage climate risks by providing direct access to new private capital and by leveraging development partner contributions. We are leading the way in innovative climate finance. (Dr Ngozi Okonjo-Iweala, Nigeria's Minister of Finance and Chair of ARC's Governing Board, speaking in September 2014, ahead of the UN Climate Summit in New York).
>
> (Artemis 2014)

The last four chapters described what has happened to money and capital in the last 30 years, and argued that financialisation could be understood as a concept describing phenomena in five domains, or in relation to: aggregate political economy; hegemonic ideology; post-liberal exceptions; governance technologies; and as a conqueror of new frontiers. But to understand financialisation in these five broad moments it is necessary to go beyond money, the political economy of markets and the material in general, to realms traditionally seen as externalities to economic thought such as ecology, the non-human world and nature. How have these financialisation processes interrelated with, recombined, and re-configured other actants and animisms; and with what consequences for constellations of social, ecological and economic assemblages in place? (Sullivan 2013b; Nancy 2001; Lohmann 2016). This implies that what is being rejected in this chapter is the traditional Marxist idea of crisis being caused by an "over-accumulation of capital" in a paradigm where "Nature" has been externalised as a "natural resource", outside of economic processes. This is an expansion of traditional political economy which allows us to see the financialisation of power as an assemblage of human/nature relations and as working across state/economy and public/private dyads, privileging neither economics nor scale. However, the chapter concludes, as a number of authors have done recently, that the ability of financialisation as a process to access and entrain nature depends on the "nature of the 'nature' being financialised" (Loftus and March 2015). The agency embedded in some things, such as water (Bakker 2003; Boelens *et al.* 2014), or oil (Labban 2010), make it hard to "attach a price tag to everything" (Smith 2008; see also Bridge 2007).

Financialisation and ecology

In ecology, the concept of financialisation has been applied to discrete and limited policy instruments, such as carbon trading, species banking or biodiversity and offset markets (see Sullivan 2011; 2013b), rather than grand theoretical change. Financialisation in this "frontier sense", of creating "new" phenomena, has been used to describe both the use of a financial instrument in the valuation of a previously uncommodified resource, (such as in carbon trading, debt for equity swaps, environmental mortgages, species, biodiversity and sustainability derivatives); and the greater use of monetary valuation of previous vernacular exchanges, such as through the titling of land markets or use rights to land. This discrete, "frontier" use of the term, refers to the critical boundary of capital accumulation as it meets the previously non-valorised world (in price terms at least), and refers to the active attrition that draws people and things into generalized commodity production on ever greater entrained scales. This definition has antecedents in concepts of primitive accumulation, or in Harvey's reframing of this as "accumulation by dispossession" (Harvey 2003, 2010; see also Sullivan 2011: 21–23; and Ferguson 2005). This work on frontier commodification is an important aspect of Marxist theories of capital accumulation more generally, as it generally concurs with the idea that general commodity production has an inbuilt tendency to expand, albeit with resistances, according to the Polanyian "double movement", such that interest-bearing money rediscovers its ties to a finite world of value in a financial crisis (Lohmann 2016: 54–55, citing McNally 2003: 12).

Thus from within the conservation literature, Sullivan applies financialisation to new markets and new products, asserting that "[f]or finance to 'operationalise' the accumulation opportunities of environmental crisis and conservation, products and commodities connecting these domains need to be created so as to open a new financialised sphere for investment, trade and speculation" (2011: 6). She cites Robertson that capital has to "see" nature in new ways (Robertson 2006: 368), "requiring that the earth-in-crisis is rethought and reworded such that it is brought further into alignment conceptually, semiotically, and materially with capital" (Sullivan 2011: 6). In this genre, the financialisation of conservation, and the environment more generally, is framed from the non-human world to serve the purposes of commodification and fetishisation in wider accumulation dynamics (see also, Igoe *et al.* 2010: 494).

However, these frontier processes do not form in isolation from the more generic processes of financialisation occurring in mainstream markets, since it is largely direct regulatory measures imposed by governments for offsetting in older resources markets which has generated demand for the "spun out" biodiversity, species and sustainability banks, funds and products. In short, Harvey, Polanyi and Moore's insistence on the requirement of "frontier theft" to accumulation may be over-stated, if our characterization of accumulation as an ever changing assemblage proves durable. Here, change is just as likely in the morphing and reforming of value as "underlying assets" and new asset classes, which, as we saw in Chapter 2, has been salient to the response to crisis. Accumulation is continued by reorganising the stock of values and assets, including virtual ones, which constitute units of capital and their derivate income streams, according to an institutional assemblage embedded in the structure and relations of class power. Thus as Lohmann has recently argued, in relation to units of "natures" "new connections are often referred to with shorthands such as 'quantification', 'abstraction', 'fragmentation' or 'monetization'". However, "such labels are clumsy synechdoches that foreshorten much of the conflict-ridden politics involved by telescoping changes in large complexes of relationships into a few, often highly-mystified, 'intellectual' zones of the process" (Lohmann 2016: 44). He cites George Henderson to the effect that the quantifiable "unit" critical to capital accumulation, "is neither unit nor thing as such, but a highly volatile set of social relations and processes" (Henderson 2004: 507; cited in Lohmann 2016: 44). With carbon emissions ever rising and mineral stocks ever depleting, circulation does not appear to be dominant over production, nor theft (and its various calculative entities and synechdoches) dominant over re-organisation, but rather all moments a consequence of these continual class reconfigurations, understood as "processes in their entirety" (Lohmann 2016: 44).

Thus the non-privileging of internal/externalities in understanding economic process is important, because empirically it becomes hard to isolate one process from another. In fact, in empirical practice, new financialised objects emerge from both within established commodified spaces and from without, as "new" products while these themselves then morph into merged elements of capitalised nature. The two most common means to use the term "financialisation" in respect to nature then mirrors this empirical reality. In other words, ways of conceptualising financialisation as old, generalised and from mainstream economy sit uncomfortably with its use for new, discrete, frontier and additional "products". But these are enmeshed since: (1) "new" products have precedents, for example in the first generation of debt-for environment swaps from the 1980s; (2) many "new" products linked to offsetting are a consequence of accumulation in "old" sites, where environmental impact must thus be similarly measured, evaluated and priced to create substitutability and commensurability between the two markets; and (3) some "new" products are rebranded or reclassified "old" companies and funds, such that eco-funds, natural capital and green bonds have etymologies in plantation, forestry and conservation companies and funds, particularly involving a re-categorisation of the underlying assets and investments of development finance institutions. Before returning to a holistic view of how financialisation frames human/non-human and nature well-being, however, let's explore the insights from the literatures on "frontiers".

Value-making at frontiers

Moore, borrowing from the Marxian concept of primitive accumulation, recently argued that capitalism still relies on "Four Cheaps" at its frontiers – of labour power, food, energy and raw materials (cited in Lohmann 2016: 44). Jason Moore is influential in transporting the concept of financialisation into ecology with his insistence on the centrality of "the penetration of finance into everyday life, and above all into the reproduction of extra-human nature" (2010: 390; see also Sullivan 2013, 2014). But then Moore goes further, to argue that not only is financialisation evident in a multi-scalar form, but that the grand scale depends on the penetration of evermore localised places for its further expansion. He argues that increases in the productivity of labour, key to the expansion of capital in Marxist terms, relies on another level of expropriation of the "outside", the unpaid work of non-humans and humans from "frontiers of uncapitalized natures" which lie "outside the circuit of capital but within reach of capitalist power" (Moore 2014: 36; cited in Lohmann 2016: 44). In Moore's terms, capital overcomes productivity crisis by finding new ways to "appropriate new streams of unpaid energy/work" and feeding these into the circuit of "capital as a whole" (Moore 2014b: 20). Indeed, he sees capitalism as a "frontier civilization" (Moore 2014a: 7), rather than just having frontiers, where "a small amount of capital [can] appropriate a very large basket of nature's gifts: cheap forests, fertile soil, workers unable to offer effective resistance, and so forth" (Moore 2011: 46). These frontiers, as Lohmann further explains, "are not pre-existing givens, but are continuously constructed just as labour power is constructed" (Lohmann 2016: 46).

In Lohmann's exhaustive historical account of these new configurations he expertly illustrates how in the process of entrainment an aspect of nature is not discovered pre-formed but changes in the process of catchment, often into evermore abstracted, generalised equivalences, or "panoplies of new equivalences" (2016: 53). Thus, before nineteenth-century thermo-dynamics, there was no abstract "energy", just "horses, fire, trade winds, lightning, the ripening of wheat and so forth" (47), in their non-interchangable forms. But by 1870:

> "energy" had become part of the currency of "nature". The commensurability of heat, kinetic energy, electricity, magnetism, and chemical energy had been cemented not just in the discourse of physicists, but also in the materiality of everyday life, in the conversion engines, factory floors, wires, pipes, travels and relationships linking goods, metals, and peoples and their territories, routines and governments.
>
> (Lohman 2016: 47)

Thus, even though he doesn't use the word, Lohmann is speaking of a whole reorganisation, a flotilla of connections in the same way as theorists would use the concepts of actants and assemblages. Similarly, from the late twentieth century the separate behaviours of traders, currencies and tectonic plates became generalised and extracted as "generalised, exchangeable risk" (ibid.: 50), and with securitisation for banks "to sever relationships with borrowers that they had had to pursue under a previous 'originate and hold' model of lending, and, increasingly, regard risk as 'external' to such relationships" (ibid.: 53).

However, in Lohmann's work, complexity is allowed for without the Marxist habit of linear progression to deepened exploitation. He notes that new entanglements are "mediated by commoners", since

> attempts to disentangle land, water and work from commons relationships in order to re-entangle them in commodity circuits are always brought up short at a certain point, necessitating moments of re-re-entanglement.
>
> (Lohmann 2016: 54; citing Polanyi's (2001) "double movement")

These entanglements pre-figure our current phase built on "successive natures of capital, each built on top of, or using materials from, previous natures", like an old building in constant renovation and repair (Lohmann 2016: 55). Thus, Lohmann explains that for EU-ETS to produce fungible units of "the carbon-cycling capacity of oceans, mountains, forests or even anthills worldwide" (ibid.: 58), nation states had to be able to agree permits and create caps, but that this "limits" or "planetary boundaries" concept belongs to the previous era" (ibid.: 58–65). In short, there are "distinct historical natures associated with various eras of capital accumulation" (ibid.: 43).

Value, frontiers and the virtual dimension

Given the new range of nature products, and building on this seminal work by Lohmann, it is apposite to explore the process by which they come into existence, particularly the role of social struggle and expertism in resisting and making the calculative and value assumptions required to enable the creation of new value entities. For example,

> the possibility of creating a marketable biodiversity offset for the mitigation of environmental harm requires a whole host of assumptions and constructs regarding "the nature of nature", accompanied by a whole other set of assumptions regarding things like development pathways, what it means to be human, the appropriateness of markets for best allocating environmental health and harm.
>
> (Bracking *et al.* 2014: 11, insight from Sian Sullivan)

In short, the commodity must be tamed and then (re)framed. The implications of the new circulating and value-accumulating entities are then iteratively felt on the nature of the commodity and on the assemblage of human/non-human/nature relationships from which it has been partially abstracted.

In Büscher's work on neo-liberal conservation the poor and nature were depicted as "'underlying assets' for what has become the 'real' source of value … namely images and symbols within the realms of branding, public relations and marketing" (Büscher 2010: 259). In his later work he argues for a "liquid nature" circulating with even less relationship to any material fixed asset (Büscher 2014). This is a characterisation of value creation that specifically fits the world of tourism and conservation, since this continues, more than other nature-based sectors, to rely on the divide of the natural world between "wild" and "resources". With the onset of industrial capitalism and colonialism non-humans became external to human life, while nature was instituted as divided between "resource" and "wild", "between (1) titled raw material to be carried over the border of 'society' to be processed or 'improved' and (2) 'protected area' supposedly quarantined from human beings" (Lohmann 2016: 48). In contrast, the current "Green Economy" corrodes this divide, in theory and practice, and doesn't consist of the nineteenth and twentieth-century style conserved examples of the whole – a national park or nature reserve. Instead, within green growth, there are new natures in "zones of 'no net loss'" wherein items are commensurated "as means to the new end of an 'averaged', 'flexible' nature" (58). Moreover, "It is through the creation of the new, 'liquid' natures of green growth that hitherto uneconomic activities presented as ecological protection are to become worthy of capital investment" (62). This might include the valuation of averaged past pollution, in order to acquire finance to mitigate it in the present, or at a larger scale, the emerging calculations of historical responsibility for global warming.

Thus where nature and people are connected through the business of tourism, value tends to exist in a more virtual form. These industries rely on images and narratives, not least the "wilderness Africa", which has spawned the expulsion of many indigenous people. For example, Nelson, writes of "environmental colonialism" based on myths and illusion (2003: 80), while Brockington has written about the power of representations of nature, particularly when combined with celebrity, which become more important than the nature itself (2008a; 2008b), culminating in what Büscher terms fictitious conservation (2012). Igoe writes of an "eco-functional" Nature seemingly "amenable to technological reorderings that will optimize economy and ecology, or at least accommodate putatively inevitable growth with minimal disruption to ecosystems and human well being" (Igoe 2013b: 43). This would be a "biophysical world made to appear eminently manageable by a global cadre of experts and professionals" (Castree and Henderson 2014: 24). The bond with nature that people want, or at least that which is presented to them, is often the idealised, romanticised one free of humans; and this symbolic nature is "the necessary and logical focus for neoliberal conservation" (Büscher 2010: 261). In another article, Büscher shows how the transfrontier conservation area (TFCA) in South Africa was turned into a marketing brand, a "brand that 'allows' nature and communities to be valued in the global marketplace" (2010: 263).

In contrast, Lohmann's work is much more adamant that the act of abstracting new nature is permanently messy and subject to continuing struggle as humans and non-humans, actants and things provide for resistance and meaning changes. It is not possible to find a calibration by which we can judge abstraction to have taken place, and perhaps Büscher's characterisation is true of the most successful experiments, where Lohmann's is more applicable to describing the historicity of human/ecology relations and their vulnerability to new forms of resistances.[1] However, Igoe's insights on how abstraction is performed through the role of virtuality and spectacle in accumulation do allow us to cognitively separate abstractions calibrated from materiality to virtuality, from abstractions related to Marxian-inspired categories of economic value.

Following work by Carolan (2005), Carrier and West (2009) on "virtual nature", Igoe uses the term "spectacle" to characterise a type of fictitious conservation, where the consumption and circulation of nature from conservation is critically removed from its sites of "production" and biophysical phenomena, where spectacle is

> a uniquely specialized and powerful form of "capital accumulated to the point that it becomes image" (Debord 1995: thesis 34), and which mystifies and mediates the relationships of its own production (thesis 4). Debord further argued that spectacle's power to transform fragments of reality into a visually pervasive totality, produced "a separate pseudo world" (thesis 2), offered in exchange for the totality of actual activities and relationship, a world of "money for contemplation only" (thesis 49).
>
> (Igoe 2013b: 38).

This concept is useful here because some of the underlying activities that make up the green economy are circulating green bonds and derivatives originally derived from REDD +, ecosystem or biodiversity offsets where the underlying "piece" of nature has been abstracted into a "park" or "conservation zone", represented in media and then turned into a commodity for contemplation and speculation. For Igoe, spectacle can be considered "part of the wider mosaic" (Igoe 2013b: 38) that Michel Foucault (1983; 2008) called techniques and technologies of government (Debord 1998: 2; Crary 2002: 456)". While Debord earlier wrote of concentrated and diffuse spectacle, in relation to Third Reich and Stalinist propaganda, and America corporate advertising respectively, Igoe isolates his third category of integrated spectacle as of particular use to understanding the spectacle of conservation (Igoe 2013b: 39–40). This is "spectacle that has integrated itself into reality to the same extent that it was describing it, and that it was reconstructing it as it was describing it" (Igoe 2013b: 40; citing Debord 1998: 9). This is apposite for the object of work here, since it connects conceptually to the ideas of performativity in economics and that the "value" of certain green economy assets and products is as much conjured by marketing, narrative and integrated spectacle, as it is from a straightforward assessment of the underlying resources.

In order to view the financialisation of capitalism, particularly as it portends to ecological frontiers, as a product of integrated spectacle, it is worth reviewing that there are "four important antecedents to spectacle: 1) forgetting, 2) abstraction, 3) reifications, and 4) proto-exchangeability" (Igoe, 2013b: 40). Forgetting how a thing is made, came into being, or its earlier "use value" function, is part of it becoming exchangeable, which precedes its reification into something more than its previous self, such as a commodity, which then assumes a degree of universality and can be exchanged for others. Thus in Igoe's terms, the conservation park is a universal representation of "ideal universal nature" (ibid.). Similarly, the green economy can be viewed as the universal branding of a set of activities that enjoy some proto-exchangeability reflected in the portfolios, and exchangeability of assets, within green firms and "green bond" funds. Iconic images such as windfarms, grasslands, blue globes held in hands, have come to signify the exchangeability of green economy assets in fund and fund-of-fund trading activity. Contemplation of image becomes the precursor of assets appreciating to functional products of speculation and trade. However, this is spectacle in that the calm serene images of green economy trade fairs belie the destruction of the activities on which some "cleaning" or "mitigation" is being rendered, such as sulphur extraction chimneys for dirty coal; which is an illustration of "Spectacle's ability to project unity and consensus where none actually exists (Debord 1998: 2)" (Igoe 2013b: 43). By claiming the normative high-ground and key signifiers of traditional environmentalism, spectacle acts to silence opposition though the all-encompassing performance of the modern, knowledge-based, expert "solution". As Igoe summarises, spectacle "provides visual articulations of nature as an eco-functional object of intervention, while concealing and marginalizing alternatives and opposition to its seemingly monolithic vision" (Igoe 2013b: 43).

If we apply the concept of spectacle to our entire human/ecology assemblage it allows for different types of value creation at different nodes, but can also be used to explain why principally private capital holders have an incentive to use green spectacle, but not necessarily an interest in funding a new just, ecologically sustainable energy and infrastructure future.

However, herein lies a problem, since the geography and temporality of trading green economy assets is re-territorialised away from the space and place of the actual activities, which are referent to the asset. In financial terms, the securitized derivatives of green bond funds are sold at scale in global stock markets, where history shows us that fund managers have little incentive to check the quality of the underlying assets. Taken back to place and space, there is evidence of non-performing, degraded and simply non-existing windfarms, offsets, carbon capture technologies and tree planting efforts. The case study of South Africa is a case in point. The materiality of a global green economy spectacle occludes the current human/nature assemblage, and the way that this territorialises pollution in concentrated areas of the Global South, while re-territorialising virtual care, and trade in pollution, in the North. Thus the materiality of a global fossil-fuels based and highly chemically intensive global production system is occluded by a normative and virtual discourse of denial and/or promise of solution, this latter performed through the green economy spectacle. In this assemblage, production in general is not made subordinate to circulation, but instead a fourth dimension of accumulation is added to provision the necessity of non-production because profits are not necessarily derived from economic activity, but from the lack of it, or denial of it: thus accumulation here is spatial, temporal and co-dependent on the production of the non-material, the spectacle and the ephemeral. How far this green economy assemblage pre-figures or reflects global political economy more generally remains to be theorised, but similarities are apparent with the complex derivatives described in chapter 2.

Thus, the key to which units of value are predominantly "virtual", "fictitious", narratively "performative" or substantive, and whether they generate derivative income at scale, is to be found in the nature of the overall assemblage in which they are situated. Or in Lohmann's (2016) terms, the particular entrainment of commoner/frontier extractive social relations that is generative of capitalist surplus. For example, it becomes clearer how a designated biodiversity offset or carbon sequestration unit can be viewed as "fictitious" when land proximate to it, that remains undesignated as a "green" asset, may be worth less, with the designation performing the difference in value. However, it is also possible to conceive of circumstances when the overall value of a nature derivative commodified into a green asset through a valuation process might end up appearing as having less value, at least in market terms, than previously, but nonetheless being of supreme value to its actual individual owner. For example, a natural resource or infrastructure fund might benefit from the ownership of a REDD + asset, despite the land value of its forest home dropping, if it simultaneously green-washed its image, added to its brand's reputation, and reduced timber access for its competitors. Here the "fictitious" value is embedded in a historical process of change that emanates from thousands of years of people/nature relations, newly romanticised in order to exclude those same vulnerable people.

The properties of things

This differential ability of financialisation to overcome the hurdles of contracting a derivative income stream from an asset or process in the present also relates to the different properties of "things". Indeed Loftus and March concur with the argument here, but in reference to "commodification" that "commodification takes a different form depending on the nature and material properties of the commodity, as well as the local institutional configurations that help or hinder capital's access to it" the latter here conceived of as an assemblage (Loftus and March 2015: 172). This has similarities to the model of how to study valuation referred to above (the LCSV protocol) excepting that institutional configuration (in Loftus and March) has been replaced by assemblage or institutional arrangement in the latter, which also then includes the role of discursive practice. This last element is a key to explain how the futures price works to control the present by managing key notions and beliefs about the "thing" in question, such that it is scarce, or particularly authentic, pure, unique or indeed useful. Buyers of the commodity need to relate to the nature of the thing as it is represented to them by sellers or price-setters, just as much, if not more so, than relating to it using their own intrinsic knowledge or need of it.

The idea that the thing itself has agency was recognised through ANT theory and animism. In terms of applying this insight to differentiated processes of financialisation, early precedents include Bakker (2003), who termed water "an uncooperative commodity", showing how the properties of water, such as its cost to transport and its framing as a natural monopoly, resist commodification (on water, see also Tricarico and Amicucci 2011). However, financialisation has occurred within the water sector, despite water's reluctance to act like a commodity, by means of the financial intermediaries and financial interests that have become involved in water infrastructure, such that "the infrastructure through which the resource [water] flows, and not the flow itself, should be the focus of attention" (Loftus and March, 2015: 175). Similarly, Labban argued in relation to oil that financialisation within oil markets exists "in parallax with oil's material properties" (2010: 545). He argues that oil trading in futures markets affects current spot prices and ideas around how scarce oil might be, such that "the perpetually shifting value of 'real' capital is a reflection of the shifting value of fictitious titles" (ibid.). Labban summarises that in the oil market, capital reproduces without intermediation in a "space-time parallax" with oil assets not moving physically, and future earnings moved to the present (2010: 542). He uses the classic Marx formula to reference his analysis (ibid.) where M-M'-M" indicates money circulating as speculation without being invested in production, and M-C-M' indicates where money is changed into commodities and then back to money. Marx termed the first "abridged" formula "money which begets money", while the second is the "general formula of capital" (Marx 1976). The former circulation within the money form alone has elsewhere been termed "profiting without producing" (Lapavitsas, 2013).

The general point is to note that some things lend themselves better than others in their ability to be used as an underlying asset for a derivatives product. However, in opposition to authors such as Knox-Hayes who conceptualise financialisation "as an *extension* of the conversion of use to exchange value in commodification" (2013: 120, emphasis added), the argument here is slightly different. Not only are the immanent properties of the thing itself to be usefully given a higher explanatory role; but the future fixing of current power structures makes financialisation a different process to commodification. Neither is necessarily linear. Commodification can be understood as the movement from a past situation when a thing had a use value, to a current situation in which it can be priced and circulated as a pacified thing, which is not to imply that this is either simple or not subject to reversal in another space or time. Financialisation, on the other hand, and particularly as it is applied to nature and the nature of things, acts to fix future derivative income streams by controlling the model of investment and its entrained obligations and recourses in the present.

For example, financialisation processes, and the critical role of financiers in decision-making in project finance, serve to securitise the derivative income from customers in PPP projects with compulsory purchase clauses, including in public–private partnerships found in the renewables sector. For example, Baker examines the experience of the South African Renewable Energy Independent Power Producer Procurement Programme (RE IPPPP), a bidding process for the procurement of privately generated, utility-scale renewable energy, wherein investment rose from just a few hundred million dollars in 2011 to US$5.7bn in 2012 and US$4.8bn in 2013 (Baker, 2015: 146). Baker concludes that there is an "incompatibility between commercial demands for 'bankability', short-term shareholder value and impatient finance and RE IPPPP's unique requirements for community ownership of projects and the realisation of economic development criteria" (ibid.). Renewable energy too is not a tamed commodity: it critically relies on feed-in tariff structures and energy regime regulators, with traditional fossil fuel and parastatals often invested with much power to control newcomers to the energy regime. Also solar and wind have different grid requirements and can compete regressively with each other.

However, these patterns cannot be explained by catch-all concepts such as speculation or the unsatisfactory epistemology of suggesting that it is possible to isolate the real and virtual as mutually exclusive. Unfortunately, most of these authors rely on these concepts, such that the question of "yes but, what is new in financialisation?", which a lay person has the prerogative to ask, is surprisingly hard to pin down. Harvey famously noted, "if we are to find anything truly distinctive (as opposed to 'capitalism as usual') in the present situation, then it is upon the financial aspects of capitalist organisation and on the role of credit that we should concentrate our gaze" (1989: 196). However, arguably, the *why* credit is causing a different structure of capital, if indeed it is, is not a question which has had an authoritative answer to date.

The problem with speculation

As Loftus and March usefully summarise, "the dominance of financial interests has an indisputable influence on the spatio-temporal dynamics of industrial capital and non-financial sectors. Furthermore, the failure to realize profits is often visited upon the 'real' economy. Thus, financialization has an inherently speculative logic based on its reliance on future claims" (Loftus and March 2015: 173). March and Purcell (2014: 17) also refer to finance representing a "speculative claim upon future profits", and Loftus and March assert that "The influence of this speculative claim on the shape and governance of specific sectors of the environment is not to be underestimated" (2015: 173). Or as Loftus and March summarise of Labban's (2010) work on oil, "The money to be made out of oil … is influenced as much by the fictions of finance as by the volumes of oil being pumped out of the ground" according to this "speculative logic" (2015: 173). However, the point that speculation can live side by side with this tendency for cost to be borne in the real economy suggests that this is not speculation in the classic sense, where sometimes investors lose money, but a form of organisation when the pattern of cost is systematically passed to someone else. Loftus and March deem this pass-on of failure as "often" occurring, but I would argue that it is part of the financial design and is nearly invariably the case. This point is discussed further below.

But first, in sum, there are three problems with the conceptualisation of financialisation from the group of authors in the *Geoforum* special issue on financialisation, in which Loftus and March (2015) provide the editorial, which have already been explored in this book. First, as the economist Fisher showed, time is not linear, so circulating capital is a loop back from expectations about the future, and this is what creates prices in the present (the apples from the orchard valuing the orchard). Thus technically, it is not so much a speculative claim on future profits, so much as a claim on income in the present whose liability and debt repayment moves into the future. Second, value does not exist in clearly marked forms that can be categorised as "M" or "C" but in tranched instruments and SPVs, which contain both simultaneously, and even serve to trade between forms of one and the other in fractions of a second while nominally owning both within the same company group. Third, the money circuit can never exist entirely without material mediation and in that sense has its own form of production. Indeed, we saw above how the financial markets are themselves dependent and produced within machines and cables and so forth. Thus, these authors perhaps (1) misuse the word "speculation"; (2) underestimate the implications of weight that should be given to the latent agency of the thing in question, even though they recognise that things are different and act differently in relation to financialisation; and (3) underestimate the role of representation and spectacle in the ability of a financialisation process to work. In the example of weather derivatives, below, the agency of the thing cannot be predicted, but it can be tamed using a calculative technology that is used to proxy for the thing and set limits to investors' liabilities and returns. In the case of carbon, it is not so much that it is commoditized, but rather that a permit to pollute is granted through the trading regime as a value proxy.

Take the central concern with speculation first. It is hard to conceive of this in the traditional sense of an investor taking a high risk, since the design of investments and finance allows for risk to be transferred to other parties in tranched funds, such that lower tier investors may lose, but rarely the higher tranches of derivatives and securities-based derivatives, funds, ETFs and index-based investors. This is, of course, in contra-distinction to the way investors represent their products in different contexts: as highly risky in circumstances when they feel the need to justify large profits; and as safe when trying to attract other pooled investors, as was illustrated in the case of the Barclays dark pool promotional literature. It is perhaps the lack of speculation that is attached to investors' returns that signals the essence of modern financialisation. Or put another way, it is in the avoidance of the incalculable risks of market asymmetry, the historical source of arbitrage, that financialisation is truly successful. It gives money holders ways of managing equity investments that not only tip the odds in their favour, but manage the full range of outcomes available to make sure that another stakeholder will pick up the bill over a number of iterations of the contract. Thus ideally, for the investor, an upper tranche of a SPV looks and acts very much like a secured rent, where rent, defined by Castree and Henderson, applies to income paid for the use of assets "created or owned by others" (2014: 31).

Castree and Henderson argue for "a more forensic sense of how productive, financial and rentier capital combine" (2014: 31) in relation to conservation capital and the work of Sullivan, Igoe and Büscher in their triptych (2013). They argue that Büscher *et al.* are wrong in suggesting that they have discovered something new about the nature of capitalism in their work on conservation, citing Johnson's view that although "we all want to say something new about something new" (2007: 96), this risks "hyperbole and mischaracterisation" (Castree and Henderson 2014: 31). Instead, they argue that the aspects of conservation capital explored by the authors, that they are "largely circulation-based, geared towards value capture, and ha[ve] cannibalistic and hypertrophic tendencies … should not surprise Marxists" (ibid.). Their verdict, and critique of the three authors, is traditional, that money cannot make money indefinitely, but will lead to crisis (ibid.), even if Marx's idea of value "embodies capitalism's non-totalising quality" (32; citing Henderson 2013). In short, everything "new" observed by Büscher *et al.*, was in fact predicted by and explained by Marx. Thus, the suggestion here, that upper tranche speculation has a rentier quality to it, runs against the grain of Marxists who view financialisation as a mode of speculation. However, the point here is not to "invent" something new, and Marx said a lot about rent too, but to note that financial risk management looks increasing like controlling all the tables in the casino.

Money from rent is a potentially sustainable move for capital to make in times of market turbulence, leaving aside this author's reticence of finding the "production/circulation" dyad very useful. There are thus two potential grounds on which "speculation", as an explanatory concept, looks misplaced. The first is that the outcomes of risk management are increasingly managed risk. The second is that, taking the project finance model as an example, the rent category applies surprisingly well to those special investor categories reserved for the bank's own insider trading desks and preferred customers, often in the dark pool. These observations are now explored further in some empirical examples of infrastructure and catastrophe bonds.

Africa's "much-needed" infrastructure and the infrastructure gap

A quick perusal of development literature could lead you to the conclusion that the only thing that is more "much-needed" in Africa than foreign direct investment, is infrastructure, with the World Bank promoting the view that there is a "gap" worth variously gigantic sounding sums of money. This is a problem that is preventing a new greener economy from emerging, although it does reflect on how finance-driven capital has developed a post-2008 "new love affair with real things" (Ouma 2014: 162). Ouma asserts that these relations should be read "from below" to understand their socio-technical logics in place (ibid.). Infrastructural builds with protected derivative income streams are both a dream come true to financiers, but also serve to grow finance. For example, Torrance's (2009) work on a new Thames Water desalination plant, showed the reordering of priorities to providing finance to the investors rather than in providing water to customers. Apparently, this plant may not produce water and may be only used in a drought, but has inflation-protected returns for institutional investors. Rather than water supply, "A more profound motivation seems to be the need for new infrastructural forms within which to ensure speculative gains" (Loftus and March 2015: 175; summarising Torrance 2009).

In fact, in South Africa, President Jacob Zuma proposed a "fast-track" for the environmental assessments of Special Infrastructure projects (SIPs), which are now managed from the Executive arm of Government in the Presidential

Infrastructure Coordinating Commission, following the passing of the controversial Infrastructure Development Act into law in 2014 (Government of the Republic of South Africa 2014). This promoted a new realm in the politics of exceptionalism due to a thinning of parliamentary oversight (Democratic Alliance 2014). However, there are a number of reasons for the popularity of infrastructure spending. First, in the absence of an industrial policy that is working to produce jobs, building something creates jobs at opportune moments in the fiscal and electoral cycle. Second, in a country with racialised inequality, the construction sector is one of the few where previously historically disadvantaged persons can gain entry as start-up costs are relatively low, so the jobs can be distributed among a constituency within an economic justice discourse, and also to key ruling party supporters in exchange for political finance. Third, public procurement and tendering processes can be further designed to assist new market entries, political support for the ruling party and to raise political finance. Fourth, justifying public expenditures on infrastructure can be done principally by talking of the beneficiaries from procurement, building and the employment created in these processes, while the actual long-run costs in loan repayment and actual sustainable jobs that remain after the construction, which are often much fewer, are downplayed. Thus, in terms of financialisation processes overall, there is also a synergistic relationship between building infrastructure; concentrating power within party-states and the greater extractivism made possible by financiers from the national economy. The whole infrastructure exercise is then made popular through a language of "mega-projects", the "Madiba Magic" of global inclusion and modernity (Desai 2015, 2016).

The example of the 2010 FIFA World Cup infrastructural funds, which built new stadiums in South Africa is another example of how risk can be transferred to future taxpayers, while short-run income streams can be guaranteed. As Desai writes of Durban after the 2010 hosting of the FIFA World Cup, and building of the new Moses Mabhida stadium: "Global finance capital … thrives in a world of large-scale investment in mega-projects, mega-events, and the short-term investment, long-term debt, and creative financing associated with them. The model also imposes a world view in which the West becomes the unit of global measurement" (Desai 2016). The Moses Mabhida stadium seats 70 000 people, where local football teams regularly draw in crowds of just a few 1000s, while its standard operating costs, excluding renovations and repair, are R88.5m a year, with only R9m retrieved from "non-bowl" activities such as shops, a gym and restaurants. The stadium must thus make over R1.5m per week to break even (the remaining R79.5m), and yet "[a]s anyone can attest who regularly passes by the great empty hulk of a building … this level of use is nowhere near being attained" (Desai 2016). Desai quotes Castells that "the flows of power generate the power of flows, whose material reality imposes itself as a natural phenomenon that cannot be controlled or predicted … People live in places, power rules through flows" (Desai 2016; citing Castells 1989: 349). Just as Loftus and March (2015) noted, it is the imprint on the ground that is perhaps what is most significant – empty stadiums and empty ports feeding investors' pockets from public taxes. In short, the "very real ways in which a material imprint from financialisation has been left in the landscape is important" (Loftus and March 2015: 175).

In a more recent "Special Infrastructure Project" (SIP), the operational plans for the Durban port expansion will require the removal of a large number – contested but in the 10s of 1,000s – of settled families in Clairwood and surrounding neighbourhoods. This US$25bn "Back of Port" (BOP) expansion plan (which includes petrochemical expansions) was named the second highest national priority in the National Development Plan 2012 (after the Waterberg-Richards Bay coal infrastructure expansion) and will take capacity at the Durban port from around 2 million to 20 million containers annually. It comes in a list falling under the Presidential Infrastructure Coordinating Commission, with the world's third and fourth largest coal-fired electricity generators at Kusile and Medupi (Desai 2015: 23). Drawn up by consultants, the impact assessments read more like promotional literature. The key impact assessment already "zones" out the people and the names of the communities affected in the title: *A Local Area Plan and Land Use Management Scheme for the Back of Port Interface Zone* (2009). They have become an "interface zone". But as Desai (2015) and Dyer (2014) summarise, the economics of investing R250bn in a container port where costs are already the highest in the world, do not make standard economic sense:

> Once more, like King Shaka airport, Moses Mabhida Stadium, and the International Convention Centre, ratepayers will have to make up the shortfall for massively underutilized infrastructure whose chief benefit is to those who get the contracts to build them and the political class who serve as the "business partners".
>
> (Desai 2015: 25)

Desai terms this "Faustian development" (27), but to oppose it is to "go against the national interest" (32).

Thus unsurprisingly, the consultants (Graham Muller Associates Consortium and UrbanEcon) who were commissioned by eThekzwini Municipality to conduct impact assessments assumed it was in the national interest a priori, such that adverse effects on persons and nature were assumed to be unavoidable and necessary, if they were mentioned at all. UrbanEcon used textbook growth multipliers to argue for surprisingly precise job creation figures of "318 279 temporary jobs created through the port construction process … 63 656 jobs during 30 year construction phase … Job creation of an additional 27 533 jobs at full operation" (Feigenbaum 2011). Meanwhile, Graham Muller Associates conducted a "status quo assessment" of the back of port area to measure the size of formal business' contribution to GDP (not jobs), thus comparing a future scenario with a status quo that will no longer exist, with the future of the proximate people affected not measured (Graham Muller Associates 2009b).

Critically, in terms of the BOP, economics failed on a number of counts (Bracking 2013b, 2013c). First, a comparative sector analysis was not carried out. Top-down planning suggests that all is possible (win-win) but the interests of different economic sectors can contradict each other, with, in this case, possible conflicts with leisure, tourism, cultural industries, sports and lifestyle industries, retail and small commercial, and light industrial ventures. A comparative counterfactual analysis was also missing that would look at the opportunity costs of investing in alternative job creating projects – as Desai points out, even if the jobs were created they would cost R1.9m each (2015: 26). Most critically, perhaps, other increases in regional capacity were not considered, such as the Bolloré Africa and CFM (ports and railway parastatal) building of Mozambique's first oil port in the city of Pemba; Grindrod, Africa's largest shipping company, and Mozambique's Maputo Port Development investing US$1.7bn over the next five years to upgrade ports; the tripling of capacity at the Maputo and Matola ports to 50 million tons by 2020 from 15 million tons; port expansion in Angola at Lobito (US$1.2bn investment by government), Cabinda, and Luanda (over US$350m); a multimillion dollar green-field port at Lamu in Kenya; and the planned US$11bn Bagomoyo port in Tanzania, which will be bigger than the Dar es Salaam and Mombasa ports, both of which are also expanding.

The externalities of the costs of the dig-out port were not costed in, including for people (social and economic impact, heritage capital) and the environment. These are significant, as a minute of the eThekwini Housing Committee notes:

> A report is to be submitted to the Housing Committee that suggests settlements for relocation to Cornubia in terms of a prioritization process. The 12 settlements requested for relocation will be included in that report. As the report currently stands there is a need of approximately 30 000 units identified for relocation to Cornubia. If the 764 structures (excluding the possibility of the "backyard shacks" in formal sites that are in the process of been quantified for Clairwood) [are added] the demand on Cornubia is further increased. The Cornubia development allows for the construction of approximately 12 000 fully subsidized housing structures. Therefore there is an oversubscription of almost 18 000 units.[2]

In other words, the municipality is expecting to need about 30 000 new houses to relocate the affected population (excluding the significant number of informal houses), and plans to do this in a new development of 12 000 that has not been built yet. On the environment Graham Muller Associates note:

> A significant area will be displaced, compensation may require remaining areas of coastal grassland such as the racecourse in addition to significant areas outside the area. The loss of habitat associated with port development may not be replaceable in the location. It may be necessary to conserve other areas within the Municipal Area.
>
> (Graham Muller Associates 2009a)

Initially, "conserving" the Clairwood racecourse was proffered as an "offset", but by August 2015, this had also controversially been transferred to developers for a logistics park, and the prospects in South Durban for its people and environment look grim (SDCEA 2014; Hallowes 2014).

In an alternative assessment of income, assets and actual employment already in the area, which were not offset as a deduction to the widely advertised jobs to be "created" by the contracted consultants, Bracking and Diga found nearly 500 jobs (491, mostly informal) existing in just 1000 representative households surveyed (Bracking *et al.* 2015: 16). Further, it was discovered that over 11.5 per cent of the residents sampled were in informal (or "illegal") settlements, which were not counted for the resettlement considerations (ibid.: 9); 23.4 per cent of households were living on less than R1,000 per month (8); 57.3 per cent cumulatively earned less than R3,000 (ibid.); and only 43.4 per cent were receiving social assistance, 87.8 per cent of which was from the Government (ibid.: 18, 19). At the time of the survey, the claimant income level for a Child Support Grant, for two people, was R2,600 suggesting that a significant portion of people who should have been able to collect assistance were not able to. In the survey, 18.1 per cent were successfully claiming Child Support, and 17.2 per cent an Old Age Pension (20). Thus, the people and their environment have been historically neglected, and are not currently "seen" by a state elite, and their contracted consultants, bent on capturing derivative income streams from construction and procurement. The poverty of the community was instead used against them to suggest that what would be lost was not worth saving, despite huge cultural, social and historical infrastructure and capital present in the neighbourhood (Bracking *et al.* 2015).

Sometimes "communities" receive more explicit attention in infrastructural planning, as in the current renewable energy sector in South Africa, where the renewables energy IPPPP model is accompanied by a government-backed power purchase agreement (PPA), and a commitment to socio-economic empowerment of historically disadvantaged communities. Typically, renewable energy project financing is based on a 70:30 debt to equity ratio of the initial capital cost of the project (Baker 2015: 149–50; citing Mendonça *et al.* 2010: 24), but in South Africa may be typically 80:20. As Baker explains, within the parameters of this programme, the more debt involved, "the lower the average cost of funding, the lower the tariff and the cheaper the project" (Baker 2015: 150). Crucially, the lenders of the finance-based debt enjoy fixed loan terms, are not liable for losses, and are in "first receipt" of the financial revenues generated, while equity investors are "more dependent" on success and returns (ibid.; citing Yescombe 2013: 13, 199). However, critically, equity shares may be "on-sold or restructured after three years" (Baker 2015: 150), and debt can be on-sold "almost immediately after commercial operations date [start] subject to the approval of the DoE [Department of Environment]" (ibid.: 154). Also, the fixed terms of the debt are at an average interest rate of 12 per cent per year for 20 years, "significantly higher" than US or European norms of 7 per cent for 10 to 15 years (ibid.: 151; citing Nelson and Shrimali 2014: 1).

The project company generally takes the form of an SPV, which under RE IPPPP must have a minimum of 40 per cent South African entity participation, a minimum black ownership level of 12 per cent with a 20 per cent target, and "a minimum of 2.5% ownership by communities living within a 50 km radius of the project site" (Baker 2015: 150), although the BEE and community categories can be merged. Although the financing for this ownership stake can come from the originating company or DFI, investments in fact vary according to the financing terms. A project developer explained to Baker that "The project will be paying off the debt for years before the equity shareholders, and hence the communities will benefit financially" at "tenors of about 15 years" (153). In fact, some debt was sold on early to insurance and pension funds, and banks are set to become, as Lohmann and Hildyard said of infrastructure generically, "loan brokers and traders" as well as lenders (ibid.: 154; citing Lohmann and Hildyard 2014: 80). Baker quotes from an interview with the Industrial Development Corporation (IDC) that:

> your private equity players will come in, de-risk it, sell it off, make their profit and then pension funds invest in it long term just for the cash flow. The private equity players are essentially selling cash flow to the pension funds. The equity shareholders make the profit because they took the risk and so they take the return.
>
> (Baker 2015: 154)

Thus, although the Department of Environment holds the right to terminate a PPA if a company fails to deliver on economic and community development, a "potential breakage event" (150), the government is also constrained to continue to enable finance to restructure the project.

However, the design of who and when incomes are paid makes sure that the local investors are last in the queue, at typically 15 to 17 odd years later. Communities are "essentially restricted" (154) in on-selling, as their percentage stake must be maintained for the company to keep its license, and the measurement criteria for the black economic empowerment (BEE) rating are complex. They are the patient investors. Baker is concerned that the new equity investors will have even less relationship with the underlying communities and that this makes the model weak as a transformatory tool. But to extrapolate further, the model allows for either of 2 outcomes: either (1) all the profit is drained in income streams such that after 18 years the communities become payable against old and depreciated windmills now worth very little, and will have to seek new credit and wait again for returns; or (2) the project is successful so the original and new upper-tranche investors issue new preferential stock in the interim, such that when the payments to communities come due communities own diluted stock, a much smaller proportion of all the stock, and again receive little. In this scenario, the proportion of the stock they own could be artificially kept at 20 per cent or some such, while the project could be "thin-capped", or artificially re-indebted, just before the share payout became due. The point is that those who control the finance largely control the finance model such that speculation is replaced by securitisation. By deferring the demands of communities to the future, they can profit in the present.

Carbon, the weather and trading in cats

Financialisation's "love affair" with real things (Ouma 2014: 162) extends to changing the way in which real things are maintained as assets into the future. Atmospheric, ecological and biological processes, which have unpredictable attributes and effects, do not, on the face of it, easily fall into financialisation logics. However, these processes affect place-bound fixed assets, and the insurance industry needs to quantify these effects in order to create an income stream. It is in this way, that weather and the changing climate have become relatively new and expanding markets for finance. The owners of an underlying asset, such as a house, which is fixed in place and might be vulnerable to damage by the weather, have traditionally bought insurance. Insurance companies then buy reinsurance, which globally applies to around 10 per cent of volume, which when aggregated may cause a reinsurer to issue an "insurance-linked security" (ILS), or more recently, a catastrophe bond (which is generally shortened to "cat" bond in the industry) to cover its whole exposure. Thus, cat bonds are a sub-category and new product developed from the wider asset class called insurance-linked securities (ILS), and represent a convergence of the reinsurance and capital markets begun in the mid 1990s (Culp 2002; World Economic Forum 2008), totalling US$40bn in bonds issued between 1997 and 2011 (Johnson 2014: 157). Catastrophe bonds then apply to generic categories such as "US wind" or "Japanese quake". The geographic liabilities, represented in cat bonds, are thus turned into "securitisation pathways" that capital market investors can access when others, such as a reinsurer or directly a city, issue cat bonds.

Through ILS and catastrophe bonds, climate change emerges as a new accumulation frontier, whereby extreme weather is made into an opportunity for capital investments. There is also secondary trading in cats. Live cat trading is where an extreme weather event is predicted and traders are betting on how bad it may be; while "dead cat" trading is where the event has happened, and the paper being traded is related to whether traders think the event will generate losses large enough to trigger a pay-out on the cat bond (Johnson 2014: 177). The growth of secondary markets would suggest that, like in ABS CDOs, generating business with the purpose of securitising it, may become a dominant logic (MacKenzie 2011; Johnson 2014: 178), albeit also acting as a "temporary financial fix for the political failure of climate governance" (Johnson 2014: 178), and "the securitization of fixed capital's place-based vulnerabilities" (ibid.: 180). In short, Johnson summarises that "[a]s the provision of catastrophe insurance has been securitized … place-bound vulnerabilities are rendered into an exploitable, diversifying asset class for financial capital" (157).

In the early 1990s, following Hurricanes Hugo and Andrew, and the Northridge CA earthquake, re/insurance companies with large exposure to catastrophes sponsored the first bond issuances, where investors receive a coupon in exchange for taking on some risk of default in the insurance regime. The first catastrophe bond was issued in 1996, (George Town Re in 1996) and the first dedicated catastrophe bond fund in 1998, although these bonds are still only a small part of the overall reinsurance and ILS markets, and are smaller than direct transfers of risk from buyers to large investment funds (IISD 2014). In total, around US$1–2bn of cat bonds were launched from 1998–2001, the market doubled to US$4bn after Hurricane Katrina, and rose to US$7.1bn in 2013 (Phillips 2014: 6).

By October 2014, the market was worth US$23 bn, after having grown by more than 25 per cent annually for much of the previous decade, compared to 10 per cent for the rest of the insurance sector (ibid.). Most catastrophe bonds are mobilised through an SPV which is normally in a secrecy jurisdiction, most often in Bermuda or the Cayman Islands, where there is no withholding tax on coupon payments to investors from the bonds collateral account. The sponsoring reinsurer, or "cedant" of the risk, sets up the SPV, which acts as an independent reinsurer to itself. The cedant pays in an initial premium to be held in a linked trust, the SPV issues notes to investors, who then pay in principle to the same trust, which then safeguards this as collateral, often doing this by investing itself in a money market fund or short-term US Treasury bonds (Johnson 2014: 165–66). A short-term floating rate is paid through to the investors plus the risk premium.

While the holding of the collateral in short-term markets is seen as a hedge against investment risk, in a full financial crisis this could erode. Cats in fact were not immune from the 2008 crisis, where hedge funds desperate for cash caused defaulting cat bonds and sell-offs in the secondary market. Lehman Brothers, in particular, was the counterparty for bonds' collateral assets in the case of four active cat bonds at that time, with all four partially defaulting with total losses of US$116m (Johnson 2014: 169; citing Trading Risk 2011). However, overall the cat bond market did not suffer badly from the 2008 crash, and 2011 marked the first year that institutional investors outnumbered dedicated catastrophe funds as buyers in the market (Johnson 2014: 158; citing Aon Benfield Securities 2011). ILS and cat bonds are highly sought-after alternative asset classes, with demand normally outstripping supply, because of low perceived correlation to broader financial market risks, benefiting too from dismal climate change predictions.

Also, as Johnson (2014: 166–167) reports, in the 15-year life of catastrophe bonds up to 2011, only a handful out of nearly 200 issued have been triggered by insurance losses, or 3 by 2014 (Phillips 2014: 7). These included Kamp Re from Zurich Financial services on US hurricane risk, but only after the infamous Hurricane Katrina, and also with the involvement of Lehman Brothers, who had exhibited "bad behaviour", with "some inappropriate assets in the cat bonds trusts" according to Barney Schauble of Nephila, a leading US cat bond investor (AllAboutAlpha 2014). Of 6 bonds related to Japanese mega-quake and tsunami of 2011, only 2 triggered, including a cat bond issued on behalf of Zenkyoren, one of the largest Japanese insurance companies, which fell to zero, as all the layers of protection were run through (IISD 2014). Institutional investors in the highest tranches of a weather derivative or catastrophe bond can also acquire full return of the principle, even if the bond triggers, although at a lesser coupon return (Johnson 2014: 167). Thus, high returns link mathematically to high risk (although arguably an inflated estimate of risk), but also to the possibility of ensuring a relatively automatic rent, which in 2013 averaged at a "mighty high" 9 per cent interest rate (Phillips 2014).

Johnson shows, in fact, that the triggering of a cat bond is just the event that keeps the market buoyant: without catastrophic damages "returns for investors fall because premium rates generally decrease and (re)insurance firms draw on internal capital or are able to access other reinsurers' capital cheaply" (Johnson 2014: 167). Ironically, more extreme weather and uncertainty about its magnitude and frequency, is growing the cat bond market, and it is just after a bond triggers that profitability is highest, where investors from capital markets input their largest volumes in order to take advantage of cat bonds as an alternative asset class with higher returns, when reinsurers are low on capital. ILS securities are desirable as they

> fashion geographic liabilities as strategic resources, uniquely desirable because of their ontological disconnection from the behaviour of financial markets. New income streams – what may be called "returns on place" – are derived by enabling purposive, scalable, and selective relationships with the geography of the built environment and geophysical hazards.
>
> (Johnson 2014: 173)

Critically, investors gain access to commodified risk and place-based premiums "without requiring them to take on the fixed costs required to originate those premiums" (ibid.: 176). These fixed costs are those of maintaining offices, marketing, product development and maintaining relationships with clients, which are done by the cedant. Of course, they also need have no ownership relationship with the actual place-based assets.

Cat bond triggers and African resilience

In 2014, Florida's Citizens Property Insurance Corporation issued a US$1.5bn cat bond, while New York's Metropolitan Transportation Authority, following a US$5bn loss from Hurricane Sandy, issued US$200m in cat bonds from its Bermuda registered MetroCat Re Ltd (Phillips 2015: 8). Both these last examples illustrate the use of cat bonds to insure places that are now hard to insure. But there are three problems with cat bonds for the poor and vulnerable. First, when the probability of an adverse event is very high, insurers have little interest, as they are unlikely to be able to charge a premium high enough to cover it. For example, when Barney Schauble of Nephila was asked what climate mitigation could be provided to the Maldives, which has a high likelihood of disappearing due to sea level rise, he answered "For the Maldives, it may be harder – buying protection against an event of quake or flood is different than responding to a scenario where a country is gradually going to be underwater" (AllAboutAlpha 2014). Second, those at risk need to be able to pay, and be reasonably responsible for the damage. In terms of anthropogenic climate change in Africa, neither of these really apply, despite the growing popularity of cat bonds among multilateral banks. Third, is the issue of who controls the calculative device that triggers the bond and makes it "fair". Phillips notes that a "wrinkle" in the use of cat bonds relates to how the bond triggers, arguing that "modelling of these parameters by independent agents plays a crucial role in determining who gets paid and when" (2014: 5). But unfortunately, the modellers are rarely independent.

Mexico was the first country to issue cat bonds in 2009 and in 2012 with the assistance of the World Bank under its MultiCat Program. The IBRD issued its own first cat bond, a three-year, US$30m transaction, in partnership with the Caribbean Catastrophe Risk Insurance Facility (CCRIF) in July 2014, linked to cyclone and earthquake risk in CCRIF countries. However, in a hedge arrangement with CCRIF, the World Bank entered into a "catastrophe swap", such that in the event the bond is triggered (and CCRIF have to pay out), "its principal will be lowered (as determined by its terms), and an equal amount will be paid to CCRIF under the swap" (Climate Change Policy and Practice 2014). Again, while CCRIF Chairman Milo Pearson, boasts that the partnership with the World Bank is "another example of CCRIF's continuing efforts to explore ways to help the countries in the Caribbean Region in building resilience to natural hazards" (ibid.), the swap facility is a direct guarantee that if his firm does not make a profit, the public bank will pay him out. If such a promise were made to the African poor and climate vulnerable it would need to be a hedge on the historical past, made by global corporations in around 1760, that if European and North American industrial pollution causes catastrophic climate change you can call in a swap deal from our governments. Of course, financialisation assumes a historically neutral past in order to allow fixing of income streams into the future, exploitation in the present, and the political requirements needed to ensure control of the global social order. As it stands these arrangements, from the perspective of the South, look more like, "We are just about to kill you. Would you like to pay for health insurance?" These ethical concerns have been made widely (see for example, Duus-Otterström and Jagers 2011). In addition, the European Insurance and Occupational Pensions Authority (EIOPA), warned in both 2013 and 2014 that the rapidly growing cat bond and related ILS market could be a source of systemic risk (EIPOPA 2013).

Nonetheless, the World Bank has an ambitious plan to roll out cat bonds across the developing world, with Turkey, Malawi, the Philippines and then "Africa". Thus, on 23 September 2014, the African Risk Capacity (ARC), an agency of the African Union launched its first Extreme Climate Facility (XCF), to coincide with the UN Climate Summit in New York. This will issue multi-year climate-change catastrophe bonds beginning in 2016, with hundreds of millions mentioned and US$1bn over 30 years, with involvement from the World Bank Treasury and early support from the Rockefeller Foundation. The ARC apparently will work to create a "fair" design for African countries by the Paris COP in 2015. Artemis advertise that these are a "tool to transfer the risks associated with climate change, while providing much-needed [that ubiquitous phrase again!] risk financing to those most exposed and at risk of severe financial losses as a result of a changing climate and weather variability" (Artemis 2014). The African Risk

Capacity (ARC) was initially set up as "a facility launched to help African Union Member States to bolster their capacities to better plan for, prepare and respond to extreme weather events and natural disasters", which in late 2014 diversified into cat bonds bespoke to "climate related risks" (ibid.). But the two outstanding issues in relation to cat bonds are how will it be decided when the bond triggers, and who will pay for "weather insurance".

Setting the "trigger" on a bond can be based on the specified losses of the issuers (as in traditional reinsurance), or estimates or proxies of losses, such as modelled loss using event parameters in a catastrophe model or index (Johnson 2014: 158; citing Hagedorn *et al.* 2009). Increasingly, however, the trigger has become embedded in a mathematical model of the weather, separately generated independently from actual reinsurance losses. Of course ILS trades are not publically registered but "over-the-counter" such that cat bond transactions are, like collateralized debt obligations, made in a world of "private facts" (MacKenzie 2008: 25). But arguably, increasingly the facts and modelling behind the "trigger" of a bond have also been privatised or made "proprietary", which seems to be particularly the case with the African cat bond plan. Companies dealing in weather derivatives exploit market opportunities by using data platforms and software that are often proprietary, thus using information asymmetries for classical arbitrage opportunities. For example, Monsanto spent US$1bn to acquire Climate Corp, a weather insurance business, which uses real-time pricing linked to weather insurance using proprietary global weather simulation models and local weather monitoring systems (AllAboutAlpha 2014). Cat bond investors also provide renewables energy sectors risk against low sun/wind/rain which would affect derivative incomes from their projects.

However, information on the weather is not a neutral commodity, but one that depends on representation and conflicted meaning, and which itself generates arbitrage opportunities in the secondary markets. For example, after the critical July 2015 pre-COP conference in Paris, *Our Common Future and Climate Change*, the conference report argued that limiting warming to less than 2 per cent is both "economically feasible" and "cost effective" (UNESCO, Future Earth and ICSU 2015). However, Kevin Anderson, an eminent climate scientist argues that this relies on predicting future application of speculative scientific innovation in "negative emissions" technologies and in changing the past. This implies that a slow evolution away from fossil fuels is possible, whereas Anderson argues that what is required is an immediate "revolutionary transition in how we use energy" (Anderson 2015: 1). He argues that the Integrated Assessment Models (IAM), used by those at the conference, of predicting climate change and its costs related to different emissions scenarios are flawed. Anderson argues instead that all carbon emissions will need to be removed from the energy system by 2050, to keep below 2 degrees of warming, a full five decades before the Intergovernmental Panel on Climate Change (IPCC's) prediction. This is a large and significant error between the science of the "policy relevant" (the IAM models) and public university science. Anderson notes that the IAM models assume that an uptake of negative carbon technologies (which take carbon out of the atmosphere) will be adopted in future, whereas most of these technologies are now only at "little more than a conceptual stage of development" (Anderson 2015: 1).

But the weather derivatives market works in relation to what is hegemonically believed about the weather, modelled into a calculative technology that probably tips the estimates of risk squarely back in the investors' interests. Ironically, however, there would probably be far more investors prepared to purchase catastrophe bonds if Anderson's view was widely believed, in so far as the price for the non-catastrophe years was extremely high to cover the payout years, and/or the investors maintained strict control of the software writing the "trigger". But Anderson's view held widely would certainly increase the supply of bonds, as it indicates higher risks for the majority global population. However, in essence perhaps, is that the "truth status" of the weather prediction is not so significant as the design of the payout trigger over time, although they are related. In fact, it is hard to attribute directly how weather news, those with sophisticated platforms to understand it, and public policy relate, but there was a peak in markets following the pre-COP Declaration in July 2015, with Artemis summarising that "July has seen the strongest returns of any month this year for the catastrophe bond market" (Artemis 2015).

The companies and trading associations promoting cat bonds are eager to promote the view that the weather can be modelled accurately and translated easily (by them) into financialised risk. Here is Artemis (a news and data analysis site for cat bonds) claiming that

> The trigger design of a catastrophe bond, with the ability to link it to actual weather or disaster conditions (parametric triggers), or an index constructed from actual weather or disaster variables (index or weather-index triggers), allows for the risk to be transferred while the capital buying the securities provides a source of contingent weather or disaster risk capital.
>
> (2014)

In other words, the indices and weather parameters are the metrics that define payouts, but their truth status in relation to real weather is secondary to the truth status of where the trigger is set by the internal calculative technology. This means that the underlying assets of the cat bond are really the weather information and calculative device that orders it, notwithstanding the consequential effects of weather on real secured assets. Here science is proposed as an unproblematic data set with, in respect of the proposed African cats:

> The XCF will be designed to be objective and data-driven, using a baseline of 30-year climatology data for Africa. Consistent meteorological information covering the entire continent is available since the start of the satellite era in the early 1980s and will be used to calculate a multi-hazard extreme climate index for each region.
>
> (Artemis 2014)

The issue of who sets the trigger baseline is critical to the fairness of the payout structure, although the wider literature does not suggest that issuers of the bonds, who will take them as debt stock, will have a say over this payout level. But the "science" of the investors certainly sounds abstracted enough:

> climate cat bonds will use a trigger structure linked to a parametric index constructed from various types of climate and weather data, which will parametrize increases in the severity and impacts of weather events, so the bonds will trigger should the index reach above pre-defined levels … The index will track increases in the frequency and magnitude of extreme weather events over and above an established baseline in each climate region.
>
> (Artemis 2014)

When a "pre-defined threshold" is reached, the African countries concerned will receive a payment (bond maturity) to "boost" adaptation, and disaster management. Just to reinforce the benevolent message, the United Nations Executive Secretary of the UN Framework Convention on Climate Change, Christiana Figueres, is quoted by Artemis, with reference to her contribution at the UN New York Climate Summit where the ARC was launched, as wishing ARC success, and as "increasing direct access to climate finance" (Artemis 2014). However, the use of "direct access" here is a travesty of its use by African negotiators to mean a right to public funding, without costly intermediaries, since African countries have very little historical responsibility for climate change.

From the perspective of the investor cat bonds can be justified morally in that they perform care and concern, and "will target the provision of additional financing to covered countries as a way to enhance their climate adaptation investments" (Artemis 2014). But this is an easy assertion to make when the investor cannot really lose. If the index does not reach the trigger point when the bond comes to maturity, the investors still get their money back as well as a yield from coupon payments. If there is a payout then the losses will be hedged across the portfolio. But repeated iterations of the trigger model act to refine probabilities, much as they do behind a roulette wheel: the payout is priced over a number of games. By controlling all the outcomes in the risk model the fund manager can ensure the win over time. With such a guaranteed return, it looks like variable rent. The only problem for the industry is persuading African countries to "insure" themselves against a problem they didn't cause: a rent to secure resilience in the face of others' pollution.

Thus, for African countries the issue must be a moral one. In purchasing what is essentially risk insurance they are acknowledging fear of events that they did not cause, and as long as things don't get too bad they will have to pay interest on the bond annually. The fairness of who sets the trigger is disputed in that the supplier of investment has more power, while even if they receive a payout it is tied to use of adaptation spending that must be in ARC's terms, using tied in suppliers in PPP arrangements. It won't be cheap, or locally owned, and will arguably increase surveillance by banks and vacate local democratic structures further in favour of the governance logics of financialisation. For example, Dr. Richard Wilcox, founding Director General of ARC said:

> XCF will ensure that African countries and the international community appropriately monitor climate shocks and will be financially prepared to implement specific adaptation measures in an effective and accountable manner, leveraging ARC's existing public-private infrastructure. The XCF allows us to leverage private capital against the risk of increased frequency of severe climate events, while using public money to fund immediate and certain adaptation requirements.
>
> (PR Newswire 2014)

Thus the whole framing of these bonds is reminiscent of the "development speak" of assistance, with "Participating countries … chosen based on criteria that include their current involvement with ARC in managing weather risks through its disaster insurance company, ARC Ltd., and having robust and investment-ready climate change adaptation plans in place" (Artemis 2015). The underlying morality of Africa paying dividends to capital investors because of a climate problem capital investors gave them is not an issue in this development speak. However, this is certainly an ethical issue for African populations, particularly when the bond trigger technology is being developed by capital holders, in an indirect relationship to actual volumes of claims, or publically owned weather data.

Insurance regimes and the future

Given the above, it is arguable that "speculation" is not the dominant process at work in financialisation processes. Rather it is the locking-in of income streams such that risk and cost is externalised away from core upper-tranche investors, who are guaranteed income streams whether the underlying assets or investments are successful or not. In this sense, it is more like rent. In terms of cat bonds, householders are paying for the continued, risk-covered, use of their house. The investors in cat bonds are receiving premiums from home owners to use their houses into an uncertain future and thus collecting an income stream for an asset they do not own. The problem for the insurance industry is persuading people to insure against losses they advertise, in the absence of either fear or a mandatory force (although many mortgage agreements include mandatory purchase clauses on home insurance). Thus, Swiss Re, a leading global reinsurance company, bemoan the uninsured property gap worldwide:

> Much of the underinsurance is due to global natural catastrophe risk, which has risen steadily over the past 40 years. In the last 10 years, cumulative total damage to global property as a result of natural disaster events was US$1.8 trillion, and about 30% of those losses were insured. In other words, the total shortfall in insurance cover – the protection gap – was US$1.3 trillion.
>
> (Swiss Re 2015)

Swiss Re model this as a "global property protection gap of US$221 billion per annum" (ibid.). Meanwhile, Lloyds have just produced a fear generating new "City Risk Index" on the GDP loss to cities they expect from weather and other disaster events, which illustrates the abstraction, measurement and packaging required to make an aggregated product for securitisation. The "City Risk Index" estimates "GDP@Risk" from 18 types of disasters to claim that of a total of US$372.56trn of GDP in its 301 cities between 2015 and 2025, US$4.56trn is "at risk", of which 71.47 per cent is in "emerging" cities and 35.20 per cent is in the "top 20" cities (Lloyds 2015a). To a modernist soundtrack, Lloyd's notes that

> By modelling and measuring these shocks [a]nd improving resilience through insurance protection [w]e can significantly reduce the financial impact of catastrophes.
>
> (Lloyds 2015b)

The insurance premium that would be paid to external investors when a city issued a cat bond, which could be registered on Lloyd's index, would ultimately be paid by tax-payers against the future use of their own homes. As Johnson summarises of the wider ILS market, "[i]t is a novel way for managers of circulating capital in search of higher profit rates to take advantage of the physical vulnerability of place-bound fixed assets and the resulting purchase of insurance coverage by asset owners" (2014: 161). Thus, "entanglements with the geophysical world" create premium flows, and thus further circulating capital (ibid.), suggesting a further move in the "capitalisation of almost everything" (Leyshon and Thrift 2007; cited in Johnson 2014: 161).

Capitalization of almost everything?

Loftus and March write of an intriguing comparison between the financialisation of weather and that of carbon that illuminates the problem of how far the nature of the thing, and the representation of what is going on, may differ between commodities. Pollard *et al.* (2008), in the collection for which Loftus and March's work is the editorial, make the astute point, repeated above, that weather derivatives are really "the commodification of information *about* nature" rather than the financialisation of the weather as such (summarised by Lofthus and March 2015: 174, emphasis in original). Historically, in the ILS market weather derivatives financialised the likelihood or not of climate impacts on business performance (Pike and Pollard 2010). However, while that is their avowed purpose, we saw above how there is an emerging disconnection between cost impacts on businesses' performance, and the calculative technology behind the triggering of a bond. However, that caveat notwithstanding, carbon trading avowedly seeks to change business, such that

> financialisation can imply a greater or lesser degree of financial intermediaries' influence over the material production of nature. In the case of

> weather derivatives, fluctuations in "nature" (changes in the weather) will influence the profits to be made *in spite of* the huge growth in a secondary market speculating on what those changes might be. Nevertheless, although partly driven by speculative gains, the intended outcome of CO_2 trading is a transformation in the production of nature (reduced greenhouse gases). For the former example, nature influences financialisation, for the latter, it is hoped that financialisation will influence the production of nature.
>
> (Lofthus and March 2015: 174, emphasis in original)

But the question to be asked here, is whether the two cases are really that different in the direction of causality, even leaving aside the obvious rejoinder of the lack of evidence that carbon trading has any impact on carbon emissions.

What the authors are suggesting is that some types of financialisation might affect the invested-in thing – this would be a type of reactivity or performativity. But arguably, all derivatives have this property in different ways to some degree. While the weather derivatives appear like an exception, as intuitively they cannot change the weather, as Pollard *et al.* (2008) made clear, they are really derivatives of weather information, which then has a direct effect on capitalised stock, particularly in agriculture. In other words, their underlying asset is not the weather at all, but weather information. The importance of information in this sense is intuitive and explains why informational software companies are spending huge amounts on cloud technologies and informational feeds in algorithmic trading software to assist the high-frequency traders manage released weather information quickly. It is in this informational dependence that these commodities are not so different, if carbon trading has no effect on levels of carbon, it too is greatly affected by news *about* carbon, particularly news about whether governments are going to restrict or allow emissions, or even more critically, re-liquidate, subsidise and grandfather fossil fuel activities through carbon trading. The carbon market is intrinsically a derivatives market for fossil-fuel based industries who are trying to hedge on the regulatory trends in pollution control (or lack of it), as well as meet their mandated caps by buying offsets if they continue to run dirty processes. Also, as Watts[3] pointed out, again it is not carbon *per se* that is financialised, but the permit to pollute in carbon, which acts like a license to access the commons. The polluters are again paying something that looks remarkably similar to a rent, to gain access to something they don't own – the air – and the right to pollute it up to mandated obligations to buy offsets – at which point access is again granted.

Conclusion

I claimed above that there were three problems in the theory of the financialisation of nature: that "speculation" does not work very well to describe what is going on in the capturing of assets for derivative profits. Also, it was claimed that credit-bearing fictitious capital is not the driver of financialisation, as many Marxists believe, since much of the money at work in financialisation is actually equity used for the purposes of extracting derivative incomes that look very much like rents. So what of the second and third problems, of the underestimated importance of the agency of the thing, and the role of spectacle to enable its capture? In the examples given above, from football stadiums, ports, and the weather, the role of speculation is low, and while the agency of the things in hand are different, they were all entrained to yield financial income streams. Also, in all cases, the representation of the thing to be built or sold drew on powerful images and tropes of modernity and spectacle, on expert science and unquestionable economics. I also argued that infrastructure lends itself particularly well to rapid class formation and its associated political corruption; while elites can sell it to a relatively uncritical public through popular images of modernity and global inclusion.

In this last sense there are surprising parallels between infrastructure, conservation and tourism in the degree of image and spectacle made possible in maps, diagrams, and artists' and computer impressions of what the future will look like, and how wondrous life will be with the new office block, housing development, port or road, often with an iconic animal in an eco-tourist backdrop. Grasslands with huge billboards of pictures of the future development stand across Africa as testament to planners' appetite to lay down concrete and invitations to buy off plan. Planning documents are also important vehicles of spectacle, with the Durban BOP development plan and new logistical transport corridor ubiquitously represented by its implementers, Transnet, by a photographic image of it already finished and set in the landscape it seeks to conquer. In this infrastructure is king, and social and environmental departments are left behind in the rush to pass the necessary agreements to develop, with environmental and social impact assessments often only done after the decision to build has been made.

These parallels across sectors as diverse as conservation, energy, and infrastructure illustrate the power of finance to entrain whole assemblages of human relationships and communities under a governance logic that enables extractable values to be driven up and out to secrecy jurisdictions. This financial outflow is accompanied by historically high dividend returns, even as domestic firms' assets are degraded, profits shrunk and corporate and sovereign indebtedness rises. But this power of financialisation to entrain other domains of human and nature lifeworlds is a power historically built from the panoplies of institutional norms, laws and risk obligations carried forward into the future for the benefit of those money-holders who simply conduct the act of investment. Preferential investment regimes rolled out under structural adjustment and bilateral investment guarantees at an intra-state level have been reinforced by regional and international trading and investment agreements that bind whole communities into what appear to be unavoidable contractual obligations, which form the foundations of the "contracted derivative income streams" of the ruling international holders of money. Over time, as we saw above, this has enabled them to extract from other institutions of money-holders, such as pension funds and firms. It turns out that the nature of the thing does not affect its entrainment differentially, insofar as capital insofar as capital seeks to escape cost relationships with all things. The empty football stadiums, abandoned toxic mine dumps, and disappeared carbon projects are all testament to the fact that capital does not need to relate to the nature of the thing, insofar as it can control the consequences of that nature in relation to its income earning streams, while disassociating from all other non-profit generating connectivity.

Notes

1 However, there is a potential difference in meaning for the concept of abstraction here: for Büscher it is a Marxian depiction of distant and reification, while for Lohmann it refers to thought categories and cognitive universalisms framing new human/nature constellations.

2 22 May 2012, Head of Housing to ECOD Housing Committee (personal communication).

3 R. Watts, draft manuscript of thesis to author, University of Manchester.

6 Illicit financial flows and exemptions from sovereignty

An astute reader will have noted that up to now this book has been describing the power of finance, rather than the financialisation of power promised in the title. The two are symbiotic. The global structure in place has had profound effects on the nature of power and governance since to do other than to be snarled in this web of finance has been confounding to ruling elites, workers and communities alike. This is not to say that there exists structurally or ideologically a bounded and well understood counterhegemonic position or class alliance that is cognisant of wanting an alternative, needing one, or otherwise wanting different. This cannot be read structurally from the nature and forces of capitalism as was once believed. Instead, what has occurred is a pattern of governance that makes the most of what is on offer, and individuals, classes and ruling elites who attempt to negotiate a bigger return to participation. Just as the third tranche investors are paid out last, least, or not at all, the community and BEE stakeholders are often reserved the third tranche position in PPPs and project financing. But even marginal participation encourages the motivation to climb, causing a widespread culture of corruption, in a liberal paradigm, or from a more strictly anthropological perspective, behaviours promoting rapid class accumulation that are mimetic and innovative of the structures, norms and governing logics that financialisation promotes. This has the consequence of rising inequality and public squalor for those who are left out. In this chapter I will first describe the consequential effects of rule by financiers in an historical capital switch to offshore and opaque SPVs and trusts of the "national" capital of African countries. Then I will explore how this has happened, before moving in the next chapter to analyse how power at all levels of government and society has become a matter conditioned by finance.

Illicit financial flows

Research by Global Financial Integrity (GFI) reveals that sub-Saharan Africa lost more than US$528bn from 2002–2013 due to corporate "trade mis-invoicing" and other financial sleights of hand (GFI 2013). This is almost double the foreign direct investment inflows to Africa during the same period – US$284bn. Elsewhere, GFI has confirmed that 60–65 per cent of Africa's illicit flows are commercially originated in practices such as trade mis-invoicing and 5 per cent are generated in acts of political corruption (ibid.). There is evidence that corporate mis-pricing funds kickbacks to office-holders in government and political parties and contributions to political party finances. However, the measurement of the contribution of each category of illicit financial flows to the overall total may in fact be misleading, as the category of corruption facilitates and leverages other flows pointing to an enmeshing of activities designated into somewhat arbitrary classifications. What is clear, however, is that IFFs are not merely the sole preserve of a pathologised political class and public administration: the vast majority by volume are moving through private sector corporate structures.

Illicit financial flows are a consequence of the inequity of the macro economy, and in turn make a large contribution to that inequity (Kar and Cartwright-Smith 2010; UNECA 2014). Illicit flows are defined as "Money that is illegally earned, transferred, or utilized" (Kar and Cartwright-Smith 2007, iv). It includes illegal capital flight where flows are specifically in violation of laws and regulations, but excludes substantively large legal or "licit" capital flight. Also, according to Global Financial Integrity, it does not currently include criminal smuggling or proceeds derived from mispriced asset swaps (see Kar and Cartwright-Smith 2007: iii–iv; ADB and GFI 2013: 1). According to UNECA and the African Union Commision, estimates are low because they don't include the proceeds of smuggling or the mispricing of services (2012b: 1). The definition includes trade mis-pricing, but there is a notorious difficulty in working out where the licit and illicit begin and end when so many trade transactions take place between parts of the same firm and where "arms-length" pricing data is unavailable. This latter context is that which defines trade pricing in much of the African natural resource sector, which is both oligopolistic and opaque (Bracking and Sharife 2014).

Baker (2005) generated the term illicit financial flows to include unrecorded capital flows from criminal corporate transfers and related practices; the proceeds of corruption; and the proceeds of trade in illegal goods and in people. While much focus goes to government corruption, Baker estimated that 60–65 per cent of IFFs globally are generated through commercial transactions in multinational corporations, particularly through trade mispricing; 30–35 per cent are criminal such as trade in drugs, weapons and people; while 5–7 per cent are generated by corruption, defined in its boundary type as the bribery of public officials. However, as Chaikin and Sharman note "corruption and money laundering are symbiotic: not only do they tend to co-occur, but more importantly the presence of one tends to create and reciprocally reinforce the incidence of the other (2009: 27). Thus many IFF components, such as transfer pricing, are facilitated by corruption, such that its low measurement might belie its importance or facilitation of the other categories (UNECA and AUC 2012b: 5).

Kar and Cartwright-Smith (2009) provided an estimation of the volume and pattern of illicit financial flows from developing countries by using a combination of the World Bank Residual model and the Trade Mis-pricing Model and two measures of net external indebtedness of the public sector based on changes in the stock of external debt (CED) and the net debt flows (NDF). They find that in 2006, developing countries lost between an estimated US$858.6bn and US$1.06

trillion in illicit financial outflows. As worrying as the global total, over the five-year period of the study 2002–2006, illicit financial flows grew at a compound rate of 18.2 per cent. Dev and Cartwright-Smith (2008) put illicit money flows from developing countries at between US$800bn and US$1 trillion by 2006 (quoted in Palan *et al.* 2010: 173). Baker (2005) argued that half of this flows out of developing and transitional economies and into major international banking centres. He further estimates that 80–90 per cent is a permanent outward transfer, but that some comes back as FDI having taken a "round trip" (Baker 2005). Illicit money annually and to date amounts to an estimated US$800m to US$1.3 trillion (Palan *et al.* 2010: 174; GFI 2014).

The banking sector

The enablers of illicit financial flows are banks,[1] using the institutional structures of secrecy jurisdictions, where secrecy jurisdictions are a central component of the basic infrastructure of a global economy of exception, although arguably becoming more significant than the "onshore economy". The significance of this is that international business companies, special purpose vehicles, and philanthropic and charitable trusts all use and interconnect their assets offshore, giving some philanthropic trusts close financial proximity to illicit financial flows. While key "politically exposed persons" (PEPs) set up family trusts in order to launder the profits of corruption, cronyism and kickbacks, these can then cross invest offshore and "clean" the money, before it round trips as "much needed" foreign direct investment. For example, Julius Malema used a "family trust" holding in an outsourced "programme management unit", a firm called On-Point, which was paid R52m in management fees from the Limpopo Road and Transport Department, to manage contracts on their behalf. On-Point then allegedly demanded to be a silent partner with the company who "wins", demanding of up to 70 per cent of profits in "management and design fees" (Amabhungane 2011). The family "Foundation" can then "gift" useful contacts, home communities and provide kickbacks for decisions in the PEPs' favour (Bracking 2015d: 236). Moreover, within these offshore company forms, and the connected family trusts, it is near impossible to tell whether "round tripping" is occurring by nationals to avoid tax, because the beneficial owners of co-investor companies are not necessarily traceable in secrecy jurisdictions.

Heggstad and Fjeldstad provide more detail on the role of the banking sector in shaping and facilitating these flows, but also highlight the problem of a paucity of research on the banking sector and capital flight in Africa. They argue that banks should not be viewed as "passive players when analysing capital flight. Banks play an active role in facilitating capital flight from Africa" (2010: 1). Although Heggstad and Fjeldstad do not analyse this explicitly, this could be because of a normative ambivalence, in some banking institutions, assigned to the practice of sending money offshore. After all, the offshore holding company is fairly ubiquitous to the business model of large-scale firms. It is not that there is no difference between illegal and "clean money"; just that it would be hard for a bank to distinguish between the two when transacting with, and sometimes when assisting in the building of, an opaque and submerged structure, often within the same company group. Heggstad and Fjeldstad note that there is not a clear distinction between illicit and licit flows, and that some authors, such as Epstein (2005: 58–65) view capital flight as a concept to include both (Heggstad and Fjeldstad 2010: 2).

Heggstad and Fjeldstad report that there is an evidenced relationship between debt and capital flight, where a "revolving door" relationship means that public loans leave the country as private assets, with sometimes up to 80 per cent of the initial value turning into flight capital (2010: 2; Boyce and Ndikumana 2001; Cerra *et al.* 2005; Ndikumana and Boyce 2008). Development projects themselves have also in the past proved to be a popular site of corrupt practice and illicit capital flight, because of the lack of competitive tendering and sometimes cosy relations between firms and DFIs (Hildyard 2000; Bracking 2001, 2007: 236–257). It reverts to regulating between "the known and the known too well" which is a complex issue that current due diligence has only begun to untangle (see Bracking 2007: 237–39). Thus, debt, misuse of official development assistance, capital flight, money laundering, illicit flows and relationships with politically exposed persons (PEPs) have all been raised as issues of concern for economic and social justice agendas.

Secrecy jurisdictions and transfer pricing

A secrecy jurisdiction is defined by its privileging of non-nationals for tax purposes and its financial opacity (NOU 2009; Bracking 2012b). Thus, at this point it is apposite to note that given the secrecy jurisdiction institutional element in the making of illicit flows, it is not possible to test the provenance of money that returns or arrives in Africa as "clean" or "dirty", since the laundering function removes knowledge of how the money was made and who owns it. But it is possible to change industrial policy, tax policy, corporate governance and domiciliary tax law in order to prevent the generation of illicit flows in the first instance. The single most important change would be to change Africa-wide tax law to embody a contributory principle of tax (like in the European Union Savings Directive of 2003) rather than the current domiciliary principle (which allows for non-sovereign domicile, double taxation agreements and tax avoidance) (Bracking *et al.* 2010). This would evaporate the raison d'être of tax havens, and make transfer pricing more difficult, doing much to therefore reduce illicit financial flows.

Illicit financial flows are nested in a set of immoral (but not necessarily illegal) corporate practices, which I have summarized elsewhere as "new forms of private sector corruption" (Bracking 2013a; 2015d: 228–229). By viewing these issues together, the shape of an economic justice agenda can be derived. This is in preference to the situation thus far, where some of these are either seen as too technical for the public to engage with, such as illicit flows, or as existing in separate compartmentalized agendas, such as tax avoidance and evasion in the "tax justice" platform, thin capitalisation in the "development" agenda; and opacity in the anti-corruption agenda. In terms of building economic justice, it would be important to open up political space for moral and normative argument by linking issues of IFFs and secrecy jurisdictions to the governance agenda and anti-corruption movement, where current power holders would find it more difficult to close down resistance by designating these issues as singularly technical or economic.

Wealth transfers

In fact, overall, the illicit financial flows agenda uses an unfortunate terminology in the form of the "IFF" acronym, which did not originate in Africa, because not all extractive practices are financial (some are in kind, although they may eventually generate a financial transfer), and nor are all wealth transfers necessarily "flows". The overall impression generated by the acronym "IFF" is thus of a somewhat technical and anodyne context in which money appears to "just move", potentially of its own accord. Of course, this is a deception and a more accurate term, if we could turn clocks back, and with the benefit of hindsight, would be "illicit wealth transfers". The word "transfer" more accurately points to a deliberate act and agency in the form of the person or organization that motivates and organizes the movement of wealth across borders. However, referring to IFFs as large flows which have equally large numbers attached arguably serves a conservative agenda, in that it does not motivate and incite sufficient cognizance or anger among a wider audience, who are either unable to comprehend scale expressed in large numbers, or who discount the results of research as of a technical nature and beyond change. In terms of political economy, money does not "just move" but requires a structure, institutional facilitation and a particular sovereign deficit in regulation combined with the existence of secrecy jurisdiction homes who provide "wealth protection". Illicit financial flows exist within a circular cause and effect loop: the extent and impact of IFFs are performative of creating and regenerating power structures, which, in turn, then cause more IFFs. In other words, the structure of power and political economy is the foundational base in which IFFs occur and in which they are, in turn, grown and perpetuated.

Political power and illicit financial flows

In terms of southern Africa at least, institutional arrangements have been authored with the governmental assistance of ruling political parties, and/or ruling political elites. This has happened in two senses: that these political parties had a requirement for financial opacity during the struggle and made early use of secrecy jurisdictions from the 1950s onward. These early hidden structures then became the forerunners of current institutional arrangements related to illicit financial flows. Second, that once in power, politically exposed persons (PEPs), either from within the party structure, the state structure, or both, have been motivated to set up internationalised structures to house illicit wealth, even where they did not exist before. These power structures, and their offshore institutional arrangements, are of two main types, depending on the history of the political party, liberation struggle and state form adopted after independence. These are first, the financial structures which originated and were developed by liberation political parties, many of which now exist in parallel to one-party states. Second, structures made by royal or familial dynasties who still rule in authoritarian states such as Lesotho or Swaziland. Both lead to the privatisation of national sovereign assets. Then there are also the family trusts and holding accounts of politically exposed persons (PEPs).

Suffice to note that these institutional arrangements that facilitate illicit financial flows are not of the bilateral once-off payment or kick-back modelled in traditional boundary corruption, which is measured for the purposes of GFI data, or which is the object to be reduced in classical anti-corruption and transparency interventions. Instead, we are analysing networked assemblages of power that are internationalized and privatized beyond the realm of the national state system. This is not to say that nation states have no role within the structure underpinning IFFs, far from it, but that the diversity of states and differences in regulatory capacity and state governance practices are used by actors in order to capture jurisdictional homes and treaty status, for the purposes of privatising sovereign and corporate sources of wealth for the few, against the interests of the many. IFFs are essentially a consequence of modern state capture caused by the logics of governance that financialisation produces.

IFFs are sourced principally in the most internationalised sectors of the national economy, in mining, agribusiness, infrastructure, energy and large-scale manufacturing. Then that wealth is moved to corporate offshore companies connected to the onshore subsidiary, or to companies registered for the purposes of providing wealth to politically connected persons, or to hybrids designed to serve both simultaneously. The pattern suggests not so much a revolving door between the private and public sectors, so much as a simultaneous, coeval, permanent dual identity and existence. Thus the institutional arrangements for facilitating IFFs, and the institutional form of the wealth storage function that they serve, are intimately related to the pattern of resources and depletions of sovereign assets. Political parties and political elites build internal financial structures that perform as a corporatised multinational alongside state power which facilitates exemptions to regulations, or privileged investment, tax and trading concessions, while managing localised dissent. This is the structure of corporate entities and political power that (simultaneously) is funded by, generates, and is characterised by illicit financial flows made up from wealth transfers.

What causes IFFs?

This question becomes pertinent when considering three underlying factors: first, that one-party or dynasty states are often extractive minerals-based economies, where vast natural resources exist in a delinked parallel economy; second, that one-party states are perceived as politically stable and relatively low risk long-term business environments for multinationals; and third, that dominant parties perceive themselves as inheritors of the rights and privileges of rule based on the role played in liberating nations from colonialism. Indeed, "intimate knowledge of the offshore was gained by 'defenders' during the struggle against colonialism and apartheid when resources outside the reach of the USA, UK and South Africa's intelligence service were needed for resistance".[2] After independence these structures proved resilient and amenable for new party-state accumulation enabled by harmful legal and financial vehicles, and "a raft of secretive associates including fiduciary nominees" (ibid.). Current offshore structures are thus (co) authored by African political elites, ruling parties and familial dynasties in partnership with international banks and global multinationals. IFFs are a measurement of how far these structures are being re-liquidated and built using current illicit financing. They then generate a further means and incentive for political and political party office holders to continue with practices of state and regulatory capture; or more accurately a move to "new forms of corruption" (Bracking 2013a).

Transfer pricing is the close relation of illicit financial flows in that it is the main conduit of their movement. A transfer price is the monetary expression of a movement of goods, services or intangibles between part of the same company that may or may not be located in different countries. Transfer pricing cannot be easily detected from consolidated company accounts or from the standards of financial data provided by public sector development finance institutions. This lack of reliable data is partly due to accounting regulations, which do not mandate the external disclosure of all corporate, and particularly intra-firm, transfers. For example, International Financial Reporting Standards (IFRS) 8 on segmental reporting and IFRS 24 on related party disclosure pay scant attention to transfer pricing. The net result is that stakeholders are not able to establish whether the companies are manipulating transfer prices to reduce global tax liability (see Mehafdi 2000). In other words, no one has been able to accurately quantify the value of the transfer of resources involving transfer prices. One attempt was the United Nations Conference on Trade and Development (UNCTAD) calculation: 44,500 MNCs with 275,000 foreign affiliations had intra-group transactions accounting for one-third of world trade which was valued at US$1.6 trillion (UNCTAD 1997).

Economic empowerment and financialised power

The mining economy of South Africa has produced a rapid accumulation of wealth for some PEPs and among senior office holders of the ruling party, the African National Congress (ANC). Patrice Motsepe was the first black South African billionaire, worth variously US$1.05bn (*Forbes* 2015) or US$2.5bn (*Cloud Nine* 2015) and the sixth wealthiest person in South Africa (and first ranked black person) (*Forbes* 2015). Second wealthiest black person in South Africa is Cyril Ramaphosa at US$450m (*Forbes* 2015) or US$550m (*Cloud Nine* 2015), brother-in-law to Motsepe, current Deputy President, whose wealth derived mostly from his investment firm Shanduka Group. Just behind them, and also beneficiaries of BEE, are Tokoyo Sexwale, Sipho Nkosi, Phuthuma Nhleko, Mathews Phosa, and Ebrahim Ebrahim. Tokoyo Sexwale headed the African

National Congress from 1994 to 2010 and is now the Non-Executive Chair of Mvelaphanda Holdings (Pty) Limited. Cyril Ramaphose is ranked 12th wealthiest person in South Africa, with Patrice Motsepe at 6th, in an otherwise all white and all male top 16 (*Forbes* 2015). More traditional business tycoons in South Africa still outweigh some of these figures, such as Nicky Oppenheimer of the De Beers Group who is said to be worth US$6.66bn and is first ranked for his personal wealth. Overall, "One-third of Africa's richest business leaders live in South Africa, including six of Africa's 23 billionaires" (*Forbes* 2015b).

For example, lesser-known figures might include Thenjiwe Mtinso, a woman who began in the black Consciousness Movement, joined the "Umkhonto weSizwe" group, was forced into exile, became a commander and then a member of the National Executive Committee of the ANC and a government ambassador post-apartheid. She is also a member of the ANC-authored Chancellor House investment company and a shareholder in that company, which has prospecting rights in over 500 sites in South Africa. The Chancellor House Mineral Resources, an investment listing, owns Wits Gold, registered to be worth R1.8bn in August 2006 (Rademeyer *et al.* 2010). Another former activist is Cheryl Carolus, now Executive Chairperson and Non-Executive Director of Gold Fields Limited, and formally Deputy Secretary-General of the ANC, a major beneficiary of BEE deals in mining through her company Petrona Development Investments. She was successful in acquiring the BEE stake in Lafarge Mining SA and De Beers Consolidated Mines. When Gold Fields mining company was accused of bribing ANC chairperson Baleka Mbete in 2013, it was Cheryl Carolus who appeared as "company spokesperson" to make public denials (Amabhungane 2013).

Layers of government and party office are associated with some form of opportunity for wealth accumulation, albeit that some of these are formalised as salary. There is an epistemological problem in merely labelling some deals as "corrupt", when black economic empowerment is legislated for in respect of greater economic justice. However, there is a conditioning part played by political connectivity in establishing who will be involved in empowerment, and where sites of accumulation, rapid forms of class formation and increased income inequality will emerge.

For example, in research in KwaZulu-Natal on the effects of Black Economic Empowerment legislation and market fairness (2013–15),[3] respondents were asked about the role of political connectivity in shaping market opportunities and procurement success. Interestingly, there were examples given to the researchers of direct personal and family gain, done with "style"; of group gain and benefits to comrades in political parties, much of which took place in the provincial, municipal and local government structures. Thus one respondent summarised that kickbacks and bribes are endemic to the public sector, but that:

> in the public sector it is endemic, but it is also extremely subtle, and it's done in a style that is really amazing, it won't be asked for directly, and it will often be done in a way that gives you the ability to not see it for what it really is. There will be the introduction of someone's sister to the company, it

> doesn't come as a bribe but as a retainer, and you basically keep someone's sister in the company, they will work, but they won't be your first choice of person for an employee, and you can't say anything if they don't come to work, they are basically there as a retainer for goodwill, and sometimes that goodwill takes months and months to come.[4]

He gives an example from KwaZulu-Natal involving premier's wives and their associates to illustrate "style".

> there would be an event, and there would be catering and t-shirts, every event, catering and t-shirts, so a contract would go out by government for one hundred thousand packets of food, and one hundred t-shirts, and these ladies would then be the deniable link, they would then get a company that they were connected with to put in a tender, let's say each t-shirt cost 10 rand, then on hundred thousand t shirt is a million rand for t-shirts, but only 50000 would actually be produced, so the company would actually only be charging for 50, I mean 500000 rand, because this person was the delegated fixer for the t-shirts they would sign off for the 50000 t-shirts as if they were 100000 t-shirts, and then the extra amount of money, the contract is paid out for the full amount, would be split, it would be paid out, how would it be split, into a bank account, no that is extremely amateurish, would it go as cash to the persons house, no, there has to be drawings from your salary in your bank account every month otherwise people start to ask questions, a lot would go to this fixer, but another amount would go to the wives of the premier, the wives of the minister, and it wouldn't go in cash, but things like negotiating a discount for a car for the daughter, getting a Gucci bag on a trip to Dubai, paying for the ticket to Dubai, having an account at a clothing store which would be settled in cash by this person, so it would be done in a style, and people don't actually talk about it as being corrupt, my brother, my sister, my home boy, we've got to look after each other, everybody else is doing it, it's us against them, and sometimes there might even be ideological reasons behind it, some of these associations based on, people who used to be in the ANC in the past, in Zapu, in the unions, I'm just using examples, in there would be some clannish explanation for why we are forming this little association, and when I say clannish I don't mean race … it's not about race, it's about how we have come a long distance together, we've fought certain fights in the unions together, we've been in a certain sect of the left in the past, so we can trade off that braaskap [really thick buddies together].[5]

There are also more indirect cases of pleasing "the dude" such as the joke about the most benefactored choir in South Africa being in the home village of a key political fixer. As the same respondent narrates:

> if you are giving under the name of social responsibility, you are giving it to a pet project of a key politician, you must pick, now this is a joke, the last

> DG of KZN [Director General of KwaZulu-Natal] was from a place called Sweet Waters, now if you gave any kind of benefits to a choir in Sweet Waters, man did that open doors for you! So that choir in Sweet Waters was probably the most benefactored choir in South Africa, and it's not like that guy was taking any money from it directly, it was just he was seen to be delivering back to his home town, that gave him a bit of, well you know what I am talking about, it's nice, to be able to be "the dude", so that sort of corporate social responsibility would pay off, that what you need those internal South African dudes to advise you on, so don't spend that money under corporate social responsibility, don't just pick the nearest decrepit person to help, you must pick people who, you know people who are able to influence tenders would want you to help, even though they are not getting something from it.

Another respondent confirmed that he was constantly pressured into kickbacks:

> Everywhere, if you want anything from top officials, you have to pay. If I have to tell how long I have battled just to have a tavern, you would be surprised. I applied for a tavern in 2005, and submitted my plans to metro. The plans were not approved until we "paid" … Then the plan was submitted to the legal board … When I made a follow-up nobody knew where the plans were … As soon as I paid, the plans and the application was found … Now, for me to be granted permission to build … for license … If you want anything done in this country, you to pay. It is a game in all levels of government. Whether it is central government, provincial government, right down to the local level.[6]

However, another respondent saw being involved with politicians or political programmes as being a source of trouble for his business, and wanted to grow with unconnected firms. He argued that:

> you can't invite politicians to participate in your business, because they have their own agendas as politicians … now we want people who are like normal business people … who will never ask you about membership of politics … if you want to buy a pack of cigarettes, buy a pack of cigarettes. You work in a shop you don't say "who did you vote for" you can't work in a shop like that. But this attitude, they want to score points for their followers. The politicians just want to get things for their voters.[7]

He spoke of a skills empowerment programme where places were distributed through political connection, whereas he thought that area quotas would have been fairer, since they would be unconnected to political parties. Interestingly though, he would still rely on councillors to collect names to fill the area quotas, suggesting that he has more faith in local government than political fixers per se. Thus he states:

> The element of being desperate is the one that makes people distort, or not obey the rules, because they are citing that they are not going to benefit throughout the whole exercise. They rather spoil it because they are not going to be beneficiaries. That is what they have cited. Even not to set up a proper criteria that is going to be fair; like how many people are involved in each area etc., if I am going to create employment [I would use] How many of you in terms of areas, KwaMashu, Ntuzuma, Inanda; you have these dividends. To KwaMashu, I am going to take 50 people; to Ntuzuma I am going to take 50 people; to Inanda, 50 people – that is a formula that works well because it doesn't have problems. You say you have the names on your own, you bring them here. I am not going to be in the community to check my friends, their names … The structures must be responsible to do that. When you come as an individual – that doesn't work, because the structures must be there. Talk to your Councillor – that's how they should sort it out.

This respondent was frustrated that he was not a big enough actor to compete in the market, when other bigger actors could buy favours:

> Money talks. If you're going to come physically, even if you don't have an appointment, if you have enough money to buy them whatever they want, give them some cash, they will, "Who is this, laani (rich guy), this tycoons". (He will say) "I want to see the Minister" … Then they start picking up the phone and doing things because they recognise me financially, that I'm doing something, I'm doing a lot of favours for them. These are the kind of things, forming areas of accessibility … climbing the ladder.[8]

His own experience was much more frustrating as he was struggling to climb the connectivity ladder:

> The government hasn't come up with, they talk of broad-based economic empowerment, all those big stuff, they wanted to prioritise black people to own such business it was absorbed and it was swallowed by nepotism, you cannot make a call to a Minister, you can find our President on Twitter on Facebook, but other people are not available, and I take a message and then no response, I was trying to contact, or you need a number they will give you a wrong number, until one of the councillors gave me the personal cell phone number of the secretary, in the first week she didn't answer as I was calling with a landline, called by cell phone, there can't be any meetings between you and the MEC [Member of the Executive Council] until it is written, then the fax number wrong, I still need that phone number.

This respondent seems to have experienced exclusion on two grounds: the economic and political. As Respondent 6 asserts, as a smaller independent business person he is losing out to the empowerment "creamy layer", failing to climb high enough to talk to the Minister. But also, as an original ANC activist from the struggle Respondent 2 explains that he is also losing out in the "struggle within a struggle" because others have taken key positions in the ANC since and want to actively exclude him.

> Because of this political struggle, there is a struggle within a struggle, the counsellors want to score some points, they think I am clever so they don't invite me, I get silenced, I get to sit at the back they take the front positions, everybody is sitting down and saying nothing, this is how they are manipulating these procedures so that they become their own outcomes, these politicians they are isolated to our access, they don't want to talk to anyone they are not told to talk to, he is busy, the minister is always busy, they don't even answer, the minister is not available he is busy, no response they behave because they are public figures they are supposed to be accessible in terms of communications, to the public but they are not.[9]

High-level corruption and immunity from prosecution

All the respondents spoke of the immunity from prosecution of high-level persons in both the public and private sectors, and of course sometimes in both at once, who were able to evade accountability or prosecution. Respondent 2, continuing from his theme of "money talks", states that the risk of prosecution for the bigger people is not there:

> I am citing elements of such behaviour because people who are well known, who have got money … it is easy for them to connect to politicians … Other businesses (are) giving kickbacks to people to senior people, so that is why you hear they are caught up in scandal … Getting money from people and then prioritising those people … Take the case of the man giving tenders for houses … He was accused of fraudulent activities, but because he is in the network of senior people, he gets a contract 175 million rand … They won't stop what they are doing … because now they become senior … so long as they accuse no one and they get the money … Now, if you are on the ground, how do you access that?[10]

In an insightful analysis Respondent 6 compares the *de jure* state of legal regulation and institutional structures existing in South Africa, with the low level of implementation and prosecution. He refers to "alluvial evidence" that can be "picked up" for potential prosecution, but also to the de facto failure of incentive for the political class to do so in practise, and to the ability of perpetrators of corruption to close down investigations or get other high ranking personnel to do this for them.

> There is over and above enough legislation. South Africa has the greatest constitution and all this wonderful legislation that governs how things work. The problem is that it is simply not enforced. Now we go back to the principals-agents problem: the principals – the people you report the misbehaviour of agents to, either don't act upon it, or for capacity purposes, I've come across arguments rooted in culture (brother needs a job, don't do him down) or it could be further, that the principal is involved in it, getting a cut. One of the unwritten rules in SA public service is this: do not steal more than your boss, and if you are stealing more than your boss, you're going to get in trouble. At a very general level, just from KZN, going back 36 months, there is over and above, enough trace evidence of corruption of premiers, premier's wives, public finance instruments, whole bunch of MECs just lying there, is alluvial, to successfully prosecute these guys, it is just not being picked up. It is there … But there is no one prepared to do that, because the person who owns such an investigation picks up all sorts of political trouble, and the interesting thing about South Africa is that we have got a way of just closing down these investigations. The political interference in internal investigations is high, and there needs to be no explanation from heads of department as to why they are stopping an internal inquiry. When it comes to the Public Prosecution, you will have the head of the NPA [National Prosecuting Authority], if the case is important enough, will simply extract the oxygen from that investigation and it will go nowhere. There is no sense of shame that if your name has been in the press you will do the Westminster thing and resign. You just brazen back because there is a lot of money involved … People don't have huge estates that they can fall back on, should they be out of politics. Many people in SA, black and white, in the political class, who were excluded by the old guys, this is the first bit of real wealth. So, if you're out of government – you can't be a disgraced Jeffrey Archer and go back to your country estate – you're out.[11]

The individualised liberal model of corruption

The liberal idea that corruption takes place on the frontiers of the public and private space, between a "private" actor who is clean or a victim, and a "public" official who is inevitably pressing for a kickback does not well reflect the reality of the financialisation of power. The liberal Weberian reform model also relies on a rationalist assumption of a benign principal–agent model and individuated incentives for change. However, neither is apparent in endemically corrupt societies. In patrimonial, clientilist and endemically corrupt regimes, with a low quality of governance institutions, forms of collusive, systemic and collectivised corruption predominate. In other words, the traditional modelling of the individual bribe-taker and bribe-payer within principal–agent theory, where the principal of a public institution lacks enough knowledge about what the agent is doing to adequately control their behaviour, is unsuitable. Instead, we have a collective action problem (Mungiu-Pippidi 2006; Persson *et al.* 2010; Rothstein 2011) since the principal, the agent and the firm or individual are more likely to be cooperating with each other, and the incentive for anyone else in either organisation or outside of it to report corruption is negligible since it would lead only to their own exclusion from the spoils, or even loss of their job or false imprisonment. The pattern of prosecution for corruption in Uganda underlines this point, where cases directly involving the presidency and key ministers have been successfully derailed by the ruling elite and scapegoats of a middle rank prosecuted instead, with in some cases the very people who were whistle-blowers in the first place prosecuted as a form of punishment for standing up against the National Resistance Movement (NRM) regime and its cronies.

For example, Asiimwe discusses the case where the now Ugandan Prime Minister Amama Mbabazi, Finance Minister Ezra Suruma and businessman Amos Nzeyi, all benefitted from the National Social Security Fund's (NSSF) inflated purchase of land owned by Mbabazi's company and held by a bank in which they all had shares, the National Bank of Commerce – even though some of the land was protected wetland and some was "fictitious" (Asiimwe 2013: 134). In this case, David Chandi Jamwa, the NSSF managing director testified to parliament that "This was the minister in charge of NSSF asking me, his subordinate, to use workers' money to pay for his friends' land … If that is not corruption, what is it?" (Chandi Jamwa 2009; cited in Asiimwe 2013: 134). However, President Museveni intervened that Chandi Jamwa had "been coached by anti-Mbabazi elements" to skew his testimony – only Chandi Jamwa went to jail, and the ministers went free (ibid).

The narratives used by the Ugandan elite to derail prosecution and legitimate such injustice share tropes with the patriotic nationalism found in other effective one-party states, such as Zimbabwe (Bracking 2009b), where persons who speak up against corruption are punished by the corrupt; they are accused verbally as having particular interests themselves, as being disloyal, unpatriotic, and as attacking "foreign investors", and "undermining growth", with personal agendas of "politics" against the (avowedly legitimate) ruling party and (apparently elected) government (see Asiimwe 2013: 133–37).

There are similar patterns in Angola, Namibia and Mozambique in the use of post-liberation nationalist rhetoric to derail attention from political elite aggrandisement. For example, in Mozambique organisations such as the *Association Wonelela* are actively tracking spending promises and the (non) appearance of the assets or infrastructure at local and provincial level (Casey 2014). However, the most senior leadership in Mozambique are working in a situation of opacity in terms of their cross-investments with foreign mineral and oil companies at a national and international scale. In fact, more generally, transparency efforts involving international and cross-border flows, including with multinational corporations, and to and from secrecy jurisdictions remains a major challenge in anti-corruption work. In the latest UK Government "UK Anti-Corruption Plan" for example, although the term "illicit financial flows" appears seven times, three are in section titles, while the four remaining mentions are circumscribed with the context solely of stolen assets, "connected to corruption" and "bribery of public officials". The 65 per cent of illicit financial flows generated and flowing in the private sector (GFI 2013) do not warrant a mention (BIS and Home Office 2014). These are the flows that are cause and consequence of high-level corruption (UNECA and AUC 2012b; UNECA 2014). The new global sustainable development goals (SDGs) in draft also painfully postpone until 2030 action on illicit flows.

Petty corruption is seen as widespread in sub-Saharan Africa, although it hasn't seen as much donor attention in recent years as "grand" or "high-level" corruption, at least since the Commission for Africa Report, *Our Common Interest* (2005) (Theobald 2008). Apart from relative neglect in favour of interest in high-level corruption and a dearth of analysis on petty corruption (Poate and Vaillant 2012: 29) there are two related problems: (1) it is nearing a consensus that much anti-corruption intervention has had little (measurable) result in the last decade (Persson *et al.* 2010; Johnsøn *et al.* 2012; DfID 2011, 2013; Norad 2011a, 2011b); and (2) the real losses and compromises to well-being that both grand and petty corruption cause remain real, substantial and acute, albeit hard to measure, for many of sub-Saharan Africa's most poor.

The Commission for Africa famously argued in *Our Common Future* that corruption served "to undermine all efforts to improve governance and foster development", and from this report onward grand corruption – the abuse of public power for private gain – was put centre stage, and attention to petty corruption put in abeyance as an unfortunate consequence (Commission for Africa 2005: 90). However, critical evaluations of anti-corruption interventions have noted its prevalence in service sectors and the rarity of specific anti-corruption support to these sectors (Norad 2011b; Poate and Vaillant 2012). During the early 2000s donors were relying on decentralisation as a relative "fix-all" for accountable service provision, before evidence built that this allowed a new generation of local brokers and new opportunities for graft (Norad 2009; cited in Transparency International 2009). Since the emphasis, then disillusionment, with decentralisation there has arguably been no further systematic strategy aimed exclusively at petty corruption. However, since basic goods are critical to poor peoples' well-being the issue of petty corruption deserves particular attention in development since it has a direct impact on everyday life. This is not to say that the macro-economic effects of grand corruption do not have an impact; just that gatekeeper providers of basic services, in their negotiation of bribes, largely determine patterns of micro-level inequality and social inclusion or exclusion.

"They have their own people they want to blame"

However, the research in South Africa suggests that, in the words of one respondent, "it's all about cliques".[12] This suggests that the individualised theoretical models of corruption at both high-level and administrative level will fail to capture the collectivised social dynamic that is foundational. This was explained recently by an impressive young businesswoman who had stopped going to BEE (Black Economic Empowerment) meetings when she realized, in her evaluation, that it was a waste of her time and a cost to her business:

> Those guys have their own people – they always have their own people – and they get the contracts over and over, even in the same bid process. R30,000, R3 million, R300 million. I don't know how they deliver on all those. And the same people who lose out always lose out, over and over. The quality of your bid doesn't matter. It's the cliques.[13]

Of course, the truth is that the "winners" don't often deliver on all the contracts. An "implementation gap", or "unfunded promise" emerges, with no obvious change in service delivery. However, management service fees, logistical and leasing fees, and inflated rents haemorrhage out from the public administration. The winners are "eating", as the businesswomen explained, "for doing nothing".

Connectivity and cliques

A successful clique works in at least three social spaces, if not four: the private, the public administration, the political party and the social network of family and friends, with no clear division between the public and private spheres. Corruption is truly collectivised. It must have a privately incorporated business, ideally with at least one shell company (management service company, special purpose vehicle or trust) preferably in a tax haven. Here is where the public officials, politicians and their relatives and friends, and people in the private sector and political parties all connect together. Of course, any individual is especially well placed in the clique if they are simultaneously a member of more than one of these institutions and so are their "comrades". For example, in the interviews with BEE business people in Durban we can see how political connectivity even acts to subvert a policy designed to deliver economic justice.[14]

> Political connectivity … enables fronting, because political connectivity is the extra amount of authority that is given to undeserving tenders, to deviate from price and to deviate from other criteria … Political connectivity allows you to cloak your claims to rent-seeking within self-serving notions of transformation, in terms of the advancement of women and people of colour. There is a lot of good work that happens where women, people of colour, and people with disabilities are advanced, I'm not disputing that. But if you have the right lingo and the right rhetoric, you are able, through political connectivity, to stake a claim to information, to public goods and monies, which if pricing were the sole criteria would have gone to someone else … It's the same thing with affirmative action. The way that affirmative action and preferential procurement work, it's not to exclude the white firm that is yet again benefitting, but to exclude the not-politically-connected black firm: that's how it works in practice. The real victims of affirmative action now are those black small entrepreneurs … who are not connected, [when] there's another black

> firm who might have outsourced the work to whites for that matter, but who are able to get that particular job because of political connectivity. Who do you know, how to register in the database, when questions are asked, who stops you from asking those questions, who threatens you, who fires the whistle-blower, who calls you a counter-revolutionary because you are raising [questions].[15]

In sum, the context is complex and processes of class formation are being wrought from constant renegotiation of actors balancing the demands of traditional authority, public administrative and party political accountability.

Boomerang deals

Khadija Sharife coined the phrase "boomerang deals" to describe a very common form of corruption. It works in a network, crosses the public/private boundary, and benefits both. The boomerang deal keeps circulating and repeating. It isn't like a "javelin deal", which is thrown just once to be caught when the "public official" leaves to go to the "private" firm that had benefitted from the contract originally organized by that person when they worked in public administration. A "boomerang deal" is instead a corruption deal that continuously comes back and forth across the boundaries of the state, contained within the clique. The "private" sector furnishes the public officials and more importantly the politically connected facilitators and beneficiaries consultancy support, kickbacks, or 'assistance' in exchange for a procurement "tap that keeps on running". But there are distinct risks to "fronting" (being the black person who "fronts" an organisation which may still be predominantly white), and being a continuous beneficiary of BEE, and also of signing off on such 'boomerang' deals – unless you have political protection. If you are a front person for a BEE consortium you can get paid very little and if a person asks for more, their position can be undermined, either in terms of tax or employment. One respondent in a very senior level of public administration, expressed the opinion that finishing a five-year term of office as Director General (DG) of a public works department was not possible if one was honest: a fake industrial tribunal would be organized to remove one from position if certain deals were not signed off.

The risk to a public official is also apparent in the changing power balance between competing cliques: "They charge people with corruption so that they can get rid of them, move them out, and then bring in their own people".[16] In other words, a successful group of people committed to benefiting from public fiscal resources is not a flat or horizontal network. It has definite features. It needs a good accountant, or indeed a high profile, nationally recognised (but not necessarily honest) accountancy company with the skills to negotiate the offshore economy. It needs a worker in the public sector in charge of signing off on a large budget, who can be bullied, bribed, threatened or enticed into joining in. If the person in that role is "blocking", then influence is exerted to have them fired. Even when the person can be persuaded to align with the clique, the risks may still return, as the clique may not need them for long, and they become the obvious "fall guy" later.

The electoral cycle and the business cycle of corruption

The electoral business cycle could also be called the corruption business cycle. This is firstly because those people in a current functioning clique are vulnerable to a loss of business if their apex politician is voted out in an election. A new person at the top might come and take their business for the benefit of "his or her own people". Second, people in public administration may themselves be absolutely free from corrupt behaviour. But they are at risk if they are in charge of public records that provide evidence of corruption. Incumbents to political office invariably want to show high levels of integrity on entry, and the records could be key to establishing control over their new territory. Three or four years later, corruption cases will emerge in the media. Some of them will be "true", and some of them will be falsely represented. Sometimes innocent people are implicated to cover the tracks of a clique or its erstwhile members who have since changed allegiance. But the public record-keeper will be at risk. Third, there is often a spike in the incidence of corruption up to an election as those in a position to benefit maximise spoils before they may be removed from office. All this means that the structure of political power, both in the government and within and between political parties, matters most to patterns of corruption and to their cost and scope. Even if the apex politician doesn't get voted out, "their own people" changes depending on the interests of the clique and their business interests as a whole. Elections where politicians change cause much more disruption to business networks, although strategic persons might successfully move allegiance just in time, or leave others in key posts to "keep the tap running".

Conclusion

This chapter showed how the political connectivity at various levels of government is the key resource needed in order to build a group, or "clique", to benefit from the financialisation of power in South Africa. My contention is that South Africa, as a case study, shares features of financialisation with other African countries, as briefly explored here. The global economy structures described in the first half of the book empower global corporates to recruit local elites into financialised business structures where the income streams move offshore. The local counterparts and joint venture partners are most often key politicians or those connected to them acting in cliques. The reward is either a direct kickback related to the derogation of public duty, the writing of regulations that favour foreign capital, or the non-implementation of a regulation that already exists. The consequence is a growth in the zones of exception available to international capital. The local counterparties benefit from a junior participation in the venture as a whole, and this mode of behaviour migrates down to all levels of government. Thus while the public sector could commit to regulation to prevent illicit financial flows, by mandating firms to improve transparency and integrity, particularly in investment agreements contracted between financial intermediaries and with public authorities, incentives to do so are conditioned by the overarching logic of financialisation as a governance technology. Under this logic, the mainstream approach to corporate governance, in southern Africa at least, centres on anaemic voluntary codes of conduct, corporate social responsibility campaigns, and transparency initiatives that can be performed as a spectacle, with little substantive effect on underlying firm behaviour (see Standing 2013; Mottiar 2014).

Notes

1 By bankers and also other professionals such as lawyers, accountants, auditors and others in the financial services industry. It is beyond the scope of this chapter to detail these, but much more research in this areas is apposite.

2 Khadija Sharife, personal communication, 2015.

3 From 2012–2015 the author and researchers, Sithembiso Myeni and Michael K Dorsey, interviewed 32 business people in KwaZulu-Natal about private sector corruption, in the context of a forensic audit of eThekwini Municipality that put irregular payments at over ZAR1.2 trillion (report by Manase & Associates; see Mbanjwa, 2012). We asked specifically about political connectivity, the regulation between the known person from the political struggle and the known too well person from one's family or village. The research was funded by the Leverhulme Trust and Chr. Michelsen Institute, and more lately by the South African National Research Foundation through the Research Chair held by the author.

4 Respondent 6, 23/8/2012, U4 Anti-Corruption Resource Centre at Chr. Michelsen Institute, and Leverhulme Centre for the Study of Value project grant no. RP2012-V-041 "Human, non-human, and environmental value systems: An impossible frontier?" 2012-2016.

5 Respondent 6, 23/8/2012. The justification is apparently partly performed by the fact that only 30,000 people would turn up to the event "There is no apparent victim, the victim is the fiscus at a later level, there is only going to be 30,000 people at that event in any case, so if the spec was for a 100,000 there would have been a waste of T-shirts, we're not going to waste T-shirts."

6 Respondent 7, 24/8/2012.

7 Respondent 2, 15/8/2012.

8 Respondent 2, 15/8/2012.

9 Respondent 6, 23/8/2012.

10 Respondent 2, 15/8/2012.

11 Respondent 6, 23/8/2012.

12 Respondent 25, 23/8/2015. Continuation of U4 and Leverhulme project with research supported by the South African Research Chairs initiative of the Department of Science and Technology and National Research Foundation of South Africa (Grant No 71220). Any opinion, finding and conclusion or recommendation expressed in this material is that of the author(s) and the NRF does not accept any liability in this regard.

13 Respondent 25, 23/8/2015.

14 Funded by the Chr. Michelsen Institute through U4, conducted for Bracking (2013c), and ongoing funded with the support of the Leverhulme Trust, see www.thestudy-ofvalue.org

15 Respondent 6, 23/8/2012.

16 Respondent 29, 27/8/2015.

7 The governance of privilege and the privilege of the governors

> Everybody eats. We all know that. But they are eating too much so it is left smeared on their faces [wipes around mouth]. Pie here, meat here – you can even see where they have been! That's not right. But vote DA [Democratic Alliance]? No way. You know how they treat black people in the Western Cape? They don't even have toilets down there.[1]

> A black man is assumed to be corrupt until proven innocent in our country. I could never join the BEE train. It would destroy my business! [interviewer, 'Why?']. I would lose all my white clients. Everyone would assume I was corrupt.[2]

We saw in the last chapter how large corporate entities make connections with high-level political persons in order to generate extractive economic entities that then shift income to secrecy jurisdictions. The organisational processes of financialisation privilege the capture of derivative income streams from fixed assets. This often leaves national companies and persons, with ownership or management relationships to those proximate assets, relatively bereft. The political economy prerogatives and practices of financialisation in specific locations lead to transfers of wealth and influencing of policy at all levels of government, even if only mimetic of the patterns of power established at the highest levels. Thus the slew of publications and evaluations from the mid 2000s that lamented the flaws and inabilities of donor anti-corruption work in practice, from theoreticians (Brown and Cloke 2005; Doig and Marquette 2005; Mungiu-Pippidi 2006) and donor departments (Johnsøn *et al.* 2012; DfID 2011; Norad 2009, 2011), isolated a central problem: that the government and society that donors wanted, of a Weberian rational-legal bureaucratic order and liberal democratic state was very far removed from the type of political regimes with which donors were negotiating, as was illustrated in the last chapter. A little later, it was also recognised, in a number of publications using the black box of "lack of political will" to explain non-results in governance reform, that not only were institutional reforms designed to "fix" states that were of a different type not working; but that more fundamentally, the elites of those countries probably didn't want that type of change in any case.

However, this has not prevented most donor interventions, up to the contemporary period in fact, focussing on institutional reforms based on moving particularist, or patron–client structures, to perform better as Weberian rational-legal bureaucracies, but with little obvious result (Theobald 2008; on Timor-Leste see Blunt 2009). Even where donors have engaged in a system of institutional reform that introduces rationality, oversight and separation of powers, research has shown that without local conviction, which is often scant, these can be rolled back very quickly once the regime changes, as Uberti showed for donor reforms of the Kosovo mining sector (2014). An evaluation report by Johnsøn *et al.* (2012) argued, based on a systematic evidence review, that anti-corruption interventions only showed positive results in relation to public financial management (PFM) reforms and mixed results for supreme audit institutions (SAIs), while there was "fair evidence" that civil service reforms, aid conditionality and anti-corruption authorities had not been effective.

A central problem of these practices is that the administrative state and the political state are relatively separate with the ruling party structures running in parallel to those of the formal state. This is common to many post-liberation Anglophone states. In this chapter we will explore the veracity of "petty corruption" in governance structures and then model what the financialisation of power looks like in domestic politics, with an emphasis on South Africa. This is not intended to imply that South Africa is an exemplar or representative case study of "Africa" in general. Rather that the author has had the privilege of undertaking research there, and it will be left to the reader to interpret how common or generic this analysis may be.

Administrative corruption

For our purposes here, administrative corruption, which is often termed "petty corruption" is defined as

> everyday abuse of entrusted power by low- or mid-level public officials in their interactions with ordinary citizens, who are often trying to access basic goods or services in places like hospitals, schools, police departments, and other agencies.
>
> (Transparency International 2009)

It involves low-level public servants including the uniformed services, who may nonetheless still be a "Big Man" in a local context, "breaking or not observing rules and procedures in return for pecuniary rewards or other forms of self-aggrandisement" (Theobald 2008: 160). The official may be influenced to perform or not perform a function, and can be rewarded by either pecuniary or non-pecuniary gifts, which would include those generated in informal social and cultural networks. These can be as diverse as school places, invitations to business functions, access to procurement deals directly or indirectly, or a job opportunity for a relative. Petty corruption undermines development because it diverts fiscal budgets to private hands. Irregularities in public procurement procedures, which in Uganda are estimated to account for the major share of lost revenues (Ntayi *et al.* 2013), can be counted in this category. The public official can also misuse or appropriate public property, create ghost workers, demand pay-back for jobs awarded to subordinates and channel jobs to relatives. As the World Bank reminded us, it can also cover not turning up for work, or doing one's work badly (World Bank 2010). In a recent study of electricity connections in Malawi, it could also cover doing something preferentially, in this case providing a residential connection, to a person believed to be politically connected, at the expense of queuing customers (Robinson and Zimmerman 2014).

In terms of the perception of the importance of this kind of corruption, it is unfortunate that the term "petty" seems to signify a lack of importance. It would probably be wise for conceptual clarity to change singularly to the more formal "administrative corruption". Arguably too, however, it is generally outsiders who write development narratives, and who would find it hard to appreciate the centrality and significance of the "little something" (Kenya), the "soft drink" (Mozambique), or various other national equivalents, to the life course of an extremely poor person. It literally makes the difference between a child being born safely or not (and potentially the life of the mother in child-birth); the longevity and quality of life for those needing anti-retroviral drugs; whether a child gets a school place; whether they can go up a grade; whether they can sit examinations or receive a certificate. For women it often means the difference between being able to access health services and family planning or not, and in rural areas, whether a woman is able to access farm extension services, seeds, land or markets. Thus petty corruption is not small; it is life-changing and life-conditioning.

In fact, the prevalence of petty corruption remains exhaustive and its effects critical to well-being and ill-being, whatever the popular perception. In large parts of Africa, it is probably accurate to describe petty corruption as endemic, pervasive and as a mediator of social inclusion/exclusion, but more often exclusion (see also Flanary and Watt 1999, on Uganda; Smith 2007 on Nigeria). For example, in recent research in Mozambique it has been established that around 10 per cent or more of the rural population are permanently excluded from public services because they have insufficient funds to pay the "soft drink" bribes. Yet even here, none of these excluded persons see an incentive to complain because this would also eliminate their hopes that one day they might be included, either as a response to a changed personal relationship, or due to a sudden rise in income (Tvedten 2014). In this circumstance, insisting on rights or causing trouble can even destroy the potential or hope that things could change or inclusion be subsequently granted. This explains the level of extreme obedience and lack of protest that outsiders find odd, even when persons are dying of curable diseases and malnutrition.

The exception to petty corruption's generalised prevalence might be in those countries that are extremely authoritarian where party or military rule decides resource allocation. However, even in this latter case, there is arguably a theoretical problem that such party states often represent the institutionalisation of patrimonialism within party structures, and then often the fusion of party and state, and thus a normalisation of petty corruption as resource allocator, rather than a distinctive model representing an alternative to the endemic administrative corruption of formal liberal state structures elsewhere. In most countries in sub-Saharan Africa it is a complex combination of politically connected person, sometimes a "broker" (see Jancsics 2013, 2014), and formal public service worker who together provide the opportunity, agency and threat of corruption to those seeking services.

Costs of corruption

Estimating the aggregate economic cost and distribution of costs of corruption is notoriously difficult given the opacity in which it occurs and that self-reported data on corruption is unreliable due to social desirability bias and fear of prosecution (see Robinson and Zimmerman 2014). In general, we know that corruption is costly to developing countries (Bardhan 1997) and is more prevalent in countries with greater inequality (Jong-Sung and Khagram 2005), but the distribution of costs is less well established. It has even been recently (re)asserted that in countries with extremely weak governance the "grease the wheels" hypothesis of corruption being positively associated with increases in overall economic efficiency may still stand (Meon and Weill 2010). However, overall costs of corruption for poor households undoubtedly remain high. A World Bank survey using data from 1999–2003 estimated that households and firms paid between US$0.6 trillion and US$1.5 trillion in bribes each year (Clarke 2011: 1122; citing Kaufmann 2005), while evidence from firms in the World Bank's *Enterprise Surveys* programme of 2006 and 2007 showed an average firm's bribe payment of between 2.5 and 4.5 per cent of sales in most low-income sub-Saharan African countries, although there is still doubt as to exact figures due to self-reporting bias and differences which occur depending on the way in which the question is asked (Clarke 2011: 1122).

Understanding the distribution of costs of corruption is even more difficult. As summarised recently by Robinson and Zimmerman (2014), some authors note that the wealthy encounter corruption more often as they have more interactions with officials (Guerrero and Rodriguez-Orwggia 2008; Hunt 2007; Hunt and Laszlo 2012); while other authors argue that the powerful and wealthy can insulate themselves from corruption at the expense of the powerless and poor (Nielsen 2006; Fadahunsi and Rosa 2002). Field experimental approaches (notably Fried *et al.* 2010; Robinson and Zimmerman 2014) have mitigated the methodological problem of self-reporting to some extent, but this research is difficult to scale up to macro-economic estimates of cost. The work on illicit financial flows, however, at aggregate scale, suggests that political corruption directly causes 5 to 10 per cent of an approximate US$1.2 trillion globally in 2012, in illegally earned and moved financial transfers, and also contributes to facilitating much of the rest, with particularly harmful effects in vulnerable economies and in African extractive economies (Global Integrity Foundation 2013; UNECA 2014).

Robinson and Zimmerman suggest that the extent of ambiguity over empirical findings on costs of corruption is due in part to the co-determinacy of the variables of power and wealth. For example, Fried *et al.* (2010) find that bribes to traffic police in Mexico, in a field experimental approach, were a high burden for the poor who were asked for a bribe more often, but that the average bribe was higher for the rich. Robinson and Zimmerman explain this as due to rich individuals being more valuable targets, but also more risky ones, who could feasibly exact more effective retribution, particularly if politically connected. In their research of bribes to traffic police and the electricity authority (ESCOM) in Malawi, they find that it is political connections that reduce exposure to corruption, and that in the absence of this, socio-economic status has no effect (Robinson and Zimmerman 2014: 1). In other words, access to political power is the critical factor that a public servant is considering at the point of asking for and setting a bribe amount. In their view "wealth only insulates one from corruption when it is seen as a proxy for political power" (ibid).

Connectivity in petty corruption

Patrimonial theories of traditional rural Africa argue that patterns of loyalty and fealty determine that material resources are "distributed and consumed as though they were the private property of the ruler" (Kelsall 2011: 77). Traditional authority relies on the exchange of (relative) security, resources and protection for networks of support (Scott 1972; Hilgers 2011: 560–570), separate from liberal governance structures, such that the rural poor must often negotiate three separate sites of power in order to access resources: the traditional authority, where "the social identity of non-elites is closely tied to the identity of the patronage network in which they are located" (North *et al.* 2009: 35); the ruling party; and the administrative state, all of which may incur a charge. The patron–client network of both the traditional authority and the ruling party govern the logics of inclusion and exclusion in a moral economy (Olivier de Sadan 1999), which in turn conditions how citizens are able to negotiate the frontier of the state, if at all. Thus, the "economic rationality of actors is 'bonded' to the social networks that enable and sustain their continuing access to resources" (Uberti, forthcoming: 14; citing Di John 2009: 145). This structure conditions service delivery, both compromising it and enabling it.

Meanwhile, in addition to petty corruption, accessing public services in post-conflict regimes and divided societies can mean pretending ethnicities or performing them, while negotiating criminal structures and threats of force (Asiimwe 2013; Orjuela 2014; Nystrand 2014). At the least, the poor are forced to amass a set of "pre-charges" related to brokerage services, which become due as a means for them to travel from their situation of relative social isolation – which is often a principal cause and consequence of poverty – through the connectivity map to someone who can assist them in the formal state, whether that be a politically connected person, or a formal administrative official, or both. In Uganda and Zimbabwe, and other African states with an authoritarian dominant ruling party, the road to public services often means acquiring a party card or at least negotiating political party structures (Asiimwe; 2013; Bracking 2005), or negotiating a structure of informal privatisation of street-level bureaucracies, as in Senegal (Blundo 2006).

This travel through "extra-state" networks often sends the nominal cost of the public service they hope to achieve sky-rocketing – even before the poor arrive at the frontier of the formal state.[3] In other words, petty corruption, in a Foucauldian sense, has become a "technology of governance" which manages the social exclusion of the poorest in a situation of scarcity. Indeed, there is often an inverse correlation between wealth and the cost of basic services. This economic injustice is not, however, necessarily recognised for what it is, with the poor in Uganda seeing the situation as "the way things are" and "largely expected" (Nystrand 2014: 821–82, 824), views shared by the rural poor in Mozambique (Tvedten 2014) and Nigeria (Smith 2007). Petty corruption is often viewed by people as something that they, and others, cannot escape, that everyone is a part of, and as something that is needed to "get by" (Nystrand 2014: 829; citing Blundo and de Sardan 2006).

Thus the relatively conservative social orders of rural Africa tend to maintain the poorest in situ, with little "liberal" knowledge of democratic entitlement or social contract. In fact, grand corruption tends to upset people more because it is seen to promote inequality (Nystrand 2014: 828–30; Uslaner 2008). It may be that getting annoyed by petty corruption is seen as a waste of time and strategically unhelpful by those concerned. Thus research in South Africa in the fisheries sector suggested that the poor could hold two views simultaneously: that petty corruption was wrong but that there was no means or point in avoiding participating (Sundström 2013). However, it could also be the case that this normative ambiguity is because complexity in rural and urban Africa troubles traditional ways of modelling political power, including theories of patrimonialism.

For example, there is growing evidence that patrimonialism doesn't "work" in an easy and assumed way in that empirical evidence shows co-ethnics and people of a ruler's home area often pay more tax than others, demonstrated in Kasara's study of agricultural taxation in 50 country-crop combinations (Kasara 2007). Under a patrimonial assumption they should be paying less (cf. Leys 1974; Bates 1983; Chandra 2004). Kasara explains that a ruler's ability to manage a home area, often through intermediaries, and the lack of political opposition often found there, (partly due to the leader's ability to suppress alternative candidates), means that votes can be "bought" more easily there than elsewhere, with a lower expenditure of resources (Kasara 2007). Given that this rate of "overtaxation" is lower in more democratic regimes suggests that while patrimonialism may instil a "psychic benefit" to co-ethics of the ruler, its material effects can be negative. Thus, Kasara's evidence proves a "remarkable anomaly [in] patterns of patronage politics in Africa: those farmers with co-ethnics in power get taxed more" (ibid.: 170). While "counterintuitive" to some extent, it "supports the intuitive idea that rulers extract the most from those who cannot evade their grasp" (ibid.). While other transfers of public investment may go to the ruler's home area, it is likely that these go to a small group of beneficiaries and to the intermediaries and local power brokers, not decreasing the degree that farmers of the area are taxed more.

Other work also suggests that there are a range of circumstances where incumbents may choose not to distribute resources to core supporters (reviewed in Kasara 2007: 159), with local-level inequalities of wealth, education and power exerting a strong influence on distribution patterns (Bardhan and Mookherjee 2000; Platteau 2004). Qualitative studies are also problematizing traditional views of how patrimonialism works (Bracking 2013a; Sundström 2013; Funder and Marani 2015). For example, while fisherpeople in South Africa often know environmental regulation officers personally, thus ensuring the trust necessary for bribing to continue, compliance decisions are nonetheless complex and the briber still views the inspector as dishonest (Sundström 2013: 454). In Bracking (2013a) business people in KwaZulu-Natal South Africa are found to largely resent the role of political connectivity in the pattern of distribution of government procurement contracts, and view BEE certification, a mandatory requirement for participation, as an unnecessary rent: "I am black in my own country. Why do I have to prove it for 15,000 rand" (the money refers to the cost of BEE auditing and registration)[4] (Bracking, forthcoming).

How leaders secure support in the localities thus deserves more study, as the distribution of patronage is not as simple as was assumed, since local economic and political inequalities seem to have a higher effect on patterns of patronage than ethnicity alone, certainly in the case of agricultural taxation, where the majority cannot be easily excluded. Indeed, types of state resources that can be enjoyed individually may have different patterns of patronage than common pool resources from which it is difficult to exclude other individuals, such as both public services and common pool natural resource regimes. For example, Funder and Marani find that in relation to local environment officers in Kenya, implementing agents of national environmental laws, officers act as bricoleurs, implementing law though personal networks, by crafting informal agreements and by delegating public authority to civil society (Funder and Marani 2015: 87). Representing the "local state" (Olivier de Sardan 2014) and implementing law as "street level bureaucrats" (Lipsky 2010), they have significant influence on the distribution and access to local goods and services. Technical officers of the local state make discrete interpretations of the law and perform governance as bricoleurs, mixing formal and informal mechanisms and practise (Funder and Marani 2015: 89). In the case of the Kenyan environment officers, they find "pragmatic solutions to the practical problem of limited budgets, time and operational scope" (ibid.: 93). These "make the state function" in the context of limited reach and capacity, where to "get the job done" means making strategic alliances with others with similar concerns and collaborative practise (ibid.).

Funder and Marani's work is a strong reminder that not all delegation of authority to non-state actors, or informally brokered agreements can be viewed as corrupt (see also Therkildsen 2014), but rather as an historic means of governance by "indirect rule" in the local African state (Funder and Marani 2015: 101). It represents a blending of legal-rational and informal relations, which some argue is essential to neopatrimonialism (Erdmann and Engel 2006), but not in circumstances that can be simplistically read as corruption. Other work on frontline bureaucrats has similar findings of "inventive practises" (Hamani (2014) on Niger courts; Mathews (2011) on Mexico; Blundo (2014) on Senegal). Bricolage here works as an institution, or practical norm, and mode of engagement between frontline bureaucrats and citizens, which can enable but also constrain communities and access to resources (Funder and Marani 2015: 103–4).

Similarly, the role of trust in corruption remains ambiguous: it is needed at a minimum level for a corrupt transaction to take place since both parties need to be sure that contracts will be honoured and that the other doesn't take recourse to the law or another authority after (Robbins 2000: 427–28). The involved citizens and officials are thus related in relationships of trust (Akpalu *et al.* 2009), despite corruption as a whole having a corrosive impact on trust (Levi *et al.* 2009; Rothstein 2011; reviewed in Sundström 2013). In Sundström's account of petty corruption in environmental compliance in the fisheries sector in South Africa the widespread belief that inspectors welcomed bribes, and that others would bribe, reduced the compliance intentions, in terms of over-fishing and allowable fish size, in research respondents, despite some viewing the consequences to fish stocks and livelihoods as negative (Sundström 2013). Corruption in fisheries certainly demands more international attention, as Standing (2008) argued, but the generic point here is that everyday corruption aggregates to problems of national and global scale, such as natural resource management and depletion, and should not be ignored as "petty", whatever the relative normativity of "captured" rural subjects.

The role of corruption in the non-delivery of public services

Public services involve the majority of persons and it is hard to either exclude people legitimately or enjoy them individually. Kasara's work (2007) would then suggest that public services would be most enjoyed by persons in more democratic circumstances and/or where there is effective political opposition. If these are absent, petty corruption could be expected to form the means to ration or exclude persons, while political patronage would not be expected to offset this substantially, excepting through local brokerage systems. Thus, to make life even more complicated for the poor, new research shows how even to access a chance at receiving public services they have to negotiate a whole frontier of middle-people and brokerage regimes (Jancsics 2014), many of which are deeply embedded in social networks (Sundström 2013; Jancsics 2014). There is also clear evidence that the cultural worth of public officials relative to other roles, such as working in the private sector, or being a politician, affects the bribe levels and mechanism of exchange (Theobald 2008; see also Jancsics (2013) on the role of social background on form of corruption in Hungary).

Thus, when officeholders are of a higher social status than businesspeople, as in the South Korea example in the 1960s, corruption became highly "elaborate systems of gift giving, banquets, entertainment, and factors keyed to the highly particular needs of officials" (Granovetter 2007: 159). By contrast, in societies such as in Latin America, where officeholders are of a lower social status than businesspeople corruption tends to be monetary and take a market-like nature (ibid.: 156–60). In complex networks it becomes hard to distinguish between the public and the private and the assumed Weberian dualism emerges as that which it is: a highly historically and geographically specific conception of corruption (Bukovansky 2006; Harrison 2006; Cheng and Zaum 2012). However, this is not to say that different cultural contexts do not have coded values around corruption. In fact, in most polities globally there is anti-corruption legislation, but this does not necessarily dictate an understanding of corruption at a local level, which "has its own morality, at least in the eyes of the local public" (Shore and Haller 2005: 8–12). It has been variously noted, for example, that while administrative corruption may be seen as "how life is", if people are charged differential levels of bribes they get much more upset because of the "unfair" treatment.

Polanyi famously stated that economic agents, in this case our citizens, act in ways designed to safeguard their social standing, their social claims and their social assets (Polanyi 2001: 65). This helps explain why pecuniary exchange doesn't have to be central or a defining absolute of administrative corruption per se, particularly if we take into account Bourdieu's observation that "capital" can be easily exchanged and circulated as "social", "cultural" and so forth and quite easily exchanged back into pecuniary reward further along in a circuit. This also helps explain the complexity of exchanges in corrupt environments. Thus, when states develop poor records of service delivery these rationalities generate patterns of behaviour that look elsewhere, to churches, charities, relatives, such that demands for accountability go quiet, or do not develop at all. In this sense, there is no service delivery problem in areas of "traditional" Africa where governments have been successful in convincing people that there is no obligation for them to deliver modern public services, and/or where people are happy with that outcome. When the state "returns" it returns back into a circuit of exchange which includes all these other actants.

This doesn't necessarily mean that increased state involvement will cause administrative corruption to grow, but it might change form, depending on the social structure in place. For example, consider Lomnitz's insight that "accepting a bribe is an acknowledgement of social inferiority, just like accepting a tip" (Lomnitz 1988: 44). This perhaps partly explains the prevalence of non-pecuniary, yet still exchange relationships, in certain parts of Africa, including KwaZulu-Natal, designed to resource persons, but which are often not monetised. This does not imply that there are no losers from these exchanges or that the acts are morally neutral: the "losers" are those who are socially and economically excluded.

Service delivery and corruption in South Africa

In South Africa, most respondents in the research conducted on corruption in eThekwini, Durban in 2012 and 2013,[5] said it was an everyday and unavoidable affair, although there is good reason to think that levels of corruption in local administration are more often suffered by historically disadvantaged and poor communities. There is evidence too, that "differential" rates of bribes are felt as unfair in that ruling party or ANC supporters are seen as privileged above others in matters such as local procurement. The forms of corruption seem to conform to Granvetter's insight, that because of the relatively high status of public officials, especially those in political appointments, corruption involves elaborate gifting, rather than direct cash.

Thus in this research the source of "bribe" and "reward" for the bribed were found to be in complex social networks, sometimes recycled in time or space, so that a favour at point "x", might only be rewarded two years later for a relative twice removed at point "y". What was surprising in this research was that network memory was very strong and it was "known" fairly instinctively or at least according to well entrenched social norms, that the gift and reward were related and consequential on each other. The dominant finding of this research, however, was that political office, or at least membership of a political party were intimately connected to economic opportunity. As one respondent noted:

> you can't get any work within eThekwini municipality unless you have political connections … Even if you know someone who is your friend, I'll make an example. If you have a friend who is an IFP [Inkatha Freedom Party], right, and you want him to get work within eThekwini, he will have to pretend that he is not an IFP. I'm making an example. Although he is my friend and I know someone … An IFP is Inkatha Freedom Party, a small opposition party … so although he will be my connection and I have a connection within eThekwini, they will turn and say no, no, no we can't help you help your friend who is not in our rank. So he will have to pretend that he is not IFP or he is very aligned with ANC. And vice versa, in areas where Inkatha has control, and vice versa in areas where NFP [National Freedom Party] has control.[6]

Or another on tenders and procurement:

> tenders cannot be accessed by people who are unemployed, regardless of qualifications, you need to buy the tender document and it is in line with the size of the tender, so you cannot afford, you borrow money from others, and you get fed up because you buy it and then you don't get it you don't win, not awarded, is like the lotto, they are selling these documents, there is nothing … you have to pay them money, but they are not offering you anything except to say you are competent.[7]

This pattern of how power translates into the lives of people is directly mimetic of how power works in financialisation processes within the global political economy. It reflects the "neoliberal anthropologics" discussed by Miller (2002) and Callon (2005). This is the direct sense in which the social order adopts a governance logic from the global political economy. Those who are higher placed in government participate in the formal and legal structure of the joint venture firm, having shares in a firm owning the underlying assets of the income streams that leave to the investors, in return for their equity or credit. These structures are then replicated to other glocalised sites of accumulation, where national money-holders seek their own loans and equity in related ventures, with the symbiotic addition of public funding.

Accountability and service delivery

This financialisation of the power of government to distribute social grants, tenders and services generates economic inequality and a lack of democratic accountability in the classical sense. In many of sub-Saharan African countries there is a disconnect between the appearance and procedures of institutional democratic life and its outcomes for the majority citizens which has promoted a normalisation of omissions, commissions and non-outcomes (Du Toit 2011, 2012; Seekings 2008; Ferguson 2007). This has two central aspects: the perennial exposure but non-prosecution of corruption and graft; and the everyday non-delivery of basic services and social protection with no basic income guarantee for work age adults. The two are of course related, since graft contributes to a comparatively low fiscal base, exacerbated by the facilitation that corrupt behaviour performs in the service of generating illicit financial flows. The low fiscal base then provides for low comparative spending on social welfare, with a further misdirection of a further amount of funds at the provincial, municipal and local levels.

These revenue losses from a low initial base are further compounded by the effects of a complex overlapping structure of power and authority. In the South African state, there are still competing logics of governance, some derivative of its contested past (see Szeftel 2004): these governmentalities are patrimonialism, the liberal institutional state, the radical "rainbow alliance" state and remaining remnants of the apartheid state, these latter particularly in planning, zoning and excessive bureaucracy. Evidence-based policy doesn't work when policy makers are not interested in evidence, and do not base their decisions in reflections within a social welfare maximisation paradigm and Weberian rationality. Instead, resources are either denied to citizens because of remnants of apartheid planning, such as "zoning" and the criminalisation of informal housing, or the use of the "development line" around Durban's central business district [CBD] beyond which citizens' rights to water, sanitation or electricity are not recognised. Or the political connectedness of persons conditions their receipt of resources as particular constituencies feel that it is their right to "eat" based in the logic of patrimonialism. Bond has recently characterised the overall state ideology as "neoliberal nationalism", with tokenistic welfare, which helps characterise this complexity (Bond 2014d), although arguably "nationalism" does not completely capture the competing logics.

In classical liberal theory, accountability is derived principally from institutions and techniques and practises of accountability at a parliamentary and central state level, such as the Public Protector, Ombudsman, and parliamentary oversight which work in an institutional context but foundationally guided by mediating values (Beetham *et al.* 2002). These traditional oversight and accountability functions are summarised in Table 7.1. The deepening of neo-liberal governance since the early 1990s, or more particularly "advanced liberal governance" has added new practices and techniques to these traditional ones (Dean 2003: 149–75; Oels 2006: 188–94). In this accountability assemblage, the technologies of advanced liberal government (Oels 2006; Dean 2003) include advanced planning, new public management, new contractualism, a reliance on market-based mechanisms, privatisation of state functions, constant audit and evidence-based policy, which have been added globally to the traditional lines of accountability found through elections and parliamentary representation. In advanced liberal government citizens, and organisations, model themselves to be calculating and responsible, competitive in a "constant strive for self-optimization" (Oels 2006: 192), "a subject whose freedom is a condition of subjection" (Dean 2003: 165). Global society is self-regulated by "technologies of agency" and "technologies of performance" (Dean 2003). The first conditions what is possible in both "participation" and resistance, that citizens and organisations conform to thin and managed deliberative spaces and processes of consultation or "new contractualism"; while the second confines the subject into constant audit, to norms, benchmarks, standards, performance indicators, quality controls, best practice and so forth that "exercise a normalizing power over the individual [and group]" (Oels 2006: 192).

Table 7.1 Accountability: making plans and keeping promises

Accountability	*Requirements*	*Institutional procedures*
Ex ante	Political equality and popular control. Rule of law, separation of powers.	Election manifesto, planning, budgeting, consultation, participation, impact assessment, safeguarding
Process	Clear lines of accountability, legal, financial and political to ensure effective and honest performance of the civil service and judicial integrity	Parliamentary scrutiny, independent public protector, ombudsman, press freedom. Independent judiciary, independent auditing process
Ex post	Strong parliamentary scrutiny powers, legally enforceable standards	Prosecution of offenders, implementation of disclosure of representative's wealth and tax. Transparent political party finance

These traditional and post-modern accountability mechanisms and governance practices are combined in South Africa and elsewhere into hybrid and complex structures of power. There are also contradictions generic to advanced liberal government that suggest its limitations, increasingly found in South Africa and elsewhere. As actors participate further in its technologies of performance and agency (Oels 2006: 192) it becomes clearer that it is not these alone that generate outcomes, but underlying positions of power (Bracking 2014). Because of this, advanced liberal government has served to confuse our understanding of accountability since while its technologies of governance are pursued as an administrative activity they do not necessarily enjoy deep roots in the practices of power and resource distribution in the political economy outside the state (Du Toit 2010, 2011),[8] or lead to consequences in the absence of political will. In other words, when *ex post* accountability is used to audit provincial government using forensic audit, and R1.3bn of irregular payments are discovered, as in the *Manase Report* on eThekwini municipality, there are no apparent consequences for the 12 councillors trading with entities in which they are a beneficial owner, excepting a small fine in a couple of cases. Advanced liberal government is sometimes not only non-performative, however proficient its participants become, but also contradicts and is displaced by alternative procedures and practices, not least those emanating from the party state (Bracking 2015c). Thus, as a consequence of corruption, competing governance logics, and the heavy technical burden of advanced liberal government, many public administrations are in a form of stasis. Public servants are balancing traditional accountability mechanisms and the newer generation of logics from advanced liberal governance (permanent audit, technical forecasting and planning requirements), all in the context of low revenue bases and competing logics of power, expressed in the demands of their political "Big Men". This has weakened the social contract still further.

However, the synergies created between financialised processes of global political economy, and national and local processes of class formation, has led to new alliances among political and business elites, and counterparties in public administrations, who may be one and the same person or people, as we saw in Chapter 6. The traditional requirement for the legitimacy of rule has, as a consequence shifted into two alternative modes of governmentality: (1) an ad hoc partial financialisation of welfare and service provision, either through direct administrative corruption or the parallel structures of Big Men and their "philanthropy"; and (2) the appearance or spectacle of care without the substance of it by any party. Many of Africa's most rapidly growing sites of class formation are accompanied by high concentrations of "clique-led" corruption, but also by apparently great acts of philanthropy – or at least that is how they are represented. Most senior ANC leaders in South Africa have a foundation or trust, as do most other presidents, often run by wives. These two modes of governmentality illustrate the power of financialisation to reshape non-economic life-worlds (see page 24), and are now discussed in turn.

Privatisation of welfare to philanthropy

The financialisation of welfare and service provision reflects financialisation logics per se; that even the poor and destitute must be entrained to produce derivative income streams. The literature on philanthro-capitalism illustrates this well. Morvaridi summarises Bourdieu that philanthro-capitalism is a transaction between "different forms of capital: economic (money and resources), social (networks or knowing influential people), cultural (linguistic and articulating on behalf of others), and symbolic (status)" (Morvaridi 2012: 1194). In this understanding capitalist philanthropists convert economic capital into symbolic capital and status, with which they can control debate, create hegemony over policy, capture parts of state regulatory capacity and return decisions and indeed the organisation of the economy itself into something that contributes to enhancing future profits. Morvaridi uses the example of the New Green Revolution in Africa to show how the Gates and Syngenta Foundations, both associated with and invested in biotechnology companies, and partnering/cross investing with Monsanto, fund prominent research institutes (including the World Food Programme, Institute of Tropical Agriculture, the universities of Harvard, Oxford, Imperial College and so forth) that promote the pro-poor properties of biotechnology and genetically modified seeds, while also "assisting" small-scale farmers to buy them with US$1.7bn in the Alliance for a Green Revolution in Africa (AGRA) programme. Here "philanthropy" buys, by means of funding "on message" research, the hegemony that genetically modified (GM) seeds are good for poor people, despite evidence to the contrary in terms of them being instrumental to small holder adverse incorporation into agribusiness. Capitalist philanthropy here exerts power and influence and locks in future profits (by capturing land, farmers and their custom) to businesses owned or invested in by the philanthropists. In 2010 the Bill and Melinda Gates Foundation purchased 500,000 shares in Monsanto, a world leader in the production of GM seeds, while giving US$47m to Monsanto to produce "water resistant maize varieties affordable for small-scale farmers" (Morvaridi 2012: 1206). Here investment in future accumulation, more strictly called venture capital, seems to have merely been reclassified as "giving", while the hegemonic market and policy structure that works in favour of producing poverty has been re-legitimised.

Similarly, Thompson, also writing in relation to AGRA, shows how this platform serves to access and privatise Africa's genetic wealth. She argues that this is being expropriated to extend processes of accumulation by dispossession and the further reach of capitalist agriculture into traditional land and agricultural systems. She then uses the concept of philanthro-capitalism to show how this is done by "replacing public agricultural sectors with private practices and control" (Thompson 2014: 389). Holmes similarly concludes that capitalist philanthropy in conservation drives neo-liberalisation. It supports processes that enable capital to make new forms of money from conservation (Holmes 2012: 185), while the associated promotion of celebrity in conservation, as persons with status, knowledge and authority (Brockington 2014) assists private economic interests in their avoidance of accountability from actual natural or environmental science. Overall, the role of philanthropy in conservation has been to support the financialisation of policy and generate market-based solutions that promote a commodification of the non-human world (Igoe and Brockington 2007; Igoe *et al.* 2010). In all these domains, philanthropy serves to provide legitimacy to elites, and allows a cultural occlusion of graft.

A spectacle of care

In terms of the second governance logic (page 142), of the spectacle of care, South Africa certainly has extensive evidence of a form of "anti-politics" (Ferguson 1996; Oels 2006), where the political is rendered excessively technical, bureaucratic but essentially performative only in the sense of generating process, but not outcomes. The poor suffer most as services are not delivered, even as planning and evaluation processes are highly productive. In other words, government non-performance in material terms sits alongside an evaluation culture where reports have to be "seen to be done" but are not "done to be seen", and where plans are like waves on a shoreline, one only just completed before a new one is penned, often with overlapping time spans – five-year plan, 2030 vision, integrated development plan and so forth. Thus in processes of procedural accountability the systems are in place in many parts of the South African state, such as in environmental impact assessments, giving the appearance of accountability, yet many major projects are agreed before the environmental impact assessment [EIA] is performed. The latter thus becomes a bought form of legitimacy but fails on its own terms to deliver accountability, a problem exacerbated by the 2014 Infrastructure Development Act, which further weakened EIAs.

This performance of government extends to the southern Africa region, where overall free basic and universal coverage is claimed in service areas where, in reality, scarcity exists. For example, in the CoBaSys research on HIV treatment systems, in Zimbabwe and Mozambique, to take just two examples, governments and some donors were claiming that antiretroviral treatment was universally available for World Health Organisation [WHO] qualifying virus blood counts of CD400 or more. But in reality, only approximately 31–33 per cent of the population could access these drugs due to petty corruption, supply stock outs and simply that patients did not have the out-of-pocket expenses to access the clinics (Machingura and Bracking 2015).

In South Africa, government functionality is busy, but often does not stretch to the actual delivery of services to large groups of excluded persons. Here, the competing logics of governance, combined with the anti-politics of technical planning and "resolutionism", have caused an unhealthy concentration of actual power within the executive and party state, while the citizens remain excluded. This circumstance is then spoken about as "the implementation gap" made up of "unfunded commitments". This poor democratic quality, expressed by service delivery outcomes, is then exacerbated as company owners say they are forced to provide poor quality goods at inflated prices to recoup the costs of paying mandatory kickbacks to corrupt politicians and government officials (Rampedi 2012). In research work on corruption in KwaZulu-Natal, the majority of business people interviewed spoke of having to buy everything in the process of working with government, from a "hook up" to the relevant person, a permit, procurement forms, and then of having to pay again to political funds (Bracking 2013c). Respondent 7 compared the *de jure* state of legal regulation and institutional structures in South Africa with the low level of implementation and prosecution. He referred to "alluvial evidence" (of corruption) that could be "picked up" if not for the lack of incentive for the political class to do so. Moreover, perpetrators of corruption are most often able to close down investigations or persuade other high-ranking personnel to do this for them.

The risks of patrimonialism are accompanied and exacerbated by increasing financialisation globally, with the South African economy vulnerable to pressures from both poor regulation internally, and abuse from global corporates (Bracking 2013a; Hay 2004). Twenty years on and the South African economy remains dominated by anti-competitive oligopolies in its major sectors. This structure, and globalisation processes, have generated new forms of corruption that are widespread in South Africa and that undermine the quality of democratic life. The openness of South Africa to the world economy is assumed to be a good thing, but it has exacerbated an *a priori* lack of corporate and state accountability, which in turn generates trade-related deindustrialisation, illicit (and licit) financial outflows, extreme competitive pressures, repeated currency crashes, artificially high interest rates, high levels of foreign debt, and an inflation-targeting regime that is pleasing mainly to bankers.

Conclusion

Financialisation contributes to current patterns of exclusion from rights and citizenship, and the resulting omissions from service delivery of large population groups locally, nationally and globally by critically exacerbating the context of people's neglect and expendability (Bracking 2013d). The financialisation of power is a critical conditioning governance logic which shapes distributional out - comes. However, neglect here is also found in historically embedded, racial and culturally referent systems of national and local power and social control (see Li 2009; Chatterjee 2008), which adds specificity to different spaces and places. There is a need to research development not from the traditional liberal perspective that rights are universal (*de jure*), but sometimes missing in practise (*de facto*) due to technical incapacities. This would be the classic development studies methodology. Instead, we need to now consider how some persons have no rights, and how this is caused by others who act in relation to them. Ideas of "surplus population" and "allowable death" (Li 2009; Mbembe 2003) have been formulated to empirically isolate those who are left out and surplus to the mainstream economy and polity, and then to analyse the best means by which the people can defend, protect and empower themselves. Local political economy and power structures are directly causal to service delivery outcomes, conditioned as they are by the social and fiscal effects of financialised political economy. At this level, there is a powerful performativity around corruption, in the idea that "everyone is doing it so I must too", an idea arguably encouraged by the un-prosecuted actions of the political elite, and the reported actions of multinational corporations in their "extract and leave" modus operandi.

Notes

1 Respondent 21, 14/7/2014, U4 Anti-Corruption Resource Centre at Chr. Michelsen Institute, and Leverhulme Centre for the Study of Value project grant no. RP2012-V-041 "Human, non-human, and environmental value systems: An impossible frontier?" 2012–2016.
2 Respondent 19, 6/9/2013.
3 For a classic tragi-comedic take on this see Sembene (1966).
4 Respondent 18, 5/9/2013.
5 See Chapter 6, n.3.
6 Respondent 11, 20/8/2013.
7 Respondent 14, 27/8/2013.
8 Neo-liberal discourses and techniques can also be used in more hybrid forms combined with other governance technologies and with flexible outcomes (Ferguson, 2009).

8 Financialised assistance, democracy and the anti-political future

In Chapter 2, the three scales of financialisation were introduced, where the term refers to the financialisation of capitalism itself; to its role in increasingly shaping everyday life and other domains; and to the importance of greater shareholder influence in corporate decision-making, although, as Christophers points out, this last theme was equally well explored by theorists who did not use the term (Henwood 1997; Lazonick and O'Sullivan 2000; Rhodes and Apeldoorn 1998, reviewed in Christophers 2015: 187–88). In this book, the thesis of the financialisation of capitalism was explored in Chapters 2 to 4, as an empirical project. In Chapters 5 to 7, the role of financialisation as a frontier (see Lake (1995) on finance as a frontier of accumulation) entraining other aspects of everyday life was explored first in relation to ecology, and then to politics and power. The third strain of theory on shareholder importance has not been covered. However, it is now apposite to review the potential weaknesses in the first and second approaches, as recently identified by Christophers, in order to work out whether this book has anything new to say, or if it hasn't, whether it can add clarity to what is already known.

"Something new about something new"?

Academics like concepts, and there is a type of life cycle that concepts tend to go through, beginning new (or more likely dusted off and rediscovered), novel, then used, then potentially over-used and then abandoned. The cycle is related to careers, citations and the commercialisation of knowledge, combined with the egotism of saying "something new about something new" (Johnson 2007: 96). So it is apposite to look at the slightly older history of a related concept – neo-liberal - ism. Ferguson's key delineation here was that neo-liberalism was used in different ways, as a "free-market fetishism"; as "arts of government"; as a "regime of [specific] practise" (Ferguson 2009; Harvey 2005); and as a "sort of 'rationality' in a Foucauldian sense" (Ferguson 2009: 170 –71; see also Hay 2004). This schema is helpful as it indicates a surprising similarity between the scales and domains of "neoliberalism" and "financialisation". It can help us understand the uses and misuses of "financialisation". Without a wide excursion into the literature on neo-liberalism, we can note that the misuse of "financialisation" is often in the "it does everything to everything" type of analysis, which is a form of fetishism Ferguson critiqued in terms of neo-liberalism. In this book I have largely combined Ferguson's last two uses, and tried to avoid the first; that is, financialisation as empirical practices conditioned by a particular rationality and form of the exercise of power by financiers. However, this is not intended to imply that financial rationality or logics are unitary or without contradiction. As Steven Collier observed in relation to neo-liberalism, the relationship between the neo-liberal political–economic project, and its specific neo-liberal techniques "is much more polymorphous and unstable than is assumed in much critical geographical work" (Collier 2005: 2; cited in Ferguson 2009: 182). The same is true of financialisation.

In a recent article, Christophers has urged that the term 'financialisation' be used with caution since it has analytic, theoretic, strategic, optic and empirical limits, the result of which is that it now appears as a 'chaotic, motley idea" (2015: 186) which can no longer confer analytical significance or coherence on any socially material phenomenon (2015: 186–7). In short he argues that promiscuous use of the term has caused the core analytic meaning to splinter, such that financialisation now only refers to a vague notion of the increased contemporary importance of finance (2015: 184). Theoretically, he claims that financialisation does not advance our understanding of capitalism's cultural and political economies, or at least any further than related theory that doesn't use the term, or any more than previous generations of writers on finance such as Arrighi, who himself drew on Fernand Braudel, and claimed no distinct novelty. Strategically, it has brought disciplines together, but this purpose is exhausted, while its optics are limiting, such that any novelty pretended for it can only be claimed if writers ignore capitalism's long durée (and Arrighi in particular), since none of the processes referred to are actually new, and spatially, they may not apply very far. In other words, overstatement of its role applies to both its scale and novelty (2015: 185). Empirically, Christophers also claims writers on financialisation critically fail to say much about finance itself, only its consequences on other things and processes.

This last is the central critique found in Christophers: he claims that much theorisation of financialisation has proceeded by exploring the consequences that the "thing" causes outside of itself, rather than by what it is and how it works. He writes:

> studies of financialization tend not to advance our understanding of money … [and] have relatively little to say about finance per se. The reason is that financialization is typically depicted as something that is "done" by finance to or within other or wider domains.
>
> (Christophers 2015: 191)

As a consequence, "[t]he object of critique is the extension of finance's rules and logics to domains where they are not welcome, not natural, and not historically normalised" rather than "capitalist finance per se" (2015b: 232). This point was taken up by Ouma (2015) and Poovey (2015) in response to Christophers (2015), with Poovey also noting the 'anti-political effects' of this consequential critique, in that the power of critique is directed to finance being in domains where it isn't welcome, rather than a critique of finance 'in place'. Here its rules are taken as a given. As a consequence of misdirected critique, Ouma (2015) and Poovey (2015) write of the 'black boxes' in analysis of financialisation, with Ouma (2015) noting the disappearance from view of micro practices and the mathematical models within markets that condition how finance and money work; while Poovey (2015) notes the understudied relationships, institutions, legal contracts and ideas that facilitate the black boxes, in particular the incomprehensibility to most of inbuilt mathematical formula and equations. In short, while financialisation's "illegitimate imperialism is castigated" it is somehow left as "unproblematic and irreproachable" in its own sphere, with its own processes "black boxed" (Christophers 2015b: 232). I too, would urge further research on these empirical weaknesses, and hope this book serves as some palliative.

The argument of the book in summary

Both Ouma (2015) and Poovey (2015) also write of the importance of time to the operation of finance, as I have done repeatedly in this book. Poovey (2015) in particular writes of the three characteristics of finance as its future orientation, its distended temporality and its inherent stochasticity as co-constituting but also contributing to the subject appearing incomprehensible. While I agree that the management of time is crucial to the management of profits, the depiction of how this works differs in this book from both Poovey and Ouma. For Ouma, relational temporality refers to finance's effort to capitalise on the future, and fix that future in place. Here, I follow Fisher more strictly, that it is the effort to define and legally fix the distribution of reward and risk *into* the future that critically enables the collecting of premiums, dividends and what often appear like rents in the present. There is no gamble on the future – money-holders try to control risk, but justify profits in its name – only a fixing of the present, which may or may not unravel, but if it does, the most powerful financiers will have sold up by then. Poovey's (2015) distended temporality is similar to this idea, but here I would argue that returns are not inherently stochastic, but fixable and controllable by the entrained assemblage of financialisation at the points of extractive connection with people and places and things. Also, it is not just the combination of Poovey's three characteristics that make the mathematical language impenetrable: they have real world effects too, in the way that ownership and debt are used to control people and places in the name of risk.

What I would like to argue is that the empirical evidence here shows that: (1) the greater influence of finance over other types of productive capital has been slowed by technical frontiers within capitalist accumulation. Circulation of money capital per se, and in particular, a greater velocity of circulation, are not now necessarily accompanied by opportunities to make enhanced profit, relative to other means of controlling time and connection. The high frequency traders have been compared to vacuum cleaners picking up cents and dimes from the trading floors,[1] so successfully have they pursued arbitrage that profit rates have shrunk, and their own markets have been undermined. The velocity of circulation, meanwhile, has increased to the physical limit of the speed of light, with stock held for seconds only before the next computer trigger to buy or sell (subject to automated risk assessment). Also, (2) banks and fund managers have thus iteratively recolonised parts of financial trading in order to regain control over the building of super-profits for preferred customers and money-holders, in dark pools and in dark trading. Thus financialisation as commonly understood, as a veritable explosion of free-forming speculation, circulation and arms-length trading in ever-expanding derivatives and fictitious capital and assets, does not correspond to the empirical evidence collected here. Instead, the real world phenomenon observable in the practice of finance is of an increase in *controlled* trading in the boardrooms of the world economy, a reassertion of capital-holders as a group to fix others in relationships of subordination, while ensuring that the logics of capitalised value are put first and privileged.

The claim here is also not that financialisation is historically novel, but that money-holders have asked of the world ever greater exceptions and special conditions in order to provide profits in the face of other sites of accumulation becoming more limited. Thus, profits from arbitrage in derivatives have shrunk as machines spot abnormal spreads and act instantly. The role of the trader in a situation of classic asymmetric information to make a quick profit at the expense of a less informed trader has gone. Or at least, the informed has become a computerised identity based on proprietary information feeds and software that gives meaning to "news" shaped for algorithmic execution. The ability of fictive capital to jump the "C" in the M-C-M' movement is limited by small margins and spreads. The answer has been, at least for capital, that in view of an increasingly unknowable future, one must take as much as one can from the present, by structuring deals where the derivative income streams start fast and large. If the thing doesn't pay for itself in the medium or long term, then this can be discounted and sold on, to local investors mostly.

If I were to try and insist that financialisation be used in respect of this deepening of control I would be making the rather arrogant assertion that I wish to lay claim to the moniker to apply to my observations, rather than to apply to those trends believed to be in existence by the bulk of those who write using the term. This would be of doubtful use in expanding knowledge of finance. However, these findings do have ramifications for the veracity of the thesis as a whole, and suggest that the long-run cycle of financialisation may be coming to an end. For example, in Chapters 2 to 4 it was established that the stock of the world's value stored as money has grown and has also grown as a proportion of the total stock of capital and in relation to productive assets, which is commensurate with the thesis. However, this is a very broad trend. It also proved difficult to place different forms of product in direct commensurability to Marxist categories of production and money capital. There is a strong sense that many forms of "derivative", such as credit default swaps between the derivatives trading desks of major banks do not exhibit deep characteristics of "moneyness". They act as a store of (potential) value but are rarely exchanged on a market, merely agreed contractually between parties. They look more like resinsurance. This lack of moneyness reflects in the controversy and widely differing estimates of the value of current global derivatives markets. Regulators simply do not know how many bilateral swaps and exposure positions, which are then hedged, are held by major banks and trading exchanges. This is exacerbated by the opaque use of swaps between firms' secrecy jurisdiction holdings, and between these and onshore balance sheets.

Fine (2010, 2014), as an exemplar of Marxist contributions (but see also Bryan *et al.* 2009; Lapavitsas 2009) theorised financialisation as the generalised subjection of economic activity to the logics of interest-bearing capital. But given the above, I have shown that is a might tautological and highly difficult to empirically establish, since near all value is interest-bearing to some degree. Also, it is not the traditional debt relationship, where a venture borrows money and agrees to interest premiums on it that is core to the configurations of investments in place. Rather, there is a role of a strategic equity investment, in partnership within a project finance assemblage, where the external "international" investors enjoy fiscal, tax, and other investment privileges at a macro regulatory scale, alongside being first in the queue for guaranteed tier one tranches of premiums or locked-down derivative income streams. The role of local power-holders to "keep the tap running" gives political elites an incentive to join in as junior partners, even as the public fiscus strains to meet the externalised profit dividends and the surrounding infrastructural and social order requirements. The power dynamic here is an entraining of things, people and non-humans into relationships in which they function as financial assets (with income streams that leave to banks and funds) (cf. Harvey 1982: 347 on financialisation as "the increasing tendency to treat the land as a pure financial asset"). But the effort of making profits appear in SPVs and in offshore trusts depends upon the asymmetric enlisting of "constitutive sociospatial others/outsides" (Christophers 2015: 198, citing literature on postcolonialism). Just as in the biblical dream of Nebuchadnezzar (Daniel 2: 41–43), finance's feet of clay are in the Global South, and not just literally in the mud excavations required for ever greater volumes of concrete.

In respect of speed of circulation, too, the "ever faster" trend of the financialisation of capitalism school was qualified: it depends how you measure it, with the added qualifier that slowing circulation can be a source of profits too. Moreover, given the complexity of the institutional forms of asset and investment, it was also argued that identifying the difference between interest-bearing or capitalised stock, and productive capital is nigh on impossible, particularly in respect of exchange traded products and indexes to the same. Relatedly, the idea that something can be real as opposed to fictive was argued to be an epistemological cul-de sac. The Marxist theory of over-accumulation leading to crisis was also rejected as a metaphor, particularly in the light of Bichler and Nitzan's illustration of how the growth of capitalised stock moved in opposite directions to the growth of value in underlying assets in firms' inventories. The idea that capitalised stock leads to increases in productivity, a falling rate of profit and the need for some value to be destroyed seems an unlikely sequence in view of a counter explanation, of when capitalised value connects with corporate stock, it is just as likely to extract or "thin-cap" that unit, reducing productivity, while causing super-profits offshore. It would then be the deterioration of assets, as Thorstein Veblen suggests, that would eventually cause a profitability crash, as owners of distal derivatives suddenly felt the cold wind of a non-performing factory or mortgage.

These changes relate to some classical aspects of money. Money-holders need to control the supply of money (restrict it) in order to maintain its value in relation to that which money can purchase. But global private-issued money has been growing relative to public-issued money, even to the extremes of totally notional bitcoin, which pressures money-holders to constantly try to ensure that their money works and will work to capture assets and income streams into the future. In other words, it is not so much that financialisation as process, is a speculative gamble made in respect to the future performance of a group of assets – that would leave much too much to chance. Rather, financialisation as process, privileges financial decision-making and the generation of guaranteed income streams in the present, because of legal agreements and project finance that is designed to reduce risk, either in the sense that it is handed on to a government, such as in a PPP agreement, or to lower tranche investors in a tiered ABS. Governments and pension funds will pay for the risks, while core money-holders lock in present-day profits by means of commitments running into the future. After a few years of contractually guaranteed income streams, they will often sell up and move on, passing stock and emerging risks as assets deteriorate to pension funds and less mobile investors.

In other words, there is an error in the way that temporality has been viewed in financialisation, although not in Fischer's first model necessarily. The value of the orchard is defined by the price of the apples. Updating Fischer, the value of the orchard as an asset or as land is irrelevant relative to the short-term income streams that can be locked down in a legal contract in respect of it. The future price of apples is increasingly a risk that is framed out of the first tranche "superior" investors' calculations, in their expectation that this temporality will take place after their exit. In a similar way, the value of the port, or the stadium, or the toll road, is defined by the price of the current year's and promised year's derivative income stream or debt obligation (not on the safety of the traveller, the necessity of a crowd, or the frequency of ships). Understood like this, it becomes clear that risk calculation in financial calculation is not associated with a direct link to a bridge falling down, or a harbour drying up, or even to anthropogenic climate change, but is formed in direct association to the chance that a derivative income stream from an owned, or more distally controlled asset, may not arrive in a SPV or tax-haven based trust, in this year, or next year.

The search for a pure beta asset class, where the asset has no correlation to market systemic risks, has led investors to bet on the weather. But it has also encouraged money-holders to control and condition an ever greater realm of ecological, human, political and social life, in a perpetual effort to externalise and distance income streams from possible human or ecological intervention. This, if there is an essence to what is out there, that requires a "financialisation" label, might be it: the constant but resisted search of finance capital for secured income streams. Christophers argues that this form of definitional practise, where the thing out there is happening, but not fully known – thus requiring that it be pinned down and captured conceptually – is like "trying to bottle the wind" (2015: 197). He asks whether we need a "single meta-concept" to assist with explanation. I would argue that it is helpful, while recognising the limits he cautions, because the ever increasing circulation of value as money is so vague as an explanation for periodic crisis. Its deficiency in economics is profound, largely because there are so few attempts at analysing capitalism's empirical core. The implications of this essence are political: how far do future generations honour the contractual deeds of their forbears in administrative office and government – particularly when written in circumstances of subordinate power?

Increasing political risk as antidote to "anti-politics"

In other words, instead of the anti-political effects of neo-liberalism being paramount and associated with financialisation, it is rather that "political risk" in finance's terms is becoming increasingly important in investors' decisions and to the future of the financialisation process. The rendering of politics into advanced liberal governance, expertism and technicality may have removed conflict in its historical form of trade union activism, although this could still change, but the political economy of financialisation offers much more potential politics than is currently realised. First, other sections of patient capital, like pension and sovereign wealth funds, are proving more "impatient" as the implications of financiers' control of markets become more evident, as the law cases against high-frequency trading indicate, or the litigation within PPP joint ventures. Second, the constant effort entailed in attempting to capture ecological processes and non-human beings, in order to fix and pacify them into assets and commodities causes constant resistance and reframing (see Lohmann 2016 in particular).

This is significant to how resistance to finance capital can be conceptualised. It is true that many writers erroneously depict financialisation as an all-powerful machinic force that appears unstoppable (note by Castree and Henderson 2014; Christophers 2015: 198), built as it is within the iron laws of the market. However, the "feet of clay" are the reliance of money-holders on their ability to carry everyone along in the project, particularly as planetary and human limits become more evident. So far, the laws and contracts that underlie the PPP agreements, the debt obligations and the distribution of risk across different asset classes and groups of competing investors have just about held up. The reinsurers absorbed large losses from the 2008 crash, but the "too big to fail" argument worked on governments to underwrite the underwriters. With no idea of how to change the system, public regulators acted to reinvigorate it. But the road of finance capital is still rocky. Consider the District Judge in America who ruled that proprietary feeds and algorithms were legitimate tools of competitive market advantage, and were immune from case law as they also performed a government regulatory function. He prolonged the life of privileged trading insiders, but the judgement itself does not make the losses to traditional pension and mutual funds, at the hands of the aggressive traders, go away. In fact, the largest bastions of Anglophone banking capital have been forced to do their business behind closed doors.

In the Global South, the limits to finance being able to write deals and design projects with the metaphorical "much-needed" FDI with terms that constantly privilege money-holders faces two limits. First, governments and populations must believe that there is no choice but to "need" FDI, but this is often not technically correct, especially since a majority is merely round-tripped to access the privileged investment environment guaranteed to non-nationals who bring "foreign" investment. Political elites are benefiting profoundly from the discursive power of the signifier of "much-needed" in realising special investment privileges. Second, insofar as the legality of the extractive arrangements and the morality of the arrangements in place continue to diverge, money holders are at risk of ever-greater episodes of revolt. It was once the case that a confirmed or irrevocable letter of credit, that was bank-backed, would always guarantee a payment, until Nigeria refused one and the ships queued at Lagos harbour for weeks (Becker 2013). It was once the case, that countries could "own" other peoples' land and legally call it a "colony" or "protectorate", until the people decided otherwise. It was once the case that no one dared rescind on a bilateral investment protection agreement, until Zimbabwe ripped up most of those applying in that country. Already a huge proportion of PPP agreements are being breached by one or other party, and ending in prolonged legal disagreements. In other words, it takes just one moment of disobedience to the law to cascade and the whole investment edifice may break, which explains the greater role of power and control that finance needs to employ, or which it at least requires to be in place on its behalf.

End game?

Thus there is a strange irony here that politics is both sidelined and muted in processes of anti-politics, and yet also emergent in the increasingly nonsensical demands made of the "feet of clay". Christophers quotes Keynes at length to show how current financialisation has limited novelty. However, the difference between the 1890s to 1930s and today, even as captured through lines chosen by Christophers to illustrate similarity, are quite striking. In the Keynes quote Christophers chooses, Keynes bemoans how the highest achievements that men (sic) are capable of are not built or done, because they would not pay according to a "bogus" and "irrelevant accountancy", where "the financial results, [are] a test of the advisability of any course of action" (Keynes 1933: 763; quoted in Christophers 2015: 192–3).

> The whole conduct of life was made into a sort of parody of an accountant's nightmare … The same rule of self-destructive financial calculation governs every walk of life. We destroy the beauty of the countryside because the unappropriated splendors of nature have no economic value. We are capable of shutting off the sun and the stars because they do not pay a dividend. London is one of the richest cities in the history of civilization, but it cannot "afford" the highest standards of achievement of which its living citizens are capable, because they do not "pay".
>
> (Keynes 1933: 763–64)

Then financiers were not willing to "mortgage the future" to build the best. But in the current phase of rule by finance, it is capital that is changing the rules of the same accountancy: they will build the least logical football stadium simply because of the value of the initial construction contracts (including politically), and the first few years of guaranteed fees, whatever the medium-term debt or overall utility of the building. Greater feats of infrastructure are now apparently possible, but only with the constant perverse effect of greater inequality, public indebtedness and no eye for financial sustainability.

Keynes argued that "once we allow ourselves to be disobedient to the test of an accountant's profit, we have begun to change our civilisation" (Keynes 1933: 765). But the issue now is who is the "we", and what type of "civilisation" are we heading for? Arguably, large money-holders are bending the rules of sustainability and the duty of care for people and the environment that suggests that you should not do now what is destructive of the future. In other words, the profit and loss account must resemble the discounted capital stock for the life of the bond or derivative. However, in structured deals, the first investors rarely plan to keep this stock past a few years, and have already planned, legislated for, or signed into a contract, their ability to disassociate risk from profit. Financial investors here are doing something much more classically about rent: taking money from someone in respect to an asset you don't own, simply because you have power over them, and can persuade them or extort them through the fear and use of force, that they should comply. Historical precedents would be the imposition of hut taxes in colonial Africa, or the "Great Hedge of India" which supported the extortion of a tax on salt. The modern equivalent would be a catastrophe bond imposed to ensure "security", but causing a division of Government the need to pay a monthly premium or "tax" for a risk it did not cause: "we will make you sick, and then make you pay health insurance, and then decide the mechanism or 'trigger' for how sick you are before we pay up".

Christophers insists that limits to financialisation exist in resistances which arise from "outside" within "the socioeconomic domain being financialized". Others are 'inside" (2015: 195). An inside resistance, in the process of finance itself, is that fixing the future in order to control the present only works when no one has an eye on what is being promised into the future, or when people think that that time is so far away that it won't affect them. It is no accident that the full costs of PPPs are hidden, or so technical that even those who negotiate them struggle with the projections. The same applies to many "development" loans in the present secured by volumetrically guaranteed supplies of raw materials to be delivered in the future. These have been favoured by Chinese capital, but with dropping commodity prices since 2012 they now exist as an increasing burden on African governments. Christophers quotes Veblen to the effect that the empirical limits of financialisation, which he himself calls "hazy", are found in the "disproportionate growth" of vendible capital by "the traffickers of capital" who "would lower the effective vitality of the community to such a degree as to jeopardize its chances of advance or even its life" (Veblen 1912: 62–65). But the actual limit would "depend" on local circumstances. Arguably, however, the limit of the growth of interest-bearing capital or finance, in relation to productive types, might also occur in the decision of a group of people to effectively say "enough", particularly in the face of legal agreements which are, by their nature, designed to take wealth from sovereign owners of it, and redistribute it to money-holders. Ownership of assets means little if the derivative income streams from them are extorted to the limit of the continued viability of the asset.

The rule of money is made in these micro practises and at the frontiers of innovation, by institutional norms that are ever changing. The New York judge could have ruled that the dark pools and the informational feeds represented anti-competitive practices, but he didn't. Instead he invoked a powerful cocktail of freedom and "Americanness": the right of those with money and power to make more money and power. The ideological effort in such decisions is critically replicated in the ideological effort of making the world in the image of Westphalia, albeit with Chinese capital. Consider, for example, what has been referred to as global civil society-making, largely in southern Africa pursued through the soft domain of philanthropy, but which logically confers on aid the attributes of venture capital. The poor and the development category themselves are remade as an asset with derivative income streams, which can be competitively captured by proximate NGOs, philanthropic trusts, aid workers and ultimately returned to big capital (Morvaridi 2012; Bosworth 2011; Bracking 2015b).

Power and politics

The simultaneous issuing of contradictory promises and policy appears to have grown as a response to the extension of neo-liberalism and financialisation, combined with narratives of reform, often selectively co-opted from activists and social movements, which intuitively cannot be met together. Governance, in this sense, has become a contradictory mesh of multi-directional appeals to many different constituencies simultaneously. For example, recent work on climate change governance and the Green Climate Fund, which focuses on the technical detail, the bureaucratic process and the foundational rationality of policies demonstrates that intuitively contradictory goals and expenditure preferences can apparently be placed together in a conflict postponing set of outcomes, particularly when framed within lengthy technical documents (Methmann 2010, 2011; Bracking 2014). Thus, for example, the seventh meeting of the Green Climate

Fund Board passed an Investment Framework policy on 21 May 2014, which promised that the Fund would only finance revenue-generating activities that were "intrinsically sound from a financial point of view", while simultaneously promising to invest in projects that "demonstrate the maximum potential for a paradigm shift towards low-carbon and climate-resilient sustainable develo - pment" (GCF 2014). Similarly, "significant allocation" to the private sector facility, sits close to a guarantee of 50 per cent of funds to adaptation, which is not traditionally a private sector priority, or even investment area. That these, and many other examples, might be contradictory technical "promises" points to policy processes in which postponement and stalling is a significant product. In fact, the production of "knowledge" itself, often at great costs in consultancy budgets, is an outcome that often substitutes for an actual policy or substantive intervention.

The movement of temporality of promises into the future, or "future fixing" is found in environmental policy and many other global policy arenas of "resolutionism", such as the current African Union effort to make a plan for 2065. In environmental policy, policy also shifts between definitions at different geographical scales. Thus, in the literature on financialisation and conservation both global and local scales are seen to interrelate and co-depend on each other, both theoretically and empirically. In the financialisation of conservation literature the two definitional nodes are in evidence – the abstract sense and discrete instrument. For example, Brockington and Duffy quote Harvey to the effect that neo-liberalism has meant "the financialisation of everything" (Brockington and Duffy 2010: 480; citing Harvey 2005: 33), but then go on to argue that actually financialisation has had limited impact in conservation, being limited to some debt for nature swaps by larger NGOs and 'interchanging of personnel" (Brockington and Duffy 2010: 480). The simultaneous movement of time and place in the generation of financialised conservation perhaps meets its extreme in the logic of offsetting, when harm in the present and local is displaced, in rhetoric and promise at least, to care in the future and distal.

The ability of governance to postpone time is related to states' abilities to promote exceptionalism for preferred constituencies, particularly to private capital in the form of multiple breaches to a unitary state sovereignty. There are imagined, virtual and exceptional spaces within the global sovereignty and domicile regime, such as trusts in tax havens, which financial firms can use in order to remain distant from social, national and political demands. Unitary sovereignty has dissembled into a frontier zone characterised by portals of exception in law and regulation, rather like an upturned colander "protecting" the sovereign space beneath, while allowing free flows to the wealthy and politically connected (Bracking 2012b). The consequent reorganisation of economic space evinced in the accompanying growth of secrecy jurisdictions has been both catalyst and consequence of financialisation, in which individual firms act as "juridically dispersed subjects … [who] have learned to take advantage of the fiction of their fragmentation by rearranging their legal existence in ways they see fit" (Palan 2002: 172). Indeed, Palan theorises tax havens as places where the "commercialisation of sovereignty" has provided for "parking lots" for firms to domicile in. The shell or holding company, or the off balance sheet "special purpose vehicle", is sited offshore, where it can hide both excess profit and excess liability. This opaque risk and liability carrying function became a chief trigger of the 2008 financial crash.

But for this corporate migration to happen, a way in, and then out, of the sovereign space had to be enabled without friction with national norms, institutions or regulation. Financialisation processes within neo-liberalism have done this, through the invention of particular company forms, such as special purpose vehicles (see Hildyard 2008), and because of the successful recruitment of most political elites into joint ventures or at least agreement with regulations deriving from the thesis of "much-needed" FDI. Thus, what is "new" in contemporary processes is the (regulated for) spacial and legal distancing of finance from both public taxation and the context of production. This latter, described in Chapter 6, is facilitated through offshore domicile, remote accounting, virtual and derivative forms, and ultimately arbitrary intra- and inter-firm accountancy systems at the whims of transfer pricing, "tax planning" mechanisms and "jurisdiction shopping". In short, financiers can largely make up what profit they make and where they notionally make it.

Corporate empires exploit this "cleverness" and "tax planning expertise" in order to make profit from their management of space and time. However, a critical divergence has developed between elite representations of the economy, echoed and articulated in neoliberalism, and the intuitive knowledge deriving from majority peoples' life-worlds. The Marxist notion of "consciousness arising from being" may yet grow into peoples' movements and unions which are strong enough to crack the clay on which financialised edifices are built.

Note

1 Comments posted online to Philips M (2013)

Bibliography

ADB and GFI (2013) *Illicit Financial Flows and The Problem of Net Resource Transfers from Africa 1980-2009*, A Joint Report by the African Development Bank and Global Financial Integrity, May.

Adebanwi, W. and Obadare, E. (2011) "The abrogation of the electorate: an emergent African phenomenon", *Democratization*, 18, 2: 311–335.

African Union Commission (2014) *African Union Election Observation Mission to the 20 May 2014 Tripartite Elections in the Republic of Malawi: Final Report*, August. Available from http://pa.au.int/en/sites/default/files/FINAL%20REPORT%20OF%20AUEOM%20TO%20MALAWI%2020%20MAY%202014%20ELECTIONS%20.pdf

Agnew, J. (1994) "The territorial trap: the geographical assumptions of international relations theory", *Review of International Political Economy*, 1: 53–80.

Agnew, J. (2005) "Sovereignty regimes: territoriality and state authority in contemporary world politics", *Annals of the Association of American Geographers*, 95, 2: 437–461.

Ahluwalia, P. (2010) "Towards (re)conciliation: the post-colonial economy of giving", *Social Identities*, 6, 1: 29–45.

Ake, C. (1996) *Development and Democracy in Africa*, Washington, DC: Brookings Institution.

Akpalu, W., Eggert, H. and Vondolia, G. K. (2009) "Enforcement of exogenous environmental regulation, social disapproval, and bribery", *Journal of Socio-Economics*, 38, 6: 940–945.

AllAboutAlpha (2014) "Catastrophe bonds and climate hedging: a talk with Barney Schauble of Nephila", 1 May. Available from http://allaboutalpha.com/blog/2014/05/01/catastrophe-bonds-and-other-weather-derivatives-profiting-from-or-hedging-the-worlds-climate-misfortunes/

Allen, J. and Pryke, M. (2013) "Financialising household water: Thames Water, MEIF, and 'ring-fenced' politics", *Cambridge Journal of Regions, Economy and Society*, 6, 3: 419–439.

Amabhungane (2011) "Malema Inc: mechanics of the silent partner", The M&G Centre for Investigative Journalism, 19 August. Available from http://amabhungane.co.za/article/2011-08-19-mechanics-of-the-silent-partner

Amabhungane (2013) "Gold fields 'graft' shaft went deeper", The M&G Centre for Investigative Journalism, 20 September. Available from http://ht.ly/p2H7q

Anderson, B. and McFarlance, C. (2011) "Assemblage and geography", *Area*, 43, 2: 124–127.

Anderson, K. (2015) "Duality in climate science" *Nature Geoscience*, 8: 898–900. Available from www.nature.com/ngeo/journal/v8/n12/full/ngeo2559.html

Angel, J. J. (2011) "The impact of special relativity on securities regulation", London: Government Office for Science. Available from www.gov.uk/government/uploads/system/uploads/attachment_data/file/289020/11-1242-dr15-impact-of-special-relativity-on-securities-regulation.pdf

Aon Benfield Securities (2011) *Insurance-linked Securities Annual Report: Consistency and Confidence*, Chicago, IL: Aon Benfield Securities.

Armah, Ayi Kwei Armah (1968) *The Beautyful Ones Are Not Yet Born*, London: Heinemann.

Arnuk, S. and Saluzzi, J. (2009) "Latency arbitrage: the real power behind predatory high frequency trading", Themis Trading LLC White Paper, 4 December. Chatham, NJ: Themis Trading LLC. Available from www.themistrading.com

Arrighi, G. (1994) *The Long Twentieth Century: Money, Power, and the Origins of Our Times*, New York: Verso.

Arsel, M. and Büscher, B. (2012), "Nature™ Inc.: changes and continuities in neoliberal conservation and market-based environmental policy" *Development and Change*, 43: 53–78.

Artemis (2014) "Climate change catastrophe bonds for Africa to be launched by ARC", 23 September. Available from www.artemis.bm/blog/2014/09/23/climate-change-catastrophe-bonds-for-africa-to-be-launched-by-arc/

Artemis (2015) "Active cat bond trading in July, as performance turns positive", 13 August. Available from www.artemis.bm/blog/2015/08/13/active-cat-bond-trading-in-july-as-performance-turns-positive/

Asiimwe, G. B. (2013) "Of extensive and elusive corruption in Uganda: neo-patronage, power, and narrow interests", *African Studies Review*, 56, 2: 129–144.

Ayers, A. J. (2006) "Demystifying democratisation: the global constitution of (neo)liberal politics in Africa", *Third World Quarterly*, 27, 2: 321–338.

Bachram, H. (2004) "climate fraud and carbon colonialism: the new trade in greenhouse gases", *Capitalism Nature Socialism*, 15, 4: 1–16.

Baker, L. (2015) "The evolving role of finance in South Africa's renewable energy sector", *Geoforum*, 64: 146–156.

Baker, R. W. (2005) *Capitalism's Achilles Heel: Dirty Money and How to Renew the Free-Market System*, Hoboken, NJ: John Wiley and Sons.

Bakker, K. (2003) "Archipelagos and networks: urbanization and water privatisation in the South", *Geographical Journal*, 169: 328–341

Bardhan, P (1997) "Corruption and development: a review of the issues", *Journal of Economic Issues*, 35, 3: 1320–1346.

Bardhan, P. and Mookherjee, D. (2000) "Capture and governance at local and national levels", *American Economic Review*, 90, 2: 135–139.

Bates, R. H. (1983) "Modernization, ethnic competition and the rationality of politics", in *State Versus Ethnic Claims: African Policy Dilemmas*, D. Rothchild and V. A. Olunsorola (eds), Boulder, CO: Westview Press.

BATS (2014) "BATS Global Markets selects Equinix's Secaucus Data Centre for BATS and Direct Edge Exchanges", 19 February. Available from www.equinix.com/company/news-and-events/press-releases/bats-global-markets-selects-equinix-secaucus-data-center/

BATS (2015a) "BATS Global Markets launches the BATS ETF marketplace, redefining the ETF industry with innovative benefits for issuers, market makers, investors", 1 October. Available from http://cdn.batstrading.com/resources/press_releases/BATS-ETF-Marketplace-FINAL.pdf

BATS (2015b) "BATS Global Markets reports record US equity and options market share in August; European equities market share reaches 25.0%", 9 September. Available from http://cdn.batstrading.com/resources/press_releases/BGM_August2015_Volume_FINAL.pdf

Bayliss, K. (2009) "Private sector participation in African infrastructure: is it worth the risk?" International Policy Centre for Inclusive Growth, Working Paper no. 55, UNDP/IPC-IG, Brasilia-DF, Brazil.

BBC News (2014) "'Too big to fail' bank rules unveiled by global regulators", BBC News, 10 November. Available from www.bbc.co.uk/news/business-29982181

Becker, R. (2013) "The Nigerian cement story", Shipping Solutions Blog, 22 December. Available from www.shippingsolutions.com/blog/the-nigerian-cement-story-2

Beetham, D. (2011) *Unelected Oligarchy: Corporate and Financial Dominance in Britain's Democracy*, Liverpool: Democratic Audit.

Beetham, D., Bracking, S., Kearton, I., and Weir, S. (2002) *International IDEA Handbook on Democracy Assessment.* The Hague, New York, London: Kluwer Law International.

Beunza, D. and Stark, D. (2004) "Tools of the trade: the socio-technology of arbitrage in a Wall Street trading room." *Industrial and Corporate Change*, 13: 369–400.

Beunza, D., MacKenzie, D., Millo, Y., and Pardo-Guerra, J. P. (2011) "Impersonal efficiency and the dangers of a fully automated securities exchange", London: Government Office for Science. Available at www.gov.uk/government/uploads/system/uploads/attachment_data/file/289015/11-1230-dr11-impersonal-efficiency-and-dangers-of-a-fully-automated-securities-exchange.pdf

Biais, B., Foucault, T. and Moinas, S. (2011) "Equilibrium fast trading", Working Paper, Toulouse School of Economics.

Bichler, S. and Nitzan, J. (2015) "Capital accumulation: fiction and reality", *Real-World Economics Review*, 72: 47–78. Available from http://bnarchives.yorku.ca/456/2/20150900_bn_capital_accumulation_fiction_and_reality_rwer.pdf

Binder, L., Coleman, J. S., LaPalombara, J., Pye, L. W., Verba, S. and Weiner, M. (1971) *Crises and Sequences in Political Development*, Princeton, NJ: Princeton University Press.

BIS and Home Office (2014) *UK Anti Corruption Plan*, London: HMSO. Available from www.gov.uk/government/uploads/system/uploads/attachment_data/file/388894/UKantiCorruptionPlan.pdf

Bloomberg News (2013) "Why should taxpayers give big banks $83 billion a year?", Bloomberg News, 20 February. Available from www.bloombergview.com/articles/2013-02-20/why-should-taxpayers-give-big-banks-83-billion-a-year-

Blundo, G. (2006) "Dealing with the local state: the informal privatization of street-level bureaucracies in Senegal", *Development and Change*, 37, 4: 799–819.

Blundo, G. (2014) "seeing like a state agent: the ethnography of reform in Senegal's forestry services", in *States at Work: Dynamics of African Bureaucracies*, T. Bierschenk and J-P Olivier de Sardan (eds), Leiden: Brill.

Blundo, G. and Olivier de Sardan, J-P. (2006) "The popular semiology of corruption", in *Everyday Corruption and the State: Citizens and Public Officials in Africa*, G. Blundo and J-P Olivier de Sardan (eds), London: Zed Books.

Blunt, P. (2009) "The political economy of accountability in Timor-Leste: Implications for public policy", *Public Administration and Development*, 29, 2: 89–100.

Boelens, R., Hoogesteger J. and Rodriguez de Francisco, J. (2014) "Commoditizing Water Territories: The Clash between Andean Water Rights Cultures and Payment for Ecosystem Services", *Capitalism Nature Socialism*, 25, 3: 84–102.

Boltanski, L. and Chiapello, E. (2007) *The New Spirit of Capitalism*, 2nd edn, London and New York: Verso.

Bond, P. (2012) "South African people power since the mid-1980s: two steps forward, one back", *Third World Quarterly*, 33, 2–2: 243–264.

Bond, P. (2014a) "Territorial alliances and emerging-market development banking: a view from subimperial South Africa", in I. Wallerstein, C. Chase-Dunn and C. Suter (eds), *Overcoming Global Inequalities: Political Economy of the World-System Annuals*, New York: Paradigm Publishers.

Bond, P. (2014b) "Can 'natural capital accounting' come of age in Africa: Part 1", Triple Crisis Blog, 9 July. Available from http://triplecrisis.com/can-natural-capital-accounting-come-of-age-in-africa-part-1/

Bond, P. (2014c) "Can 'natural capital accounting' come of age in Africa: Part II", Triple Crisis Blog, 2 July. Available from http://triplecrisis.com/can-natural-capital-accounting-come-of-age-in-africa-part-2/

Bond, P. (2014d) "Talk left, walk right" in South African social policy: Tokenistic extension of state welfare versus bottom-up commoning of services", *Transformation: Critical Perspectives on Southern Africa*, 86: 48–77.

Bosworth, D. (2011) "The cultural contradictions of philanthrocapitalism", *Society*, 48, 5: 382–388.

Boyce, J. K. and Ndikumana, L. (2001) "Is Africa a net creditor? New estimates of capital flight from severely indebted sub-Saharan African countries, 1970–96", *Journal of Development Studies*, 38: 27–56.

Bracking, S. (2001) "The Lesotho Highlands corruption trial: who has been airbrushed from the dock?" *Review of African Political Economy*, 28, 88: 302–306.

Bracking, S. (2005) "Development denied: autocratic militarism in post-election Zimbabwe", *Review of African Political Economy*, 32, 104/5: 341–357.

Bracking, S. (2007) *Corruption and Development*, Houndsmills: Palgrave Macmillan.

Bracking, S. (2009a) *Money and Power: Great Predators in the Political Economy of Development*, London and New York: Pluto Press.

Bracking, S. (2009b) "Political economies of corruption beyond liberalism: an interpretative view of Zimbabwe", *Singapore Journal of Tropical Geography*, 30, 1: 35-51.

Bracking, S. (2010) "Democratisation through power-sharing: is 'riding the tiger' a necessary evil or unfortunate distraction?", *The Constitution*, 10, 1: 1–14.

Bracking, S. (2012a) "How do investors value environmental harm/care? Private Equity Funds, Development finance institutions and the partial financialization of nature-based industries", *Development and Change*, 43, 1, 271–293.

Bracking, S. (2012b) "Secrecy jurisdictions and economic development in Africa: the role of sovereign spaces of exception in producing private wealth and public poverty", *Economy and Society* 41, 4: 615–637.

Bracking, S. (2013a) "A Qualitative reframing of private sector corruption: considerations from the natural resource sector in South Africa", Chr. Michelsen Institute, *U4 Issue*, 2013: 7. Available from www.u4.no/publications/a-qualitative-reframing-of-private-sector-corruption-considerations-from-the-natural-resource-sectors-in-south-africa/

Bracking, S. (2013b) "Durban Port's poverty, consumerism, enoughness", *The Africa Report*, 29 April. Available from www.theafricareport.com/Columns/durban-ports-poverty-consumerism-enoughness.html

Bracking, S. (2013c) "Heading for a crash without seatbelts", *The Mercury (KwaZulu-Natal)*, 5 July: 7.

Bracking, S. (2013d) “Rights-less in the land of the rainbow nation”, *The Africa Report*, 20 March. Available at www.theafricareport.com/Columns/right-less-the-land-of-the-rainbow-nation.html

Bracking, S. (2015a) “Performativity in the green economy: how far does climate finance create a fictive economy?”, *Third World Quarterly*, 36, 12: 2337–2357.

Bracking, S. (2015b) *Philanthropy and Development in Southern Africa*, Pretoria: Southern Africa Trust. Available from www.southernafricatrust.org/philanthropy-development-in-southern-africa/

Bracking, S. (2015c) “The anti-politics of climate finance: the creation and performativity of the green climate fund”, *Antipode* 47, 2: 281–302.

Bracking, S. (2015d) “Corruption and development: the mutable edges of morality in modern markets”, in *Routledge Handbook of Political Corruption*, Paul Heywood (ed.), London and New York: Routledge.

Bracking, S (forthcoming), “Where economic justice policy and rentier markets collide: the history and experience of BB-BEE in KwaZulu-Natal, South Africa”.

Bracking, S. and Sharife, K. (2014), “Rough and polished: a case study of the diamond pricing and valuation system”, Leverhulme Centre for the Study of Value, Working Paper Series, 4. Available from http://thestudyofvalue.org/wp-content/uploads/2014/05/WP4-Bracking-Sharife-Rough-and-polished-15May.pdf

Bracking, S., Brockington, D., Bond, P., Büscher, B., Igoe, J. J., Sullivan, S. and Woodhouse, P. (2014) “Initial research design: ‘Human, non-human and environmental value systems: an impossible frontier?’” Leverhulme Centre for the Study of Value, Working Paper Series, 1. Available from http://thestudyofvalue.org/wp-content/uploads/2013/11/WP1-Initial-Research-Design-final.pdf

Bracking, S. and Diga, K. with Pia Falschebner, Mandy Lombo, Tawonga Rushambwa and Ayanda Tshabalala (2015) “Clairwood Survey: community views of the value of Clairwood in the context of current development plans for Durban port expansion Research, Report 2015 No 1 ”, University of KwaZulu-Natal and Leverhulme Centre for the Study of Value. Available from https://appliedpovertyreduction.files.wordpress.com/2015/01/emailing-clairwood_qual_report-finished-minus-frequency-table1.pdf

Branch, D. and Cheeseman, N. (2008) “Democratization, sequencing, and state failure in Africa: lessons from Kenya”, *African Affairs*, 108, 430: 1–26.

Braudel, F. (1982) *Civilization and Capitalism, 15th–18th Century: The Wheels of Commerce*, Berkeley, CA: University of California Press.

Brenner, R. (2006). *The Economics of Global Turbulence*, London: Verso.

Bridge, C. (2007) “Acts of enclosure: claim staking and land conversion in Guyana’s gold fields”, in N. Heynen, J. McCarthy, S. Prudham and P. Robbins (eds), *Neoliberal Environments: False Promises and Unnatural Consequences*, London and New York: Routledge.

Brockington, D. (2008a) “Celebrity conservation: interpreting the Irwins”, *Media International Australia*, 127: 96–108.

Brockington, D. (2008b) “Powerful environmentalisms. conservation, celebrity and capitalism”, *Media, Culture and Society*, 30, 4: 551–568.

Brockington, D. and Duffy, R. (2010) “Capitalisam and conservation: the production and reproduction of biodiversity conservation”, *Antipode*, 42, 3: 469–484.

Brogaard, J. A., Hendershott, T. and Riordan, R. (2014) “High frequency trading and price discovery”, *Review of Financial Studies*, 27, 8: 2267–2306.

Brown, E. and Cloke, J. (2005) “Neoliberal reform, governance and corruption in Central America: exploring the Nicaraguan case”, *Political Geography*, 24, 5: 601–630.

Bryan, D., Martin, R., and Rafferty, M. (2009) "Financialization and Marx: giving labor and capital a financial makeover", *Review of Radical Political Economics*, 41: 458–472.

Bukovansky, M. (2006) "The hollowness of anti-corruption discourse", *Review of International Political Economy*, 13, 2: 181–209.

Burbach, R. and Flynn, P. (1980) *Agribusiness in the Americas*, New York: Monthly Review Press.

Büscher, B. (2010) "Derivative nature: interrogating the value of conservation in 'Boundless Southern Africa'", *Third World Quarterly*, 31, 2: 259–276.

Büscher, B. (2012) "The political economy of Africa's natural resources and the 'Great financial crisis'", *Journal of Economic and Social Geography*, 103, 2: 136–149.

Büscher, B. (2013) "Nature on the move: The value and circulation of liquid nature and the emergence of fictitious conservation", *New Proposals: Journal of Marxism and Interdisciplinary Inquiry*, 6, 1–2: 20–36.

Büscher, B. (2014) "Selling success: constructing value in conservation and development", *World Development*, 57: 79–90.

Büscher, B. and Igoe, J. (2013) "Prosuming conservation: producing/consuming nature and the material base of speculative capitalism", *Journal of Consumer Culture*: 1–23.

Büscher, B. and Arsel, M. (2012) "Neoliberal conservation and uneven geographical development: exploring the changing nature of capitalist modernity in nature-society interactions", Special feature of *Journal of Economic and Social Geography*, 103, 2: 129–195.

Butterman, W. C. and Amey, E. B. III (2002) *US Geological Survey, Mineral Commodity Profiles: Gold*, Open-File Report 02-303. US Department of the Interior and US Geological Survey.

Callon, M. (1998) *The Laws of the Markets*, Oxford: Blackwell.

Callon, M. (2005) "Why virtualism paves the way to political impotence: Callon replies to Miller", *Economic Sociology European Electronic Newsletter*, 6, 2.

Callon, M. (2007) "What does it mean to say economics is performative?" in D. MacKenzie, F. Muniesa and L. Siu (eds), *Do Economists Make Markets? On the Performativity of Economics*, Princeton, NJ: Princeton University Press.

Callon, M. and Muniesa, F. (2005) "Economic markets as calculative collective devises", *Organization Studies,* 26(8): 1229–50.

Cameron, A. and Palan, R. (2004) *The "Imagined Economies" of Globalization*, London: Sage.

Carolan, M. S. (2005) "Society, Biology and Ecology", *Organization and Environment*, 18, 3: 393–421.

Carothers, T. (2007) "How democracies emerge: the 'sequencing' fallacy", *Journal of Democracy*, 18: 13–27.

Carrier, J. G. and West, P. (2009) *Virtualism, Governance and Practice*, New York: Berghahn.

Carruthers, B. G. and Stinchcombe, A. L. (1999) "The social structure of liquidity: flexibility, markets, and states", *Theory and Society*, 28, 3: 353–382.

Casey, R. (2014) "Irish researcher visits Mozambique in advance of a defining election", *Irish Examiner*, 18 October. Available from www.irishexaminer.com/viewpoints/analysis/irish-researcher-visits-mozambique-in-advance-of-a-defining-election-291826.html

Carver, L. (2015) *Measuring the value of what? An ethnographic account of the transformation of 'Nature' under the DEFRA biodiversity offsetting metric.* The University of

Manchester, School of Environment, Education and Development, Leverhulme Centre for the Study of Value.
Castells, M. (1989) *The Informational City: Information, Technology, Economic Restructuring and the Urban-Regional Process*, Oxford: Blackwell.
Castree, N. (2006) "Commentary: from neoliberalism to neoliberalisation: consolations, confusions, and necessary illusions", *Environment and Planning A*, 38: 1–6.
Castree, N. (2010a) "Neoliberalism and the biophysical world 1: what 'neoliberalism' is and what difference nature makes to it", *Geography Compass 4*, 12: 1725–1733.
Castree, N. (2010b) "Neoliberalism and the biophysical world 2: theorising the neoliberalisation of nature." *Geography Compass 4*, 12: 1734–1746.
Castree, N. (2010c) "Crisis, continuity and change: neoliberalism, the left and the future of capitalism", *Antipode*, 41, s1: 185–213.
Castree, N. (2011) 'Neoliberalism and the biophysical environment: a synthesis and evaluation of the research', *Environment and Society: Advances in Research*, 1(1): 5–45.
Castree, N. and Henderson, G. (2014) "The capitalist mode of conservation, neoliberalism and the ecology of value", *New Proposals: Journal of Marxism and Interdisciplinary Inquiry*, 7, 1:16–37.
Cerra, V. Rishi, M. and Saxena, S. C. (2005) "Robbing the riches: capital flight, institutions and instability", IMF Working Paper WP/05/199.
CFTC and SEC (2010) Findings regarding the market events of May 6, 2010. Report of the Staffs of the CFTC and SEC to the Joint Advisory Committee on Emerging Regulatory Issues, US Commodity Futures Trading Commission and the US Securities and Exchange Commission, Washington. Available from www.sec.gov/news/studies/2010/marketevents-report.pdf
Chaboud, A. P., Chiquoine, B., Hjalmarsson, E. and Vega, C. (2014) "Rise of the machines: algorithmic trading in the foreign exchange market", *Journal of Finance*, 69, 5.
Chaikin, D. and Sharman, J. C. (2009) *Corruption and Money Laundering*, New York: Palgrave Macmillan.
Chandi Jamwa, D. (2009) "NSSF: Jamwa exposes Suruma, Nzeyi trickery", *The Independent* (Kampala), February 28.
Chandra, K. (2004) *Why Ethnic Parties Succeed: Patronage and Ethnic Headcounts in India*, Cambridge, Cambridge University Press.
Chang, H-J. (1994) *The Political Economy of Industrial Policy*, London, Macmillan.
Chatterjee, P. (2008) "Democracy and economic transformation in India", *Economic & Political Weekly*, 43, 16: 53–62.
Cheng, C. and Zaum, D. (2012), "Introduction: key themes in peacebuilding and corruption", *International Peacebuilding*, 15, 3: 301–309.
Chomsky, N. (1993) *Year 501: The Conquest Continues*, Montreal and New York: Black Rose Books.
Christian Aid and Tax Justice Network (2014) *Africa Rising? Inequalities and the Essential Role of Fair Taxation.* Available from www.christianaid.org.uk/images/Africa-tax-and-inequality-report-Feb2014.pdf
Christophers, B. (2012) "Anaemic geographies of financialisation", *New Political Economy*, 17, 3: 271–291.
Christophers, B. (2015) "The limits to financialization", *Dialogues in Human Geography*, 5, 2: 183–200.
Chua, A. (2004) *World on Fire: How Exporting Free Market Democracy Breeds Ethnic Hatred and Global Instability*. New York: Knopf.

CIA Factbook (2014), *World Tables*. Available from www.cia.gov/library/publications/the-world-factbook/rankorder/2079rank.html

Clarke, G. (2011) "How petty is petty corruption? Evidence from firm surveys in Africa", *World Development*, 39, 7: 1122–1132.

Climate Bonds Initiative (2014) *Bonds and Climate Change: The State of the Market in 2014*, London: Climate Bonds Initiative. Available from www.climatebonds.net/files/files/-CB-HSBC-15July2014-A4-final.pdf

Climate Change Policy and Practice (2014) "World Bank issues first catastrophe bond", IISD reporting services. Available from: http://climate-l.iisd.org/news/world-bank-issues-first-catastrophe-bond/

Cloud Nine Bulletin (2015) "Top five wealthiest blacks in South Africa 2015", *Cloud Nine Bulletin*, 20 March. Available from http://cloudninebulletin.co.za/top-five-wealthiest-blacks-in-south-africa-2015/

Collier, S. J. (2005) "The spatial forms and social norms of 'actually existing neoliberalism': toward a substantive analytics", International Affairs Working Paper, New York: New School University.

Collier, S. J. and Ong, A. (2008) *Global Assemblages: Technology, Politics, and Ethics as Anthropological Problems*. Oxford: Wiley-Blackwell.

Comerton-Forde, C. and Putnins, T. J. (2015) "Dark trading and price discovery", *Journal of Financial Economics*. Available from http://papers.ssrn.com/sol3/papers.cfm?abstract_id=2183392

Commission for Africa (2005) *Our Common Future*. Available from www.commissionforafrica.info/2005-report

Congressional Budget Office (2013) "Report on the Troubled Asset Relief Program", US Government, 23 May. Available from www.cbo.gov/sites/default/files/cbofiles/attachments/44256_TARP.pdf

Conroy-Krutz, J. and Logan, C. (2011) "Museveni and the 2011 Ugandan elections: did the money matter?", Afrobarometer, Working Paper 135.

Crary, J. (2002) "Spectacle, attention, and counter-memory", in *Guy Debord and the Situationist International*, Tom McDonough (ed.), Cambridge, MA: MIT Press.

Crotty, J. (2009) "Structural causes of the global financial crisis: a critical assessment of the 'new financial architecture'", *Cambridge Journal of Economics*, 33: 563–580.

Culp, C. (2002) The Art of Risk Management: Alternative Risk Transfer, Capital Structure, and the Convergence of Insurance and Capital Markets, New York: John Wiley & Sons.

Dean, M. (2003) [1999] *Governmentality: Power and Rule in Modern Society*, London: Sage Publications.

Dean, M. (2006) "A political mythology of world order: Carl Schmitt's nomos", *Theory Culture and Society: Explorations in Critical Social Science*, 23: 1–21.

Debord, G. (1995) *The Society of the Spectacle*, New York: Zone Books.

Debord, G. (1998) *Comments on the Society of the Spectacle*, London: Verso.

DeLanda, M. (2006) *A New Philosophy of Society: Assemblage Theory and Social Complexity*, London: Continuum.

Deleuze, G. and Guattari, F. (1987) *A Thousand Plateaus: Capitalism and Schizophrenia*, trans. Brian Massumi, London: Continuum.

Democratic Alliance (2014) "No parliamentary oversight over infrastructure spend could lead to corruption and undermine growth", Democratic Alliance, Cape Town, 25 February. Available from www.da.org.za/2014/02/no-parliamentary-oversight-over-infrastructure-spend-could-lead-to-corruption-and-undermine-growth/

Desai, A. (2015) "Of Faustian Pacts and mega-projects: the politics and economics of the port expansion in the south basin of Durban, South Africa", *Capitalism Nature Socialism*, 26, 1: 18–34.

Desai, A. (2016) "Between Madiba magic and spectacular capitalism: the FIFA World Cup in South Africa", in *Mega-Events and Globalization: Capital and Spectacle in a Changing World Order*, R. Gruneau and J. Horne (eds), Abingdon: Routledge.

Dev, K. and Cartright-Smith, D. (2008) "Illicit financial flows from developing countries: 2002–2006", Washington DC: Global Financial Integrity.

DfID (2011) "DFID's governance portfolio review: summary review of DFID's governance portfolio, 2004–2009", London: Department for International Development. Available from www.gov.uk/government/uploads/system/uploads/attachment_data/file/67458/governance-portfolio.pdf

DfID (2013) "Joint evaluation of support to anti-corruption efforts 2002–2009, Independent report", 31 January, London: Department for International Development. Available from www.gov.uk/government/publications/joint-evaluation-of-support-to-anti-corruption-efforts-2002-2009

Diga, K. and Bracking, S. (2015) "Descriptive statistics: the developmental value of the Durban port expansion project", Research Report 2015 No 2, Leverhulme Centre for the Study of Value, University of Manchester and Chair in Appiled Poverty Reduction Assessment, University of KwaZulu-Natal. Available from https://appliedpovertyreduction.files.wordpress.com/2015/01/technical-paper-2-final.pdf

Doig, A. and Marquette, H. (2005) 'Corruption and democratisation: the litmus test of international donor agency intentions?', *Futures*, 37: 199–213.

Dore, R. (2008) 'Financialization of the Global Economy', *Industrial and Corporate Change*, 17: 1097–1112.

Du Toit, A. (2011) "Nasruddin's key: poverty measurement and the government of marginal populations", Paper presented at the conference on Marginality and Extreme Poverty: Towards Inclusive Development for and with the Poorest, Center for Development Research (ZEF) University of Bonn, Germany, June 20–22.

Du Toit, A (2012) "The trouble with poverty: reflections on South Africa's anti-poverty consensus", Working Paper 22, Institute for Poverty, Land and Agrarian Studies (PLAAS), University of the Western Cape, Bellville.

Duffield, M. (2001) "Governing the borderlands: decoding the power of aid", *Disasters*, 25, 4: 308–320.

Duhigg, C. (2009) "Stock traders find speed pays, in milliseconds", *New York Times*, 23 July. Available at: www.nytimes.com/2009/07/24/business/24trading.html?_r=0

Durbin, M. (2010) *All About High-Frequency Trading*, New York: McGraw-Hill.

Duus-Otterström, G. and Jagers, S. C. (2011) "Why (most) climate insurance schemes are a bad idea", *Environmental Politics*, 20, 3: 322–339.

Dyer, J. (2014) "The consequences of Durban's proposed port development", presentation at the University of KwaZulu-Natal's Centre for Civil Society, Durban.

EIOPA (2013) "Second half-year financial stability report 2013", Frankfurt: European Insurance and Occupational Pensions Authority. Available from https://eiopa.europa.eu/Pages/SearchResults.aspx?k=filename:EIOPA_Financial_Stability_Report_-_2013_1H_01.pdf

Environmental Finance (2014a) "A review of the green market in 2014", Environmental Finance.com. Available from www.environmental-finance.com/content/analysis/a-review-of-the-green-market-in-2014.html

Environmental Finance (2014b) "Bond investors ponder fifty shades of green",

Environmental Finance.com. Available from www.environmental-finance.com/content/analysis/bond-investors-ponder-fifty-shades-of-green.html

Environmental Finance (2014c) "Is GDF's green bond issue really green?", Environmental Finance.com. Available from www.environmental-finance.com/content/analysis/is-gdf%E2%80%99s-green-bond-issue-really-green.html

Environmental Finance (2014d) "The rise of the green bond index", Environmental Finance.com. Available from www.environmental-finance.com/content/analysis/the-rise-of-the-green-bond-index.html

Environmental Finance (2015a) "Barclays and MSCI launch review of green bond index rules", Environmental Finance.com. Available from www.environmental-finance.com/content/news/barclays-and-msci-launch-review-of-green-bond-index-rules.html

Environmental Finance (2015b) "State Street launches world's first index-linked green bond fund", Environmental Finance.com.

Epstein, G. (2005) "Introduction: financialization and the world economy", in *Financialization and the World Economy*, G. Epstein (ed.), Northampton, MA: Edward Elgar.

Epstein, G. and Jayadev, A. (2005) "The rise of rentier incomes in OECD countries: financialization, central bank policy and labor solidarity", in *Financialization and the World Economy*, G. Epstein (ed.), Northampton, MA: Edward Elgar.

Equinix (2014) "BATS Global Markets selects Equinix's Secaucus Data Center for BATS and Direct Edge Exchanges", 19 February, Equinix. Available from www.equinix.com/company/news-and-events/press-releases/bats-global-markets-selects-equinix-secaucus-data-center/

Equinix (2015a) "New York data centers", Redwood City, CA: Equinix. Available from www.equinix.com/locations/united-states-colocation/new-york-data-centers/

Equinix (2015b) "NY4 New York: network interconnection specifications", Redwood City, CA: Equinix. Available from www.equinix.com/locations/united-states-colocation/new-york-data-centers/ny4/

Equinix (2015c) "Expand worldwide", Redwood City, CA: Equinix. Available from www.equinix.com/

Erdmann, G. and Engel, U. (2006) "Neopatrimonialism revisited: beyond a catch-all concept", GIGA Working Papers No.16, Leipzig.

Ewing, J. (2014) "Financial Stability Board to propose stricter capital rules for global banks", *The New York Times*, 10 November. Available from http://dealbook.nytimes.com/2014/11/10/financial-stability-board-to-propose-stricter-capital-rules-for-global-banks/?_r=0

Fadahunsi, A. and Rosa, P. (2002) "Entrepreneurship and illegality: insights from the Nigerian cross-border trade", *Journal of Business Venturing*, 17, 5: 397–429.

Feigenbaum, T. (2011) "Measuring anticipated economic impact of dig-out port development: order of magnitude study", 16 March, UrbanEcon, Durban.

Ferguson, J. (1990) *The "Anti-Politics" Machine, Development, Depolitisization and Bureaucratic Power in Lesotho*, Minneapolis, MN: University of Minnesota Press.

Ferguson, J. (1994) "The anti-politics machine: development and bureaucratic power in Lesotho", *The Ecologist*, 24, 5: 176–181.

Ferguson, J. (2005) "Seeing like an oil company: space, security, and global capital in neoliberal Africa", *American Anthropologist*, 107, 3: 377–382.

Ferguson, J. (2006) *Global Shadows: Africa in the Neoliberal World Order*. Durham, NC: Duke University Press.

Ferguson, J. (2007) "Formalities of poverty: thinking about social assistance in neoliberal South Africa", *African Studies Review*, 50, 2: 71–86.

Ferguson, J. (2009) "The uses of neoliberalism", *Antipode*, 41, s1: 166–184.

Financial Stability Board (2011) "Potential financial stability issues arising from recent trends in Exchange-Traded Funds (ETFs)", Basel: Financial Stability Board. Available from www.fsb.org/wp-content/uploads/r_110412b.pdf

Financial Stability Board (2014) "Adequacy of loss-absorbing capacity of global systemically important banks in resolution: consultative document", Basel: Financial Stability Board. Available from www.financialstabilityboard.org/wp-content/uploads/TLAC-Condoc-6-Nov-2014-FINAL.pdf

Fine, B. (2010) "Locating financialisation", *Historical Materialism*, 18: 97–116.

Fine, B. (2014) "Financialization from a Marxist perspective", *International Journal of Political Economy*, 42, 4: 47–66.

Fisher, I. (1907) *The Rate of Interest*, New York: Macmillan.

Flanary, R. and Watt, D. (1999) "The state of corruption: A case study of Uganda", *Third World Quarterly*, 20, 3: 515–536.

Folkman, P., Froud, J., Johal, S. and Williams, K. (2007) "Working for themselves? Capital Market intermediaries and present day capitalism", *Business History*, 49, 4: 552–572.

Forbes (2015a) "South Africa's richest: gallery", *Forbes*, 18 November. Available from www.forbes.com/pictures/gfgl45emmh/1-nicky-oppenheimer/

Forbes (2015b) "Why South Africa tops Africa's 50 richest in 2015", *Forbes*, 18 November. Available from www.forbes.com/sites/katevinton/2015/11/18/why-south-africa-tops-africas-50-richest-in-2015/

Foster, V. and Briceno-Garmendia, C. (eds) (2010) *Africa's Infrastructure: A Time for Transformation*, Washington, DC: The World Bank. Available from http://siteresources.worldbank.org/INTAFRICA/Resources/aicd_overview_english_no-embargo.pdf

Foucault, M. (1979) *Discipline and Punish: The Birth of the Prison*, New York: Vintage Books.

Foucault, M. (1980) *Power/Knowledge: Selected Interviews and Other Writings 1972-1977*, Colin Gordon (ed.), London: Harvester.

Foucault, M. (1997) "The birth of biopolitics", in *Michel Foucault, Ethics: Subjectivity and Truth*, Paul Rabinow (ed.), New York: The New Press.

Foucault, M. (2004b) [1979] *Geschichte der Gouvernementalität II: Die Geburt der Biopolitik, Vorlesung am College de France 1978–1979*, M. Sennelart (ed.), Frankfurt: Suhrkamp Verlag.

Foucault, M. (2008) *Segurança, território, população: curso dado no Collège de France (1977–1978)*, M. Senellart (ed.), trans. E. Brandão, São Paulo: Martins Fontes.

Foucault, M. (2013) *Politics, Philosophy, Culture: Interviews and Other Writings, 1977–1984*, L. Kritzman (ed.), London: Routledge.

Fraser, N. and Gordon, L. (1994) "A genealogy of 'dependency': tracing a keyword of the US welfare state", *Signs*, 19, 2: 309–336.

Fredriksen, A. (2014) "Emergency shelter topologies: locating humanitarian space in mobile and material practice", *Environment and Planning D: Society and Space*, 32, 1: 147–162.

Fredriksen, A. and Sullivan, S. (2014) "Actor Network Theory (ANT)", LCSV Working Paper No. 2: A conceptual map for the study of value: An initial mapping of concepts for the project "Human, non-human and environmental value systems: an impossible frontier?", Leverhulme Centre for the Study of Value, University of Manchester. Available from http://thestudyofvalue.org/wp-content/uploads/2013/11/WP2-A-conceptual-map.pdf

Fredriksen, A., Bracking, S., Greco, E., Igoe, J. J., Morgan, R. and Sian Sullivan (2014) LCSV Working Paper No. 2: A conceptual map for the study of value: An initial mapping of concepts for the project "Human, non-human and environmental value systems: an impossible frontier?", Leverhulme Centre for the Study of Value, University of Manchester. Available from http://thestudyofvalue.org/wp-content/uploads/2013/11/WP2-A-conceptual-map.pdf

Fried, B. J., Lagunes, P. and Venkataramani, A. (2010) "Corruption and inequality at the crossroad: a multimethod study of bribery and discrimination in Latin America", *Latin American Research Review*, 45, 1: 76–97.

Froud, J., Haslam, C., Johal, S. and Williams, K. (2000), "Financialisation and shareholder value: consultancy moves, management promises", *Economy and Society*, 29: 80–120.

Funder, M. and Marani, M. (2015) "Local bureaucrats as bricoleurs: The everyday implementation practices of county environment officers in rural Kenya", *International Journal of the Commons*, 9, 1: 87–106.

Global Financial Integrity (2013) "Illicit financial flows". Available from www.gfintegrity.org/issue/illicit-financial-flows/

Goldfarb, Z. A. (2010) "Report examines May's 'flash crash,' expresses concern over high-speed trading", *Washington Post*, 1 October. Available from www.washingtonpost.com/wp-dyn/content/article/2010/10/01/AR2010100103969.html?sid=ST2010100107554

Goldman, R. and Papson, S. (2006) "Capital's brandscapes", *Journal of Consumer Culture*, 6: 327–353.

Goodchild, P. (2012) "What is Wrong with the Global Financial System?", *Journal of Interdisciplinary Economics*, 24, 7: 7–28.

Goodman, D. Sorj, B. and Wilkinson, J. (1984) "Agro-industry, state policy and rural social structures: recent analyses of proletarianisation in Brazilian agriculture", in *Proletarianisation in the Third World: Studies in the Creation of a Labour Force Under Dependent Capitalism*, B. Munslow and H. Finch (eds), Abingdon: Routledge.

Gowan, P. (2009) "Crisis in the heartland: consequences of the new Wall Street system", *New Left Review*, 55: 5–29.

Graham Muller Associates (2009a) "Composite summary and strategic issues – final draft March 2009: A Local area plan and land use management scheme for the Back of Port Interface Zone", Durban: Graham Muller Associates.

Graham Muller Associates (2009b) "Addendum b: status quo assessment", Durban: Graham Muller Associates.

Graham, P. (2007) *Hypercapitalism: New Media, Language, and Social Perceptions of Value*. New York: Peter Lang.

Graham, Y. (2012) "Towards an agenda for social justice philanthropy in Africa in a time of global restructuring", Southern Africa Trust, mimeo.

Gramsci, A. (1971) *Selections from the Prison Notebooks*. London: Lawrence and Wishart.

Granovetter, M. (2007) "The social construction of corruption", in *On Capitalism*, V. Nee and R. Swedberg (eds), Stanford: Stanford University Press.

Green Climate Fund (GCF) (2014) "Investment framework". Available from http://gcfund.net/fileadmin/00_customer/documents/MOB201406-7th/GCF_B07_06_Investment_Framework140509__fin_20140509.pdf

Green Climate Fund (GCF) (2015) "Status of pledges for GCFs initial resource mobilization (IRM)." Available from http://news.gcfund.org/wp-content/uploads/2015/04/release_GCF_2015_contributions_status_30_april_2015.pdf

Guerrero, M. A. and Rodriguez-Oreggia, E. (2008) "On the individual decisions to commit corruption: a methodological complement", *Journal of Economic and Social Behaviour*, 65, 2: 357–372.

Guttmann, R. (2008) "A primer on finance-led capitalism and its crisis", *Revue de la Regulation*, 3/4, 1–19.

Hagedorn, D., Heigl, C., Mueller, A. and Seidler, G. (2009) "Choice of triggers", in *The Handbook of Insurance-Linked Securities*, P. Barrieu and L. Albertini (eds), Chichester: Wiley.

Hallowes, D. (2014) *Planning Poverty: The NDP and the Infrastructure of Destruction*. Pietermaritzburg: GroundWork.

Hamani, O. (2014) "'We make do and keep going!' Inventive practices and ordered informality in the functioning of the district courts in Niamey and Zinder (Niger)", in *States at Work: Dynamics of African Bureaucracies*, T. Bierschenk and J-P Olivier de Sardan (eds), Leiden: Brill.

Hanke, S. H. (2012) "It's the money supply, stupid", *Globe Asia*, July. Available from www.cato.org/publications/commentary/its-money-supply-stupid

Harrison, E. (2006) "Unpacking the anti-corruption agenda: dilemmas for anthropologists", *Oxford Development Studies*, 34, 1: 15–29.

Harvey, D. (1982) *The Limits to Capital*, Chicago, IL: University of Chicago Press.

Harvey, D. (1989) *The Condition of Postmodernity*, Oxford: Blackwell.

Harvey, D. (2003) *The New Imperialism*, Oxford: Oxford University Press.

Harvey, D. (2005) *A Brief History Of Neoliberalism*, Oxford: Oxford University Press.

Harvey, D. (2006) "Neo-liberalism as creative destruction", *Geografiska Annaler*, 88B, 2: 145–158.

Harvey, D. (2008) *The Communist Manifesto: Karl Marx and Friedrich Engels*, London: Pluto Press.

Harvey, D. (2010) *The Enigma of Capital: and the Crisis of Capitalism*, London: Profile Books.

Harvey, D. (2013) *A Companion To Marx's* Capital *(Vol. 2)*. New York: Verso.

Hasbrouck, J. and Saar, G. (2013) "Low-latency trading", *Journal of Financial Markets*, 16, 4: 637–770.

Haufler, V. (1997) *Dangerous Commerce: Insurance and the Management of International Risk*, Ithaca and London: Cornell University Press.

Hay, C. (2004) "The normalizing role of rationalist assumptions in the institutional embedding of neoliberalism", *Economy and Society*, 33, 4: 500–527.

Heggstad, K. and Fjeldstad, O-H. (2010) "How banks assist capital flight from Africa: a literature review", CMI Report R 2010:6, Bergen: Chr. Michelsen Institute. Available from www.cmi.no/publications/file/3750-how-banks-assist-capital-flight-from-africa.pdf

Heller, M. (2014) "Global bank regulator calls for larger capital cushions", *CFO*, 10 November. Available from ww2.cfo.com/regulation/2014/11/global-bank-regulator-calls-larger-capital-cushions/

Hendershott, T., Charles, J. M. and Menkveld, A. J. (2011) "Does algorithmic trading improve liquidity?" *Journal of Finance*, 66: 1–33.

Henderson, B., Jegadeesh, N. and Weisbach, M. (2006) "World markets for raising new capital", *Journal of Financial Economics*, 82, 1: 63–101.

Henderson, G. (2004) "'Free food', the local production of worth, and the circuit of decommodification: a value theory of the surplus", *Environment and Planning D: Society and Space*, 22, 4: 485–512.

Henderson, G. (2013) *Value in Marx: The Persistence of Value in a More-Than-Capitalist World*, Minneapolis: University of Minnesota Press.

Henry, J. (2012) "The price of offshore revisited", Tax Justice Network. Available from www.taxjustice.net/wp-content/uploads/2014/04/Price_of_Offshore_Revisited_120722.pdf

Henwood, D. (1997) "Talking about work", *Monthly Review*, 49, 3: 18–30.

Herbst, M. (2013) "The bank bailout cost US taxpayers nothing? Think again", *The Guardian*, 28 May. Available from www.theguardian.com/commentisfree/2013/may/28/bank-bailout-cost-taxpayers

Hewitt, M. (2011) "Quantitative easing is nothing new", *DollarDaze*, 30 January. Available from http://dollardaze.org/blog/?post_id=00762&cat_id=20

Hildyard, N. (2000) "Underwriting corruption: Britain's role in promoting corruption, cronyism and graft", London: The Corner House. Available from www.thecornerhouse.org.uk/resource/underwriting-corruption

Hildyard, N. (2008) "A (crumbling) wall of money: financial bricolage, derivatives and power", London: The Corner House. Available from www.thecornerhouse.org.uk/summary.shtml?x=562658

Hildyard, N. (2016) *Licensed Larceny Infrastructure: Accumulation and the Global South*, Manchester: Manchester University Press.

Hilferding, R. (1910) *Das Finanzkapital. Eine Studie über die jüngste Entwicklung des Kapitalismus*, (Marx-Studien, vol. III), Vienna: Wiener Volksbuchhandlung.

Hilgers, T. (2011) "Clientelism and conceptual stretching: differentiating among concepts and among analytical levels", *Theory and Society*, 40, 5: 567–588.

Hirschey, N. H. (2013) "Do high frequency traders anticipate buying and selling pressure?" Working paper, LBS.

Holert, T. (2012) "'A live monster that is fruitful and multiples': capitalism as poisoned rat?", *e-flux*, 36. Available from www.e-flux.com/journal/%E2%80%9Ca-live-monster-that-is-fruitful-and-multiplies%E2%80%9D-capitalism-as-poisoned-rat/

Holmes, G. (2012) "Biodiversity for billionaires: capitalism, conservation and the role of philanthropy in saving/selling nature", *Development and Change*, 43, 1: 185–203.

Hunt, J. (2007) "How corruption hits people when they are down", *Journal of Development Economics*, 84, 2: 574–589.

Hunt, J. and Laszlo, S. (2012) "Is bribery really regressive? Bribery's costs, benefits, and mechanisms", *World Development*, 40, 2: 355–372.

Huntington, S. P. (1968) *Political Order in Changing Societies*, New Haven, CT: Yale University Press.

Ibrahim Index of African Governance (2014) *2014 Summary Report with Key Findings*, London and Dakar: Mo Ibrahim Foundation. Available from www.moibrahimfoundation.org/iiag-resources/

ICSID (2010) In the proceedings between Suez, Sociedad General de Aguas de Barcelona S. A., and Vivendi Universal S. A. (Claimants) and the Argentine Republic (Respondent): decision on liability. ICSID Case No. ARB/03/19 Washington, DC: International Centre for Settlement of Investment Disputes, 30 July. Available from www.italaw.com/documents/SuezVivendiAWGDecisiononLiability.pdf

Igoe, J. (2010) "The spectacle of nature in the global economy of appearances anthropological engagements with the spectacular mediations of transnational conservation", *Critique of Anthropology*, 30, 3: 375–397.

Igoe, J. (2013a) "Consume, connect, conserve: consumer spectacle and the technical mediation of neoliberal conservation's aesthetic of redemption and repair", *Human Geography*, 6, 1: 16–28.

Igoe, J. (2013b) "Nature on the move II: contemplation becomes speculation", *New Proposals: Journal of Marxism and Interdisciplinary Inquiry*, 6, 1–2: 37–49.

Igoe, J. and Brockington, D. (2007) "Neoliberal conservation: a brief introduction", *Conservation and Society*, 5, 4: 432–449.

Igoe, J., Neves, K. and Brockington, D. (2010) "A spectacular eco-tour around the historic bloc: theorising the convergence of biodiversity conservation and capitalist expansion", *Antipode*, 42, 3: 486–512.

IISD (2014) "World Bank issues first catastrophe bond", *Climate Change Policy and Practice*, 8 July. Available from http://climate-l.iisd.org/news/world-bank-issues-first-catastrophe-bond/

IMF (2011) *Global Financial Stability Report: Durable Financial Stability: Getting There from Here*, Washington, DC: International Monetary Fund. Available from www.imf.org/external/pubs/ft/gfsr/2011/01/pdf/text.pdf

IMF (2014) *Global Financial Stability Report: Moving from Liquidity to Growth-Driven Markets, World Economic and Financial Surveys*, Washington, DC: International Monetary Fund. Available from www.imf.org/external/pubs/FT/GFSR/2014/01/pdf/text.pdf

Index Mundi (2014) "World economy profile 2014", Index Mundi.com. Available from www.indexmundi.com/world/economy_profile.html

International Organisation of Securities Commissions (IOSCO) (2011) "Regulatory issues raised by the impact of technological changes on market integrity and efficiency" Technical Committee of the International Organisation of Securities Commissions. Available from www.iosco.org/library/pubdocs/pdf/IOSCOPD354.pdf

Iqbal, Z. (2011) "Zambia presidential election: setting an example for Africa", International Institute for Justice and Development, 7 October. Available from http://iijd.org/news/entry/Zambia-Presidential-Election-Setting-an-Example-for-Africa

Jancsics, D. (2013) "Petty corruption in Central and Eastern Europe: the clients's perspective", *Crime, Law and Social Change*, 60: 319–341

Jancsics, D. (2014) "'A friend gave me a phone number': brokerage in low-level corruption", *International Journal of Law, Crime and Justice*, 20: 1–20.

Johnsøn, J., Taxell, N. and Zaum, D. (2012) "Mapping evidence gaps in anti-corruption: Assessing the state of the operationally relevant evidence on donors' actions and approaches to reducing corruption", Chr. Michelsen Institute, *U4 Issue*, 2012: 7. Available from www.cmi.no/publications/publication/?4624=mapping-evidence-gaps-in-anti-corruption

Johnson, L. (2014) "Geographies of securitized catastrophe risk and the implications of climate change", *Economic Geography*, 90, 2: 155–185.

Johnson, R. (2007) "Post-hegemony? I don't think so". *Theory, Culture and Society*, 24, 3: 95–110

Johnson, S. (2014) "China's growing power over South Africa", *Market Realist*, 17 December. Available from http://marketrealist.com/2014/12/chinas-growing-power-south-africa/

Johnston, D. and Saad-Filho, A. (2007) *Neoliberalism: A Critical Reader*, London: Pluto Press.

Jones, C. (2013) *Can the Market Speak?* London: Zero Books.

Jong-Sung, Y. and Khagram, S. (2005), "A comparative study of inequality and corruption", *American Sociological Review*, 70, 1: 136–157.

Kar, D. and Cartwright Smith, D. (2007) *Illicit Financial Flows*, Washington, DC: GFI.

Kar, D. and Cartwright Smith, D. (2009) *Illicit Financial Flows from Developing Countries: 2002–2006*, Washington, DC: GFI.

Kar, D. and Cartwright Smith, D. (2010) *Illicit Financial Flows From Africa: Hidden Resources for Development*, Washington, DC: GFI.

Kar, D. and Freitas, S. (2012). *Illicit Financial Flows from Developing Countries: 2001–2010*, Washington, DC: GFI.

Kasara, K. (2007) "Tax me if you can: ethnic geography, democracy, and the taxation of agriculture in Africa", *American Political Science Review*, 101, 1: 159–172.

Kaufmann, D. (2005) "Myths and realities about governance and corruption" in *Global Competitiveness Report 2005–6*, A. Lopez-Claros, M. E. Porter and K. Schwab (eds), Oxford: Oxford University Press.

Kelleher, J. (2014) "What is bitcoin's intrinsic value?" *Investopedia.com*, 18 September. Available from www.investopedia.com/articles/investing/091814/what-bitcoins-intrinsic-value.asp

Kelsall, T. (2011) "Rethinking the relationship between neo-patrimonialism and economic development in Africa", *IDS Bulletin*, 42, 2: 76–87.

Kerr, N. N. (2011) "Perceptions versus reality: assessing popular evaluations of election quality in Africa", Afrobarometer, Working Paper 137.

Keynes, J. (1933) "National self-sufficiency", *The Yale Review* 22: 755–769.

Knox-Hayes, J. (2013) "The spatial and temporal dynamics of value in financialisation: analysis of the infrastructure of carbon markets", *Geoforum*, 50: 117–128.

Kohl-Arenas, E. (2011) "Governing poverty amidst plenty: participatory development and private philanthropy", *Geography Compass*, 5: 811–824.

Korf, B. (2007) "Antinomies of generosity: moral geographies and post-tsunami aid in Southeast Asia", *Geoforum*, 38, 2: 366–378.

Krippner, G. (2004) "What is financialisation", Department of Sociology, UCLA, mimeo.

Krippner, G. (2005) 'The financialization of the American economy', *Socio-Economic Review*, 3: 173–208.

Labban, M. (2010) "Oil in parallax: scarcity, markets, and the financialization of accumulation", *Geoforum* 41, 541–552.

Lake, R. (1995) "Spatial fix 2: the sequel", *Urban Geography*, 16: 189–191.

Langley, P. (2007) "The uncertain subjects of Anglo-American financialization", *Cultural Critique*, 65: 66–91.

Langley, P. (2008) "Financialization and the consumer credit boom", *Competition and Change*, 12: 133–147.

Lapavitsas, C. (2009) "Financialised capitalism: crisis and financial expropriation", *Historical Materialism*, 17: 114–148.

Lapavitsas, C. (2013) *Profiting Without Producing: How Finance Exploits Us All*, London: Verso.

Latour, B. (1986) "Visualization and cognition: thinking with eyes and hands" in *Knowledge and Society: Studies in the Sociology of Culture Past and Present*, H. Kuklick (ed.), Greenwich, CT: JAI Press.

Latour, B. (1999) *Politiques de la nature: Comment faire entrer les sciences en démocratie*, Paris: La Découverte.

Latour, B. (2005) *Reasembling the Social: An Introduction to Actor-Network Theory*. Oxford: Oxford University Press.

Law, J. (1999) 'After ANT: complexity, naming and topology', in *Actor Network Theory and After*, J. Law and J. Hasard (eds), Malden, MA: Blackwell.

Lazonick, W. and O'Sullivan, M. (2000) "Maximizing shareholder value: a new ideology for corporate governance", *Economy and Society*, 29: 13–35.

Leander, A. (2008) "Securing Sovereignty by Governing Security through Markets", in *Sovereignty Games: Instrumentalizing State Sovereignty in Europe and Beyond*, R. Adler-Nissen and T. Gammeltoft-Hansen (eds), New York: Palgrave Macmillan.

Lee, B. and LiPuma, E. (2002) "Cultures of circulation: the imaginations of modernity", *Public Culture*, 14, 1: 191–213.

Lee, B. and LiPuma, E. (2005) "Financial derivatives and the rise of circulation", *Economy and Society*, 34: 404–427.

Lee, R., Clark, G., Pollard, J. and Leyshon, A. (2009) "The remit of financial geography: before and after the crisis", *Journal of Economic Geography*, 9: 723–747.

Leinweber, D. (2009) *Nerds on Wall Street: Math, Machines, and Wired Markets*, Hoboken, NJ: Wiley.

Lenglet, M. (2011) "Conflicting codes and codings: how algorithmic trading is reshaping financial regulation", *Theory, Culture and Society*, 28: 44–66.

Levi, M., Sacks, A. and Tyler, T. (2009) "Conceptualizing legitimacy, measuring legitimizing beliefs", *American Behavioral Scientist*, 53, 3: 354–375.

Lewis, M. (2015) *Flash Boys: A Wall Street Revolt*, New York: W. W. Norton & Company.

Leys, C. (1974) *Underdevelopment in Kenya: The Political Economy of Neo-Colonialism, 1964–1971*, Berkeley, CA: University of California Press.

Leyshon, A. and Thrift, N. (2007) "The capitalization of almost everything", *Theory, Culture & Society*, 24: 97–115.

Li, T. (2010) 'To make live or let die? Rural dispossession and the protection of surplus populations', *Antipode*, 41, 1: 66–93.

Lipsky, M. (2010) *Street-Level Bureaucracy: Dilemmas of the Individual in Public Service*, New York: Russell Sage Foundation.

LiPuma, E. and Lee, B. (2004) *Financial Derivatives and the Globalization of Risk*, Durham, NC: Duke University Press.

Lloyds (2015a) *Lloyds' City Risk Index 2015–2012*, London: Lloyds. Available from www.lloyds.com/cityriskindex/

Lloyds (2015b) *Cities Risk Index*, London: Lloyds. Available from https://youtu.be/0KQpJtBchwg

Loftus, A. and March, H. (2015) "Financialising nature?", *Geoforum*, 60: 172–175.

Lohmann, L. (2014) "An alternative to 'alternatives'", *World Rainforest Movement Bulletin*, December: 1–3.

Lohmann, L. (2016) "What is the 'green' in 'green growth'?" in *Green Growth: Political Ideology, Political Economy and the Alternatives*, G. Dale, M. V. Mathai and J. A. Puppim de Oliveira (eds), London: Zed Books.

Lohmann, L. and Hildyard, N. (2014) "Energy, work and finance". Sturminster Newton: The Corner House. Available from www.thecornerhouse.org.uk/resource/energy-work-and-finance

Lomnitz, L. (1988) "Informal exchange networks in formal systems: a theoretical model", *American Anthropologist*, 90, 1: 42–55.

Lukes, S. (ed.) (1986) *Power*, Oxford: Blackwell.

MacDonald, C. (2008) *Green, Inc.* Guildford: Lyons.

Machingura, F. and Bracking, S. (2015) "HIV Treatment and biopolitics", Working Paper, Leverhulme Centre of the Study of Value, University of Manchester.

MacKenzie, D. (2009) "Making things the same: gases, emission rights and the politics of carbon markets", *Accounting, Organizations and Society*, 34, 3–4: 440–455.

MacKenzie, D. (2011) "The credit crisis as a problem in the sociology of knowledge", *American Journal of Sociology*, 116, 6: 1778–1841.

MacKenzie, D., Beunza, D., Millo, Y. and Pardo-Guerra, J. P. (2012) "Drilling through the Allegheny Mountains", *Journal of Cultural Economy*, 5, 3: 279–296.

Mamudi, S. (2015) "Dark pools were the losers as US markets saw volume spurt", *Bloomberg Business*, 24 August. Available from www.bloomberg.com/news/articles/2015-08-24/dark-pools-are-the-losers-as-exchanges-get-huge-volume-from-rout

Marazzi, C. (2011a) *The Violence of Financial Capitalism,* Los Angeles: Semiotext(e).

Marazzi, C. (2011b) *Capital and Affects: The Politics of the Language Economy*, Los Angeles: MIT Press.

March, H. and Purcell, T. (2014) "The muddy waters of financialisation and new accumulation strategies in the global water industry: the case of AGBAR", *Geoforum* 53: 11–20.

Martin, R. (2002) *Financialization of Daily Life*, Philadelphia, PA: Temple University Press.

Martinez, V. H. and Roşu, I. (2011) "High frequency traders, news and volatility", Working Paper, HEC.

Marx, K. (1894). *Capital. A Critique of Political Economy – Vol. 3: The Process of Capitalist Production as a Whole*, F. Engels (ed.), New York: International Publishers.

Marx, K. (1975) *Collected Works*, trans. R. Dixon *et al.*, New York: International Publishers.

Marx, K. (1976) *Capital: Volume I*, London: Penguin Books.

Marx, K. (1978) *Capital: Volume II*, London: Penguin Books.

Mathews, A. S. (2011) *Instituting Nature: Authority, Expertise and Power in Mexican Forests*. Cambridge, MA: MIT Press.

Mauss, M. (1924) [1990] *The Gift: The Form and Reason for Exchange in Archaic Societies*, trans. W. D. Halls, London: Routledge.

Mbanjwa, B. (2012) "The Manase report unpacked", *IOL*, 8th February. Available from www.iol.co.za/dailynews/news/the-manase-report-unpacked-1.1229867

Mbembe, A. (2003) "Necropolitics", *Public Culture*, 15, 1: 11–40.

Mcbride, S. and Merolli, J. (2013) "Alternatives to austerity? Post-crisis policy advice from global institutions", *Global Social Policy*, 13, 3: 299–320.

McCrank, J. (2014) "Dark markets may be more harmful than high-frequency trading" Reuters, 7 April. Available from www.reuters.com/article/us-markets-darkpools-analysis-idUSBREA3605M20140407

McNally, D. (2003) "Beyond the false infinity of capital: dialectics and self-mediation in Marx's theory of freedom", in *New Dialectics and Political Economy*, R. Albritton and J. Simoulidis (eds), Basingstoke: Palgrave Macmillan.

Mehafdi, M. (2000) "The ethics of international transfer pricing", *The Journal of Business Ethics*, 28, 2: 365–381.

Mendonça, M., Jacobs, D. and Sovacool, B. (2010) *Powering the Green Economy: The Feed-in Tariff Handbook*, London: Earthscan.

Meon, P-G. and Weill, L. (2010) "Is Corruption an Efficient Grease?", *World Development*, 38, 3: 244–259.

Methmann, C. P. (2010) "'Climate protection' as empty signifier: a discourse theoretical perspective on climate mainstreaming in world politics", *Millennium: Journal of International Studies*, 39, 2: 345–372.

Methmann, C. P. (2011) "The sky is the limit: global warming as global governmentality", *European Journal of International Relations*, 19, 1: 69–91.

Miller, D. (1997) *Capitalism: An Ethnographic Approach*, Oxford: Berg.

Miller, D. (1998) "A theory of virtualism" in *A New Political Economy*, J. Carrier and D. Miller (eds), Oxford: Berg.

Miller, D. (2002) "Turning Callon the right way up", *Economy and Society*, 31, 2: 218–33.

Moore, J. (2008) "ecological crises and the agrarian question in world-historical perspective", *Monthly Review*, 60, 6: 54–63.

Moore, J. (2010) "The end of the road? Agricultural revolutions in the capitalist world-ecology, 1450–2010", *Journal of Agrarian Change*, 10, 3: 389–413.

Moore, J. (2011) "Wall Street is a way of organising nature: An interview with Jason Moore", *Upping the Anti: A Journal of Theory and Action*, 12. Available from www.jasonwmoore.com/uploads/Moore__Wall_Street_is_a_Way_of_Organizing_Nature__2011.pdf

Moore, J. (2014a) "The Capitalocene, part II: abstract social nature and the limits to capital". Available from www.jasonwmoore.com/Essays.html

Moore, J. (2014b) "The end of cheap nature. or how I learned to stop worrying about 'the' environment and love the crisis of capitalism", in *Structures of the World Political Economy and the Future of Global Conflict and Cooperation*, C. Suter and C. Chase-Dunn (eds), Berlin: LIT.

Morningstar Advisor (2011) "The weighting game and other puzzles of indexing", *Morningstar Advisor*, February/March. Available from www.nxtbook.com/nxtbooks/morningstar/advisor_20110203/index.php?startid=52#/54

Morvaridi, B. (2012) "Capitalist philanthropy and hegemonic partnerships", *Third World Quarterly*, 33, 7: 1191–1210.

Mottiar, S. (2014) "Philanthropy and development in Southern Africa: philanthropy and resource governance", Pretoria: Southern Africa Trust. Available from www.southernafricatrust.org/wp-content/uploads/2015/04/Paper-One-Philanthropy-and-Resource-Governance.pdf

Mungiu-Pippidi, A. (2006) "Corruption, diagnosis and treatment", *Journal of Democracy*, 17, 3: 86–99.

Muniesa, F. (2005) "Contenir le marché: la transition de la criée à la cotation électronique à la Bourse de Paris", *Sociologie du Travail*, 47, 4: 485–501.

Muniesa, F. (2007) "Market technologies and the pragmatics of prices", *Economy and Society*, 36, 3: 377–395.

Murray, S. J. (2006). "Thanatopolitics: on the use of death for mobilizing political life", *Polygraph: International Journal of Politics and Culture*, 18: 191–215.

Nadal, A. and Aguayo, F. (2014) "Leonardo's sailors: A review of the economic analysis of wildlife trade", LCSV Working Paper No. 6, Leverhulme Centre for the Study of Value, University of Manchester. Available from http://thestudyofvalue.org/publications/#6

Nancy, J.-L. (2001) "The two secrets of the fetish", *Diacritics*, 31, 2: 3–8.

Narang, M (2010) "Tradeworx, Inc. public commentary on SEC market structure concept release", submission to Securities and Exchange Commission, 21 April. Available at www.sec.gov/comments/s7-02-10/s70210-129.pdf

National Audit Office (2011) "The Comptroller and Auditor General's Report on Accounts to the House of Commons: The financial stability interventions. An extract from the Certificate and Report of the Comptroller and Auditor General on HM Treasury Annual Report and Accounts 2010-11" (HC 984 July 2011), London: HM Treasury. Available from www.nao.org.uk/wp-content/uploads/2011/07/HMT_account_2010_2011.pdf

National Audit Office (2014) "Taxpayer support for UK banks: FAQs", London: National Audit Office. Available from www.nao.org.uk/highlights/taxpayer-support-for-uk-banks-faqs/

Ndikumana, L. and Boyce, J. (2008) "New estimates of capital flight from sub-Saharan African countries: linkages with external borrowing and policy options", Working Paper 166, Political Economy Research Institute, University of Massachusetts, Amherst.

Ndikumana, L. and Boyce, J. (eds) (2012) "Africa's capital losses: what can be done?", *Concerned Africa Scholars Bulletin*, 87.

Nel, A. (2014) "Sequestering Market Environmentalism: Geographies of Carbon Forestry and Unevenness in Uganda", PhD Thesis submitted to the University of Otago.

Nel, A. (2015) "Assembling value in carbon forestry", LCSV Working Paper No. 10, Leverhulme Centre for the Study of Value, University of Manchester. Available from http://thestudyofvalue.org/wp-content/uploads/2015/01/WP-10_Nel-2015-Assembling-value-in-carbon-forestry.pdf

Nelson, D., Shrimali, G. (2014) "Finance mechanisms for lowering the cost of renewable energy in rapidly developing countries", London: Climate Policy Initiative.

Nelson, R. H. (2003) "Environmental colonialism. 'Saving' Africa from Africans", *The Independent Review*, 8: 65–86.

Nielsen, V. L. (2006) "Are street-level bureaucrats compelled or enticed to cope?", *Public Administration*, 84, 4: 861–889.

Nitzan, J. and Bichler, S. (2009) *Capital as Power: A Study of Order and Creorder*, Abingdon: Routledge.

Nitzan, J.and Bichler, S. (2015) 'US capital accumulation: fiction vs. reality', *Real-World Economics Review*, 72: 66. Available from www.academia.edu/16376633/Capital_Accumulation_Fiction_and_Reality

Norad (2011a) "Joint evaluation of support to anti-corruption efforts 2002–2009, evaluation report", Oslo: Norwegian Agency for Development Cooperation. Available from www.oecd.org/countries/zambia/48912166.pdf

Norad (2011b) "Contextual choices in fighting corruption: lessons learned", Oslo: Norwegian Agency for Development Cooperation. Available from www.oecd.org/countries/zambia/48912957.pdf

North, D. C., Wallis, J. J. and Weingast, B. R. (2009) *Violence and Social Orders: A Conceptual Framework for Understanding Recorded Human History*, Cambridge: Cambridge University Press.

NOU (2009) "Tax havens and development: status, analyses and measures", Government Commission on Capital Flight from Poor Countries, Oslo: Norwegian Agency for Development Cooperation. Available from www.u4.no/recommended-reading/tax-havens-and-development-status-analyses-and-measures/

Ntayi, J. P., Ngoboka., P. and Kakooza, C. S. (2013) "Moral schemas and corruption in ugandan public procurement", *Journal of Business Ethics*, 112: 417–436.

Nystrand, M. J. (2014) "Petty and grand corruption and the conflict dynamics in Northern Uganda", *Third World Quarterly*, 35, 5: 821–835.

O'Connor, A. (2001) *Poverty Knowledge: Social Science, Social Policy and the Poor in Twentieth-century US History*, Princeton, NJ: Princeton University Press.

O'Connor, J. (1998) *Natural Causes: Essays in Ecological Marxism*, New York: Guilford Press

OECD (2013) "Aid Activities targeting environmental objectives", OECD.Stat. Available from https://stats.oecd.org/Index.aspx?DataSetCode=RIOMARKERS

OECD (2014a) "Aid to developing countries rebounds in 2013 to reach an all-time high", OECD, 9 April. Available from www.oecd.org/newsroom/aid-to-developing-countries-rebounds-in-2013-to-reach-an-all-time-high.htm

Oels, A. (2006) "Rendering climate change governable: from biopower to advanced liberal government?", *Journal of Environmental Policy and Planning*, 7, 3: 185–207.

Olivier de Sardan, J-P. (1999) "A moral economy of corruption in Africa?", *The Journal of Modern African Studies*, 37, 1: 25–52.

Olivier de Sardan, J-P. (2014) "The delivery state in Africa: interface bureaucrats, professional cultures and the bureaucratic mode of governance", in *States at Work: Dynamics of African Bureaucracies*, T. Bierschenk and J-P. Olivier de Sardan (eds), Leiden: Brill.

Ong, A. (2006) *Neoliberalism as Exception: Mutations in Citizenship and Sovereignty*, Durham, NC: Duke University Press.

Orhangazi, O. (2008) *Financialization and the US Economy*, Northampton, MA: Edward Elgar.

Orjuela, C. (2014) "Corruption and identity politics in divided societies", *Third World Quarterly*, 35, 5: 753–769.

Ouma, S. (2014) "Situating global finance in the Land Rush Debate: a critical review", *Geoforum*, 57: 162–166.

Ouma, S. (2015) "Getting in between M and M, or How farmland further debunks financialisation", *Dialogues in Human Geography*, 5, 2: 225–228.

Palan, R. (2002) "Tax havens and the commercialization of state sovereignty", *International Organization* 56, 1: 151–176.

Palan, R., Murphy, R. and Chavagneux, C. (2010) *Tax Havens: How Globalization Really Works*. Ithaca, NY: Cornell University Press.

Panitch, L. and Gindin, S. (2003) "Global capitalism and American empire", in *Socialist Register 2004: The New Imperial Challenge*, L. Panitch and C. Leys (eds), London: Merlin Press.

Panitch, L. and Gindin, S. (2008) "Finance and American empire", in *American Empire and the Political Economy of Global Finance*, L. Panitch and M. Konings (eds), New York: Palgrave Macmillan.

Pardo-Guerra, J. P. (2010) "Creating flows of interpersonal bits: the automation of the London Stock Exchange, c.1955–90", *Economy and Society*, 39: 84–109.

Parku, S. (2014) "Who says elections in Ghana are free and fair?" Afrobarometer, Policy Paper 15.

Peltz, M. (2010) "Inside the machine: a journey into the world of high frequency trading", *Institutional Investor*, 14 June. Available from www.institutionalinvestor.com/article/2595257/inside-the-machine-a-journey-into-the-world-of-high-frequency-trading.html?ArticleId=2595257&p=1#/.VrTRq1nCt8E

Persson, A., Rothstein, B., Teorell, J. (2010) "The failure of anti-corruption policies: a theoretical mischaracterization of the problem", QoG Working Paper 19, University of Gothenburg, Quality of Government Institute. Available from www.qog.pol.gu.se/digitalAssets/1350/1350163_2010_19_persson_rothstein_teorell.pdf

Petajisto, A. (2011) "The index premium and its hidden cost for index funds", *Journal of Empirical Finance*, 18: 271–288.

Peters, J. (2011) "The rise of finance and the decline of organised labour in the advanced capitalist countries", *New Political Economy*, 16: 73–99.

Philips, M. (2013) "How the robots lost: high-frequency trading's rise and fall", *Bloomberg Business,* 6 June. Available from www.bloomberg.com/bw/articles/2013-06-06/how-the-robots-lost-high-frequency-tradings-rise-and-fall

Phillips, L. (2014) "Cat bonds: cashing in on catastrophe", *Road to Paris*, 18 November. Available from http://roadtoparis.info/2014/11/18/cat-bonds-cashing-catastrophe/

Picardo, E. (2014a) "An introduction to dark pools", *Investopedia.com*, 2 September. Available from www.investopedia.com/articles/markets/050614/introduction-dark-pools.asp

Picardo, E. (2014b) "You'd better know your high-frequency trading terminology", *Investopedia.com*, 2 September. Available from www.investopedia.com/articles/active-trading/042414/youd-better-know-your-highfrequency-trading-terminology.asp

Pike, A. and Pollard, J. (2010) "Economic geographies of financialization", *Economic Geography*, 86, 1: 29–51.

Pitluck, A. Z. (2011) "Distributed execution in illiquid times: an alternative explanation of trading in stock markets", *Economy and Society*, 40: 26–55.

Platteau, J-P. (2004) "Monitoring elite capture in community-driven development", *Development and Change*, 35, 2: 223–246.

Poate, D. and Vaillant, C. (2012) "Joint evaluation of support to anti-corruption efforts 2002–2009", Oslo: Norwegian Agency for Development Cooperation. Available from www.sida.se/globalassets/publications/import/pdf/en/joint-evaluation-of-support-to-anti-corruption-efforts-synthesis-2002-2009_3297.pdf

Pogge, T. (2002) *World Poverty and Human Rights: Cosmopolitan Responsibilities and Reforms*, Cambridge: Polity Press.

Pogge, T. (2005) "World poverty and human rights", *Ethics and International Affairs*, 19, 1: 1–7.

Pogge, T. (2008) *World Poverty and Human Rights: Cosmopolitan Responsibilities and Reforms*, 2nd edn, Cambridge: Polity Press.

Pogge, T. (2010) *Politics as Usual: What Lies behind the Pro-Poor Rhetoric*, Cambridge: Polity Press.

Polanyi, K. (2001) [1944], *The Great Transformation*, 2nd edn, Boston, MA: Beacon.

Pollard, J.S., Oldfield, J., Randalls, S., Thornes, J.E., (2008) "Firm finances, weather derivatives and geography", *Geoforum* 39, 616–624.

Poovey, M. (2015) "On the 'limits to financialisation'", *Dialogues in Human Geography*, 5, 2: 220–224.

PR Newswire (2014) "Africa to issue over $1 billion dollars in climate change bonds", 22 September. Available from www.prnewswire.com/news-releases/africa-to-issue-over-1-billion-dollars-in-climate-change-bonds-276391261.html

Preda, A. (2009) "Brief encounters: calculation and the interaction order of anonymous electronic markets", *Accounting, Organizations and Society*, 34: 675–693.

Preece, R. (2012) *Dark Pools, Internalization, and Equity Market Quality*, Charlottesville, VA: CFA Institute. Available from www.cfapubs.org/doi/pdf/10.2469/ccb.v2012.n5.1

Prudham, S. (2007) "The fictions of autonomous invention: accumulation by dispossession, commodification and life patents in Canada", *Antipode*, 39, 3: 406–429.

Prudham, S. (2008) "Tall among the trees: Organizing against globalist forestry in rural British Columbia", *Journal of Rural Studies*, 24, 2: 182–196.

Rabbitts, F. (2012) "Child sponsorship, ordinary ethics and the geographies of charity", *Geoforum*, 43: 926–936.

Rademeyer, J., Pauw, J. and Trench, A. (2010) "Ruling party's cash cow at centre of yet another controversy", *City Press*, 22 November.

Ramaswamy, S. (2011) "Market structures and systemic risks of exchange-traded funds", Working Paper 343, Basel: Bank for International Settlements.

Rampedi, P. (2012) "BEE firms 'forced to pay bribes'", *The Mercury*, 28 August: 1.

Rhodes, M. and Apeldoorn, B. (1998) "Capital unbound? The transformation of European corporate governance", *Journal of European Public Policy*, 5: 406–427.

Robbins, P. (2000) "The rotten institution: corruption in natural resource management", *Political Geography*, 19: 423–443.

Roberts, J. (2010) "The state, empire and imperialism", *Current Sociology*, 58, 6: 833–858.

Roberts, M. (2015) "Debt, demand and depression", blog. Available from https://thenextrecession.wordpress.com/2015/10/18/debt-demand-and-depression/

Robertson, M. (2006) "Nature that capital can see: science, state and market in the commodification of ecosystem services", *Environment and Planning D: Society and Space* 24: 367–387.

Robertson, M. (2007) "Discovering price in all the wrong places: the work of commodity definition and price under neoliberal environmental policy", *Antipode*, 39, 3: 507.

Robinson, A. L. and Zimmerman, B. A. (2014) "Who subsidizes corruption? A field experiment on corruption, discrimination, and marginalization", mimeo.

Rodrik, D. (2008) *One Economics, Many Recipes: Globalization, Institutions, and Economic Growth*, Princeton, NJ: Princeton University Press.

Rossi, M. (2014) "Increased scrutiny of high-frequency trading", *Harvard Law School Forum on Corporate Governance and Financial Regulation*, 23rd May. Available from https://corpgov.law.harvard.edu/2014/05/23/increased-scrutiny-of-high-frequency-trading/

Rothstein, B. (2011) *Quality of Government: Corruption, Social Trust and Inequality in an International Perspective*. Chicago, IL: University of Chicago Press.

Rubino, J. (2011) "Emerging threat funds?", *CFA Magazine*, September/October. Available from www.cfapubs.org/doi/pdf/10.2469/cfm.v22.n5.7

Saul, J. S. (1997) "'For fear of being condemned as old fashioned': liberal democracy vs. popular democracy in sub-Saharan Africa", *Review of African Political Economy*, 24, 73: 339–353.

Scott, J. C. (1972) *Comparative Political Corruption*, Englewood Cliffs, NJ: Prentice-Hall.

SDCEA (South Durban Community Environmental Alliance) (2014) Comments on the deepening, lengthening, and widening of berth 203 to 205, pier 2, container terminal, and Port of Durban – Amended EIA Report, Durban: SDCEA.

SEC (2008) "Exchange-traded funds", SEC Release Nos. 33-8901, IC-28193, 73 Fed. Reg. 14618, 11 March.

SEC (2010) "Concept release on equity market structure", Federal Register 75/13, 21 January.

Seekings, J. (2008) "Deserving individuals and groups: the post-apartheid state's justification of the shape of South Africa's system of social assistance", *Transformations*, 68.

Sembene, O. (1966) *The Money-Order*, Paris: Presence Africaine.

Sharife, K. (2011), *Tax Us If You Can: Why Africa Should Stand Up for Tax Justice*, Nairobi: Tax Justice Network Africa.

Sharife, K. (2013a) "Disappearing Diamonds", 100 Reporters, 20 February. Available from http://100r.org/2013/02/disappearing-diamonds/

Sharife, K. (2013b) "Made in China: the secret of Mugabe's election success", 100 Reporters, 28 October. Available from http://100r.org/2013/10/made-in-china-the-secret-of-mugabes-election-success/

Sharife, K. and Grobler, J. (2013) "Kimberley's Illicit Process", *World Policy Journal*, Winter 2013/2014. Available from www.worldpolicy.org/journal/winter2013/kimberleys-illicit-process

Shaviro, S. (2009) *Without Criteria: Kant, Whitehead, Deleuze, and Aesthetics*, Cambridge, MA: The MIT Press.

Shaxson, N. (2007) *Poisoned Wells: The Dirty Politics of African Oil*, Basingstoke: Palgrave Macmillan.

Shaxson, N. (2011) *Treasure Islands: Uncovering the Damage of Offshore Banking and Tax Havens*, Basingstoke: Palgrave Macmillan.

Sheng, A. (2009) "Global imbalances demand global fiscal system", East Asia Forum, 28 October. Available from www.eastasiaforum.org/2009/10/28/global-imbalances-demand-global-fiscal-system/

Shore, C. and Haller, D. (2005) *Corruption: Anthropological Perspectives*, London: Pluto Press.

Sikka, P. (2014) "Break the stranglehold of shareholders", *The Guardian*, 11 December. Available from www.theguardian.com/commentisfree/2014/dec/11/break-stranglehold-shareholders-company-funding-key-decisions

Smith, D. J. (2007) *A Culture of Corruption: Everyday Deception and Popular Discontent in Nigeria*, Princeton, NJ: Princeton University Press.

Smith, N. (2008) *Uneven Development: Nature, Capital and the Production of Space*. Athens, GA: University of Georgia Press.

Source UK (2015) "Source exchange traded products". Available from www.source etf.com/

Sparke, M. (1994) "White mythologies and anemic geographies: a review", *Environment and Planning D: Society and Space*, 12: 105–123.

Sparke, M. (2005) *In the Space of Theory: Postfoundational Geographies of the Nation-State*. Minneapolis, MN: University of Minnesota Press.

Standing, A. (2008) "Corruption and industrial fishing in Africa", *U4 Issue* 2008:7, Bergen: Chr. Michelsen Institute.

Standing, A. (2013) "Political corruption: the implications of a neo-republican approach", CMI Working Paper, Chr. Michelsen Institute, Bergen.

Stiglitz, J. (1992) "Alternative tactics and strategies in economic development", in *New Directions in Development Economics*, A. K. Dutt and K. Jameson (eds), Aldershot: Edward Elgar.

Stockhammer, E. (2004) "Financialisation and the slowdown of accumulation", *Cambridge Journal of Economics*, 28: 719–741.

Stockhammer, E. (2010) "Financialisation and the global economy", Working Paper 240, Political Economy Research Institute, University of Massachusetts, Amhurst.

Straus, R. R. (2014) "Jittery stock market lurches into the red again after growth fears see £46BN wiped off leading UK shares in one day", *This is Money*, 15 October. Available from www.thisismoney.co.uk/money/markets/article-2794322/carnage-world-s-markets-sees-46billion-wiped-value-uk-shares-just-one-day.html

Sullivan, S. (2011) "Banking nature? the financialisation of environmental conservation", Working Paper 8, Open Anthropology Cooperative Press, London. Available from http://eprints.bbk.ac.uk/6063/1/Sullivan-Banking-Nature.pdf

Sullivan, S. (2013a) "Nature on the move III: (Re)countenancing an animate nature", *New Proposals: Journal of Marxism and Interdisciplinary Inquiry*, 6, 1–2: 50–71.

Sullivan, S. (2013b) "Banking nature? The spectacular financialisation of environmental conservation", *Antipode*, 45, 1: 198–217.

Sullivan, S. (2014) "Commodity fetishism", LCSV Working Paper No. 2: A conceptual map for the study of value: An initial mapping of concepts for the project "Human, non-human and environmental value systems: an impossible frontier?", Leverhulme Centre for the Study of Value, University of Manchester. Available from http://thestudyofvalue.org/wp-content/uploads/2013/11/WP2-A-conceptual-map.pdf

Sullivan, S., Igoe, J. and Buscher, B. (2013) "Introducing nature on the move: a triptych", *New Proposals: Journal of Marxism and Interdisciplinary Inquiry*, 6, 1–2: 15–19

Sundström, A. (2013) "Corruption in the commons: Why bribery hampers enforcement of environmental regulations in South African fisheries", *International Journal of the Commons*, 7, 2: 454–472.

Swiss Re (2015) "Underinsurance in property is a global, and growing, challenge, says latest Swiss Re sigma study", 14 September, Zurich: Swiss Re. Available from www.swissre.com/media/news_releases/Underinsurance_in_property_is_a_global_and_growing_challenge_says_latest_Swiss_Re_isigmai_study.html

Szeftel, M. (2004) "Two cheers? South African democracy's first decade", *Review of African Political Economy*, 31, 100: 193–202.

Taussig, M. (1987) *Shamanism, Colonialism and the Wild Man: A Study in Terror and Healing*. Chicago, IL: Chicago University Press.

Temperton, P. (2007) "Trading with the help of 'guerrillas' and 'snipers'", *The Financial Times*, 19 March. Available from www.ft.com/cms/s/1/a465e85a-d5be-11db-a5c6-000b5df10621.html#axzz3zKEDkjaC

Theobald, R. (2008) "Polishing up the steel frame: will more bureaucracy help contain the problem of petty corruption in sub-Saharan Africa?" *Commonwealth and Comparative Politics*, 46, 2: 157–176.

Therkildsen, O. (2014) "Working in neopatrimonial settings: public sector staff perceptions in Tanzania and Uganda", in *States at Work: Dynamics of African Bureaucracies*, T. Bierschenk and J-P. Olivier de Sardan (eds), Leiden: Brill.

Thompson, C. (2014) "Philanthrocapitalism: appropriation of Africa's genetic wealth", *Review of African Political Economy*, 41, 141: 389–405.

Torrance, M. (2009) "The rise of a global infrastructure market through relational investing", *Economic Geography*, 85, 1: 75–97.

The Trading Mesh (2015) "McKay Brothers International launches lowest known latency microwave routes from Interxion London", *The Trading Mesh*, 24 June. Available from www.thetradingmesh.com/pg/newsfeeds/mckaybothers/item/691326/mckay-brothers-international-launches-lowest-known-latency-microwave-routes-from-interxion-london

Trading Risk (2011) "Kamp Re posts 75 percent loss at closure", *Trading Risk Newsletter*, 12 January.

Transparency International (2009) *The Anti-Corruption Plain Language Guide*. Berlin: Transparency International.

Tricarico, A. and Amicucci, C, (2011) "Financialisation of water", note from conference on "Financialisation of natural resources", Paris, 28–29 October. Available from www.fame2012.org/en/2011/12/16/financialisation-of-water/

Trotman, A. (2015) "Barclays facing new dark pool fraud allegations", *The Telegraph*, 21 January. Available from www.telegraph.co.uk/finance/newsbysector/banksandfinance/11361612/Barclays-facing-new-dark-pool-fraud-allegations.html

Tsing, A. L. (2000) "Inside the economy of appearances", *Public Culture*, 12, 1: 115–144.

Tsing, A. L. (2005) *Friction: An Ethnography of Global Connection*, Princeton, NJ: Princeton University Press.

Tvedten, I. (2014) "'Goats eat where they are tied up': illicit and habitual corruption in Mozambique", Chr. Michelsen Institute, mimeo.

Uberti, L. (2014) "Is separation of powers a remedy for the resource curse? Firm-Licensing, corruption and mining development in post-war Kosovo", *New Political Economy*, 19, 5: 695–722.

Uberti, L. (forthcoming) "Can institutional reforms reduce corruption? Economic theory and patron-client politics in developing countries", *Development and Change*.

UNCTAD (1997) *World Investment Report: Trends and Determinants*. Geneva: United Nations. Available from http://unctad.org/en/Docs/wir1998_en.pdf

UNCTAD (2012) *Economic Development in Africa Report 2012: Structural Transformation and Sustainable Development in Africa*, Geneva: United Nations. Available from http://unctad.org/en/PublicationsLibrary/aldcafrica2012_embargo_en.pdf

UNECA and AUC (2012a) *Economic Report on Africa 2012: Unleashing Africa's Potential as a Pole of Global Growth*, Addis Ababa: UNECA. Available from www.uneca.org/sites/default/files/PublicationFiles/era2012_eng_fin.pdf

UNECA and AUC (2012b) "High Level Panel on Illicit Financial Flows from Africa: scale and development challenges", Background Document, October, Addis Ababa: UNECA.

UNECA (2014) *Illicit Financial Flows: Report of the High Level Panel on Illicit Financial Flows from Africa*, Addis Ababa: UNECA. Available from www.uneca.org/sites/default/files/PublicationFiles/iff_main_report_26feb_en.pdf

UNESCO, Future Earth and ICSU (2015) "Our common future under climate change: outcome statement by CFCC15 Scientific Committee", 10 July. Available from http://poolo.kermeet.com/Data/kmewexV7/block/F_bedaa0dbe3d01a517f0fa7eb11d4b1a4559fae1ae868b.pdf

UNEP (2011) *Towards a Green Economy: Pathways to Sustainable Development and Poverty Eradication: A Synthesis for Policy Makers*, Nairobi: United Nations Environment Programme. Available from www.ipu.org/splze/rio+20/rpt-unep.pdf

United States District Court, Southern District of New York (2015), Barclays Liquidity Cross and High Frequency Trading Litigation, 26th August, Case 1:14-md-02589-JMF Document 50. Available from https://cryptome.org/2015/08/flash-boys-050.pdf

Uslaner, E. M. (2008) *Corruption, Inequality, and the Rule of Law: The Bulging Pocket Makes the Easy Life*, Cambridge: Cambridge University Press.

Veblen, T. (1912) *The Theory of Business Enterprise*, New York: Charles Scribner's.

Weber, M. (1930) [1905] *The Protestant Ethic and the Spirit of Capitalism*, trans. T. Parsons, London: George Allen & Unwin.

Whitfield, D. (2014) "PPP wealth machine: UK and global trends in trading project ownership", Research Report 6, European Services Strategy Unit. Available from www.european-services-strategy.org.uk/ppp-database/ppp-equity-database/ppp-wealth-machine-parts-1-8.pdf

Williams, J. (2014) "COP blog: the role of the Green Climate Fund in providing the missing 'clean trillion'", Environmental Finance.com, 17 December. Available from www.environmental-finance.com/content/analysis/cop-blog-the-role-of-the-green-climate-fund-in-providing-the-missing-clean-trillion.html

World Bank (2010) *Silent and Lethal: How Quiet Corruption Undermines Africa's Development Efforts, World Development Indictors 2010*, Washington, DC: World Bank.

World Bank (2014a) "World development indicators". Available from http://data.worldbank.org/indicator/BX.KLT.DINV.CD.WD/countries/1W?display=graph

World Bank (2014b) "World development indicators: broad money (% of GDP), broad money (IFS line 35L..ZK)".

World Bank (2014c) "Market capitalization of listed companies (current US$)". Available from http://data.worldbank.org/indicator/CM.MKT.LCAP.CD
World Bank (2014d) "Stocks traded, total value (% of GDP)". Available from http://data.worldbank.org/indicator/CM.MKT.TRAD.GD.ZS/countries?display=graph
World Bank (2015) "Table of Gini Coefficient". Available from https://data.world bank.org/indicator/SI.POV.GINI/
World Economic Forum (2008) "Convergence of insurance and capital markets", WEF Working Papers. Geneva: World Economic Forum.
World Federation of Exchanges (2014) "2013 WFE market highlights". Available from www.world-exchanges.org/insight/reports/world-federation-exchanges-publishes-2013-global-market-highlights
World Hunger Education Service (2013) *2013 World Hunger and Poverty Facts and Statistics*. Washington, DC: World Hunger Education Service. Available from www.worldhunger.org/articles/Learn/world%20hunger%20facts%202002.htm
Yescombe, E. R. (2013) *Principles of Project Finance*, London: Academic Press.
Young, R. (1990) *White Mythologies: Writing History and the West*, London: Routledge.
Zaloom, C. (2006) *Out of the Pits: Trading and Technology from Chicago to London*, Chicago, IL: Chicago University Press.
Zhu, H. (2013) "Do dark pools harm price discovery?", *The Review of Financial Studies*, 27, 3: 747–789.

Index